DISSERTATIONS IN NINETEENTH-CENTURY AMERICAN POLITICAL AND SOCIAL HISTORY

Editor
RONALD P. FORMISANO
Clark University

A Garland Series

Region, Economy, and Party

The Roots of Policy Formation in Pennsylvania, 1820–1860

ANN MARIE DYKSTRA

GARLAND PUBLISHING, INC.
NEW YORK & LONDON 1989

Library of Congress Cataloging-in-Publication Data

Dykstra, Ann Marie.
Religion, economy, and party: the roots of policy formation in Pennsylvania, 1820–1860/ Ann Marie Dykstra.
p. cm.—(Dissertations in nineteenth-century American political and social history)
Includes bibliographical references.
ISBN 0–8240–4065–1 (alk. paper)
1. Pennsylvania—Economic policy. 2. Pennsylvania—Economic conditions—Regional disparities. 3. Pennsylvania. General Assembly—History—19th century. 4. Pennsylvania—Politics and government—Decision making. I. Title. II. Series.
HC107.P4D94 1990
338.9748'009'034—dc20 89–48047

Printed on acid-free, 250-year-life paper
Manufactured in the United States of America

PREFACE

Many people have helped bring this dissertation to conclusion. While at the University of Utah, I received excellent training and guidance from Ray Gunn and Ed Davies. Ray's seminars in Jacksonian America focused my attention on these years, and his influence led me to study politics and eventually, the state legislature. Ed gave me my first exposure to quantitative methods and to Pennsylvania history. I am grateful to both for having the initial confidence in me and for their continued encouragement.

The history department at the University of Pittsburgh allowed me to continue my studies through various fellowships and research grants. Sam Hays further influenced and shaped this thesis through his wonderfully creative approach to history. Above all, I am grateful to him for proving what an exciting discipline history can be. Van Beck Hall was the first to use many of the techniques adopted in this study in his work on Massachusetts and Virginia; his guidance was invaluable. Susan Hansen provided an important interdisciplinary perspective and her interest and support were greatly appreciated.

A special word of thanks must go to Ted Muller. Through Ted, I was able to work on The Atlas of Pennsylvania for several summers. I became more familiar with many aspects of Pennsylvania's past, and in the process, saw the value in adopting a geographical approach for my own work.

Ted was extremely generous with his time and patience as he exposed me to the world of historical geography.

I am also very grateful to my parents for their love and support. My father's interest in law and politics and my mother's love of numbers have clearly passed on to a second generation.

And finally, it is doubtful that this study would have been completed without the constant encouragement of my husband, Gary. Not only were his artistic skills called into play for the production of the final maps, but his patience, affection and sense of humor sustained me through the darker hours. In many ways, this dissertation is as much a part of him as it is of myself.

TABLE OF CONTENTS

LIST OF TABLES

LIST OF FIGURES

CHAPTER ONE

THE POLITICAL RESPONSE TO ECONOMIC CHANGE: STATE LEGISLATURES IN ANTEBELLUM AMERICA

The formation of state economic policy is one of the most important chapters in nineteenth century American political history. During the antebellum years in particular, state legislatures kept pace with the momentous transformation of a pre-industrial to an industrial society by constructing transportation networks, establishing adequate banking and financial institutions, and creating thousands of business corporations. The task confronting state legislatures was not an easy one. Not all areas of society developed at the same rate, nor did all sectors of the economy see the future in exactly the same light. As a result, antebellum representatives were confronted with a variety of demands that came from every corner of their state. These often conflicting requests were resolved in the halls of the state assemblies by an outpouring of legislation that created a central role for the state in the process of economic development.

Given the importance of state legislatures in these critical decades of American economic growth, it is surprising how little attention has been paid to them of late. The most thorough treatment of these institutions was completed nearly four decades ago. As the federal government became increasingly involved in the economy in the post-World War II years, works such as Louis Hartz's

Economic Policy and Democratic Thought: Pennsylvania, 1776-1860 and Oscar and Mary Handlin's Commonwealth: A Study of the Role of Government in the American Economy, Masschusetts, 1774-1861 were written to demonstrate the tradition of an active government in America's past.[1] These studies argued that antebellum state legislatures were not guided by laissez faire theories. On the contrary, their participation in the economy stemmed logically from the colonial mercantile principle which expected the government actively to promote economic growth for the good of the state.

The extent of government involvement in the economy varied significantly from state to state. In the early decades of the nineteenth century, there was no clear distinction between the public and private spheres of economic life. Some states created quasi-public organizations by investing heavily in private corporations that were designed to serve the common weal. Pennsylvania, New York, and Ohio became even more integrally involved through their publicly financed and administered transportation systems. Massachusetts, on the other hand, chose a less active role, but continued to guide the economic development of the state through charter and regulatory legislation.

In most cases, state involvement reached its zenith in the 1830s. Proliferation of corporate charters and other privileges made it harder to justify state actions in terms of a generalized public interest. By the eve of the Civil War, most states had retreated from active economic participation as the development of corporate policy created a more distinct private sector of the economy.

After the publication of these studies, attention shifted away from the importance of antebellum state legislatures. Scholars who looked at the issues debated and enacted by these assemblies usually did so within a political party framework. The emergence of the Democrat and Whig parties during the 1830s is heralded as the first truly national party system.[2] Rodney O. Davis, Herbert Ershkowitz and William G. Shade, Peter Levine, Marc Kruman, and Douglas Bowers have used roll-call analysis of state legislatures to examine the extent of party loyalty and to determine if real differences existed between Democrats and Whigs in the 1830s and 1840s.[3] These studies have revealed much about the activities of state governments. Yet for the most part, legislative debates and economic issues, in particular, have been used primarily as vehicles to test the tenacity of party divisions. The evolution of policies and their relationship to one another are frequently obscured.

Recently, L. Ray Gunn and Ballard Campbell have turned the focus back to the state legislature itself. More importantly, they have explored the relationship between legislative activity and the larger society. In his examination of the antebellum New York legislature, Gunn argues that political development lagged behind the pace of social and economic change. Overwhelmed by the demands of a rapidly developing economy, legislators were increasingly unable to respond effectively. As a result, the state resorted to enacting policies such as general incorporation laws which removed important decision-making powers from the public arena, thereby contributing to the creation of a more active, private economic sphere.[4]

Campbell's study of midwestern legislatures in the late nineteenth century is an ambitious attempt to examine political change in a broader environmental context. The voting patterns of the representatives were correlated with their party affiliation, personal characteristics, and the socio-economic composition of their districts. In analyzing the broad spectrum of legislative activity, the author found that voting alignments shifted with the issue at hand and were the product of a variety of economic and cultural factors. On the whole, Campbell concluded, state legislatures were very responsible representative institutions that fulfilled an important role throughout the nineteenth century.[5]

It is time to build upon the traditions of the post-war scholars and apply new methodologies to arrive at a better understanding of the relationship between political change and economic development in antebellum America. State legislatures were the centers of policy innovation during these years and the most active level of government. Smaller than the nation, yet larger than isolated communities, these assemblies performed a vital integrating, middle-level function as they created policies to direct and promote the rapid, yet uneven pace of economic growth.[6]

II

This study focuses on the formation of economic policy in antebellum Pennsylvania and relates the process of legislative decision-making directly to the patterns of economic development in Pennsylvania's legislative districts.[7] Pennsylvania is an ideal state to study the influence of differing rates of economic growth on the activities and policies of the state legislature. The physical geography of the state is extremely diverse ranging from the rocky, mountainous sections of the anthracite country, to the rich limestone soils of the counties in the southeastern corner of the state, to the dense forests of the Allegheny Plateau. This varied topography meant that some areas of the state were already quite populated by the early nineteenth century while others remained totally unsettled and little explored until the 1830s.

The physiographical heterogeneity of the commonwealth translated into a very diversified economy. Agriculture remained the dominant economic activity throughout the antebellum years as Pennsylvania continually ranked among the top producers of wheat, corn and other staple products. Yet it was also during these decades that the state emerged as an important manufacturing center, a development that was due in no small part to the abundance of such valuable resources as anthracite coal and lumber. By 1860, Pennsylvania was the nation's leading producer of metals and lumber and ranked among the top three states in the production of machinery, food products, glass, textiles and leather.

The state aided and promoted this economic development. Pennsylvania confronted the commercial barriers posed by rugged topography early on as the legislature actively attempted to create a suitable and efficient transportation network. The commonwealth is most famous, or infamous as the case may be, for the construction of the ambitious publicly-owned and administered internal improvements system. Initial plans called only for the construction of a major east-west canal designed to facilitate access to the Ohio Valley. In the end, the network included numerous branch lines which extended to nearly every corner of the state. The construction of this system along with the state subsidy of other routes stretched the budget beyond any reasonable capacity and created prolonged and serious financial problems for the commonwealth. The state also promoted a banking system through direct financial involvement and an increasingly lenient charter policy. The number of charters granted for banking and business purposes increased markedly so that by 1860, the corporation had become generally accepted as the preferred and preeminent form of business organization.

In the House of Representatives, between forty and fifty percent of all laws passed as well as of all roll-calls taken during each session dealt with Pennsylvania's economy.[8] The foremost task of the state legislators was to allocate public resources and privileges to various individuals and groups. As the pace of economic growth quickened, legislators were deluged with an astronomical number of petitions asking for everything from financial subsidization or direct public ownership for some endeavors to corporate charters to aid the strictly private efforts of others. The patterns of policy-making which emerged did not reflect a broad design or long-range plan. Policy was incremental, fragmented and highly decentralized. The state legislature, in other words, became a central clearing house where the disparate demands from hundreds of individual citizens and communities were debated, compromised, resolved, and ultimately enacted as laws.[9]

The distributive character of policy meant that hundreds of roll-calls were taken on very specific, often minute points of political economy. These roll-calls are an extremely valuable source that provide a direct link between political decision-making and the broader society. The positions taken by individual representatives can be related directly to the economic characteristics of their legislative districts. In this way, we can begin to evaluate the association between the uneven rates of economic growth and the formation of state policy.[10]

In the past, most scholars have used roll-call analysis primarily to determine the extent of partisan stability. Patterns of legislative behavior, however, can and should be established irrespective of politial party affiliation. Party development was extremely erratic during the early decades of the nineteenth century, and many issues simply do not fit the partisan mold. Adopting a strictly party analysis of politics gives short shrift to wider societal forces that merit independent examination. "Patterns of social and economic development out of which political impulses spring," argues Samuel P. Hays

> cannot be understood more than dimly if subordinated as explanatory features of more dominant factors of the political party. . . . A more satisfactory treatment requires that society be reconstructed on its own terms, independent of its confined context as an explanatory variable, so that one can observe the impulses which reach out from individual and institutional endeavor into the wider political world. Those social and economic processes take place independent of party; political impulses in the eras of both pre-party years and the years of party decline were no less intense and real than in periods of high party development.[11]

The primary focus of this study is not party, but regional, economic and commercial patterns which shaped Pennsylvania's development in the antebellum period. The role of political parties and the emergence of the high degree of party discipline which Joel Silbey has termed "the partisan imperative," become all the more interesting in light of these various socio-economc trends.[12] While parties did, indeed, perform an important role in shaping and formulating economic policy, it is their relationship to and their origin in these regional, economic and commercial developments that is ultimately of greatest import. Parties, like policies, were reflections of significant divisions within the broader society.

III

Previous attempts to uncover important socio-economic distinctions which underscored legislative conflict have centered on personal differences among the elected representatives. These distinctions may or may not reflect similar divisions within the constitutencies. But there are other drawbacks. To begin with, there is ample evidence to suggest that most legislators were local elites. Hence, differences between these men on factors such as wealth, occupation, or level of education, were limited. Secondly, all accounts indicate that legislative turnover, particularly in the lower houses of state legislatures, was very high, especially in states like Pennsylvania where these officials were elected annually.[13] It seemed, therefore, much more logical and profitable to focus not on the characteristics of the individual representatives, but on the districts themselves.[14] Studies by political scientists have likewise concluded that constituency factors such as wealth, education, and industrialization are better predictors of policy outcomes than political factors such as partisan affiliation or popular electoral behavior.[15]

Relating legislative behavior to the districts required some way of describing the uneven and diversified patterns of economic development in Pennsylvania. Some areas of the commonwealth quickly emerged as manufacturing centers. Some were fortuitously situated upon major transportation routes and were well integrated into a wider commercial network. Abundant natural resources provided a ready-made economic advantage for some sections of the state while other areas remained sparsely settled, highly dependent upon agriculture, and relatively isolated from larger market forces. Antebellum Pennsylvania, then, was composed of many economies, and the elected representatives' demands and preconceptions were shaped, to a large degree, by their district's peculiar economic experience.

In an attempt to capture these patterns of economic development, Pennsylvania's legislative districts were categorized in two separate ways. Using the county (which was also the basis for defining the districts) as the primary unit of analysis, the commonwealth was first divided into seven geographical regions. The idea of region is admittedly a tricky one, and the definition of precise geographical boundaries presents a formidable task. Yet very distinct regional patterns of economic development did exist in antebellum Pennsylvania. A clearly discernible trend toward regional crop specialization, for example, was the result of variations in climate and soil composition. The newly-emerging industrial areas had ready access to new fuel sources which came from adjacent regions with abundant reserves of natural resources. These patterns of regional development, moreover, were reinforced by the commonwealth's rivers which continued to direct and structure the flow of goods and communications throughout the antebellum period. Each of these seven regions underwent a unique type of economic development during this era, and the characteristics which set each region apart from the others should be expected to create shared interests and a common outlook that would, in turn, be translated into political action by the region's representatives in Harrisburg.

The significance of these regional distinctions has not been overlooked by other students of Pennsylvania history. Literature on Pennsylvania politics has stressed the importance of sectionalism in the treatment of the legislative and party battles of the period and frequently attributed persistent political conflict to irreconcilable regional differences.[16] These works, however, generally highlighted noteworthy conflicts. Sectionalism, or regionalism, deserves a much more systematic examination across a broad spectrum of economic issues.

While the regions provided a static way of describing antebellum Pennsylvania, it was also necessary to be able to analyze how the commonwealth's economy changed over the four decades and to detect patterns within regions in terms of variations in levels of economic development. Rather than relying on a single measure to describe economic growth, a wide variety of variables were combined to give the most complete picture possible of each county's relative level of development and commercial involvement at four different points in time.[17] Census data were used extensively to describe each county's economic mix. Percapita production figures on a variety of agricultural products and manufactured goods indicated the extent of these economic activities, and tax assessments of real and personal property provided a contemporary view of each county's relative level of wealth.

How well was each community integrated into a wider communications and financial network? Banking data showing the amount circulating in the form of loans demonstrated the relative prosperity of the county, and also revealed how dependent the community had become on finance capital for continued growth. Postal data were relied upon to indicate the commercial orientation of each county. Records which listed the annual amount of mail passing through each post office demonstrated which communities were in constant contact with wider markets and broader commercial opportunities, and which remained relatively isolated.

All of these variables were then combined into a single index number for each county, for each decade under consideration, and then ordinally ranked. The four resulting continua were divided into five commercial-economic groups. It was thus possible to obtain a sense of each county's <u>relative</u> level of development and its change during the antebellum period. In addition, the county ranks were averaged together to create five commercial-economic aggregate groups. This second set of groups indicated which counties remained consistently among the most developed, which the least developed, and which in between. The regions and both sets of commercial-economic groups then became the basis for analyzing legislative behavior during the 1828-29, 1838-39, 1849 and 1859 sessions of the Pennsylvania House of Representatives.

These regional and multi-dimensional descriptions of economic life permit a much broader, yet more subtle type of socio-economic influence than that set forth by the Progressives or by Arthur M. Schlesinger, Jr. in The Age of Jackson.[18] The question is not one of individual self-aggrandizement, or of the "haves" versus the "have-nots." Pennsylvania society was much too varied and complex for such simple dichotomies. The approach used in this study implies that as the counties underwent various patterns of commercial and economic development, the members of the community, and particularly the members of the local elite who tended to represent the county in Harrisburg, developed a shared outlook which was rooted in their particular regional and economic experience. This perception was, in turn, translated into political expression through petitions to the state legislature and to policy through the legislator's voting behavior in the House of Representatives.[19]

IV

Pennsylvania legislators were remarkably consistent when they cast their votes on economic issues. Within each session, they displayed persistent regional and commercial-economic group positions on controversial policies. On some issues, such as internal improvements, the greatest support remained in the same regions and in the same commercial-economic groups throughout all four sessions. Support for banking and business endeavors, on the other hand, shifted markedly during the twenty years after the 1828-29 session in direct response to changes in the larger economy. Regional self-interest occasionally operated as a clear influence, yet continuous patterns of obvious sectional aggrandizement are not as evident or as pervasive as historians have argued. A representative's behavior was shaped just as much by the level of commercial and economic development in his county as by the characteristics of the broader region in which it was located.

The political parties, which emerged during the 1830s, were products of Pennsylvania's varied economy. They attempted to harness regional, commercial and economic impulses and give them greater cohesion and more concrete, direct political expression. In some instances, in some areas, and on some issues, they did so with a good deal of success. The party cohesion levels and their consistent position on certain types of policies, in fact, attests to the potency of parties as important integrating legislative institutions. Party positions on these economic issues, moreover, demonstrate that party rhetoric and party platforms were not merely hollow words. The Whigs were, indeed, the more fervent advocates of economic progress while the Democrats remained more reluctant to support change through the use of government involvement in the economy.

Although the Democrats were the dominant party in Pennsylvania throughout the 1830s and 1840s, many of the economic policies enacted seemed much more in line with Whig party doctrine than with official Democratic pronouncements. Democratic support of many controversial economic issues came, in most instances, only in the eleventh hour, or on the final votes on many economic bills. Whig representatives tended to come from districts with fairly uniform commercial and economic outlooks which facilitated the development of a more consistent and cohesive legislative position. The Democrats, on the other hand, came from counties with much more disparate regional and commercial-economic characteristics. Democratic members who joined the Whigs, thus ensuring the enactment of their policies tended to represent counties with qualities that were strikingly similar to those of the Whig districts. Those counties which sent representatives to Harrisburg who consistently supported pro-banking, business or transportation legislation, moreover, go far in explaining the sources of Republican party support in Pennsylvania in the late 1850s.

The Pennsylvania legislature, then, served as a laboratory for political and economic change during the antebellum decades. As a rapidly diversifying economy generated increasingly varied and numerous demands, Pennsylvania representatives responded by passing an increasing number of laws and experimenting with new political techniques that together resulted in a markedly expanded role for the state. The policies developed during these years reflect the incredible variation and conflict within the commonwealth's economy. The persistence and strength of voting patterns indicate that representatives had developed a clear perception of their county's needs, a vision of the future, and some conception of the appropriate role of government in attaining both. They behaved accordingly when they cast their roll-call votes on a wide array of economic policies.

FOOTNOTES

[1] Oscar Handlin and Mary Flug Handlin, Commonwealth; A Study of the Role of Government in the American Economy: Massachusetts, 1774-1861 (New York: New York University Press, 1947); Louis Hartz, Economic Policy and Democratic Thought: Pennsylvania, 1776-1860 (Cambridge: Harvard University Press, 1948; reprint ed. Chicago: Quadrangle Paperback Books, Inc. 1968). See also, Milton Sydney Heath, Constructive Liberalism: The Role of the State in Economic Development in Georgia to 1860 (Cambridge: Harvard University Press, 1954); James Neal Primm, Economic Policy in the Development of a Western State: Missouri, 1820-1860 (Cambridge: Harvard University Press, 1954). For a discussion of these works, see Harry N. Scheiber, "Government and the Economy: Studies of the 'Commonwealth' Policy in Nineteenth Century America," Journal of Interdisciplinary History 3 (Summer 1972): 135-51.

Those who have focused on specific policies passed by state governments include Carter Goodrich, Government Promotion of American Canals and Railroads, 1800-1890 (New York: Columbia University Press, 1960); and Harry N. Scheiber, Ohio Canal Era: A Case Study of Government and the Economy, 1820-1861 (Athens, Ohio, 1969). James Roger Sharp, The Jacksonians Versus the Banks: Politics in the States after the Panic of 1837 (New York: Columbia University Press, 1970); and William G. Shade, Banks or No Banks: The Money Issue in Western Politics, 1832-1865 (Detroit: Wayne State University Press, 1972) have contributed to our knowledge of banking policies in the states. Both studies, however, are more concerned with attitudes toward banks among constituencies and do not concentrate on the development of banking policy in the state legislature.

For a discussion of the importance of the state legislature in nineteenth century America, see Ballard Campbell, "The State Legislature in American History: A Review Essay," Historical Methods Newsletter 9 (September 1976): 185-87.

[2] Richard P. McCormick, The Second American Party System: Party Formation in the Jacksonian Era (Chapel Hill: University of North Carolina Press, 1966).

[3] Douglas E. Bowers, "The Pennsylvania Legislature, 1815-1860: A Study of Democracy at Work," (Ph.D. dissertation, University of Chicago, 1974); Rodney O. Davis, "Illinois Legislators and Jacksonian Democracy, 1834-1841," (Ph.D. dissertation, University of Iowa, 1966); Rodney O. Davis, "Partisanship in Jacksonian State Politics: Party Divisions in the Illionis Legislature, 1834-1841," in Robert Swierenga, Quantification in History (New York, 1970):

149-62; Herbert Ershkowitz and William G. Shade, "Consensus or Conflict? Political Behavior of State Legislative Parties during the Jacksonian Era," Journal of American History 58 (December 1971): 591-621; Marc W. Kruman, Parties and Politics in North Carolina: 1836-1865 (Baton Rouge: Louisiana State University Press, 1983); Peter D. Levine, The Behavior of State Legislative Parties in the Jacksonian Era: New Jersey, 1829-1844 (Rutherford-Teaneck, N.J.: Fairleigh Dickenson Press, 1977); Peter D. Levine, "State Legislative Parties in the Jacksonian Era: New Jersey, 1829-1844," Journal of American History 62 (December 1975): 591-608.

[4]L. Ray Gunn, "Crisis of Authority in the Antebellum States: New York, 1820-1860," Review of Politics 41 (April 1979):273-97; "The New York State Legislature: A Developmental Perspective," Social Science History 4 (August 1980): 267-94; "Political Implications of General Incorporation Laws in New York to 1860," Mid-America 59 (October 1977): 171-91.

Douglas E. Bowers, "The Pennsylvania Legislature," looks broadly at the activities of the Pennsylvania General Assembly including daily legislative practices and the development of the standing committee system. Little attempt, however, is made to relate these developments to broader social and economic changes. More recently, Bowers has turned his attention to an examination of lobbying in antebellum Pennsylvania. See Douglas E. Bowers, "From Logrolling to Corruption: The Development of Lobbying in Pennsylvania, 1815-1861," Journal of the Early Republic 3 (Winter 1983): 439-74.

[5]Ballard Campbell, Representative Democracy: Public Policy and Midwestern Legislatures in the Late Nineteenth Century (Cambridge: Harvard University Press, 1980).

[6]See Samuel P. Hays, "Political Parties and the Community-Society Continuum," in William Nisbet Chambers and Walter Dean Burnham, The American Party Systems: Stages of Political Development, 2nd ed. (New York: Oxford University Press, 1975), pp. 152-181, for a discussion of the different levels of political life.

[7]This study does not examine the influence of ethno-cultural characteristics on the policy process. Given the saliency of econmic issues during the antebellum years, I felt it was more important first to test the validity of sectional and economic interests on the formation of transportation, banking and business legislation.

[8]These figures are based upon an average of the four sessions analyzed in this study. See Table 5.

[9]For a discussion of "distributive" policies in antebellum state legislatures, see Bowers, "From Logrolling to Corruption, pp. 473-4; Bowers, "The Pennsylvania Legislature;" Gunn, "Crisis of Authority," pp. 284-85; Gunn, "The New York State Legislature," pp. 270-71; Theodore J. Lowi, "Business, Public Policy, Case Studies, and Political Theories," World Politics 16 (July 1964): 677-715; Richard L. McCormick, "The Party Period and Public Policy: An Expoloratory Hypothesis," Journal of American History 56 (September 1979): 279-98; pp. 283-85; Harry N. Scheiber, "Federalism and the American Economic Order, 1789-1910," Law and Society Review 10 (Fall 1975): 88-89.

[10]For the most part, I have only relied upon Rice Indexes of Cohesion and simple percentage calculations in employing roll-call analysis in this study. More sophisticated techniques like the index of likeness (or index of difference) and Guttman scaling, while certainly valuable, are much more readily adaptable to two-party analysis. This study analyzed legislative behavior for seven regions, five commercial-economic groups, five commercial-economic aggregate groups, as well as political parties. As a result, the index of likeness was not particularly appropriate.

I consciously chose not to use Guttman scaling in an attempt to gain a better and more detailed understanding of the issues involved. Guttman scaling combines a series of roll-call votes on a related issue in order to provide a single measure of an individual legislator's position. While combining related votes certainly has its merits, it also frequently obscures important voting patterns within the issue categories themselves. A consistent effort was made in this study to break-down the issues within each broad classification as far as possible and to analyze voting patterns along these lines.

[11]Samuel P. Hays, "Politics and Society: Beyond the Political Party," in Paul Kleppner et al., eds., The Evolution of American Electoral Systems (Westport, Conn.: Greenwood Press, 1982), p.

[12]Joel H. Silbey, The Partisan Imperative: The Dynamics of American Politics Before the Civil War (New York: Oxford University Press, 1985).

[13]See, for example, Edward J. Davies, II, "Political Careers and Social Origins of Pennsylvania Legislators, 1848-1853, 1870-1875, 1890-1895," (University of Utah, 1985); Levine, Behavior of State Legislative Parties, pp. 64-90.

[14]Van Beck Hall, Politics Without Parties: Massachusetts, 1780-91 (Pittsburgh: University of Pittsburgh Press, 1972), also chose to focus on the

characteristics of the districts rather than on the representatives.

[15]The terms of the debate were first set by Richard E. Dawson and James A. Robinson, "Inter-Party Competition, Economic Variables, and Welfare Policies in the American States," Journal of Politics 25 (May 1963): 265-89; Thomas R. Dye, "Politics versus Econmics: The Development of the Literature on Policy Determination," Policy Studies Journal 7 (1979): 652-662; J. H. Fenton and D. W. Chamberlayne, "The Literature Dealing with the Relationships between Policy Processes, Socioeconomic Conditions, and Public Policies in the American States: A Bibliographic Essay," Polity 1 (Spring 1969): 388-404; Richard I. Hofferbert, "Socioeconomic Dimensions of the American States, 1890-1960," Midwest Journal of Political Science 12 (1968): 405-409; Richard I. Hofferbert, "State and Community Policy Studies: A Review of Comparative Input-Output Analysis," Political Science Annual 3 (1972): 3-72. More recently, political scientists have begun once again to examine the impact of political factors. See Jack M. Treadway, Public Policy Making in the American States (New York: Praeger, 1985).

[16]Hartz, Economic Policy and Democratic Thought; Philip Klein, Pennsylvania Politics, 1817-1832: A Game Without Rules (Philadelphia: Historical Society of Pennsylvania, 1940); Charles M. Snyder, The Jacksonian Heritage: Pennsyvlania Politics, 1833-1848 (Harrisburg: Pennsylvania Historical and Museum Commission, 1958).

[17]A very similar approach was used by Hall, Politics Without Parties, and E. Willard Miller, An Economic Atlas of Pennsylvania (Harrisburg: Commonwealth of Pennsyvlania, State Planning Board, 1964). See also Linda Pritchard, "Religious Change in a Developing Region: The Social Contexts of Evangelicalism in Western New York and the Upper Ohio Valley during the Mid-Nineteenth Century" (Ph.D. dissertation, University of Pittsburgh, 1980).

18Arthur M. Schlesinger, Jr. The Age of Jackson (Boston: Little, Brown & Co., 1945). For a discussion of the influence of the Progressive historians, see Edward Pessen, Jacksonian Society: Society, Personality and Politics, revised ed. (Homewood, Illinois: The Dorsey Press, 1978), pp. 351-58.

[19]Donald Ratcliffe, "Politics in Jacksonian Ohio: Reflections on the Ethnocultural Interpretation," Ohio History 88 (1979): 5-35, argues along the same lines. Although he is looking at voting rather than legislative behavior, he found that economic factors "took the form not of socioeconomic class interests or antagonisms but of

communal responses to the varying economic experiences undergone by the different regions of Ohio." (quote, p. 9)

CHAPTER TWO

THE SEVEN GEOGRAPHICAL REGIONS OF ANTEBELLUM PENNSYLVANIA

Pennsylvania underwent rapid economic expansion during the antebellum decades. In 1820, the pre-industrial traditions and relationships of the colonial period still dominated. By 1860, the state had clearly launched its Industrial Revolution. Not all Pennsylvanians, however, experienced the same degree or type of economic transformation. Some areas of the state had already become highly industrialized and were well entrenched in a wider, multi-state economic and commercial network. Other areas were not even settled until the 1820s or 1830s and remained in essentially frontier, semi-subsistence conditions until mid-century. These varying rates of economic change heavily influenced the policy decisions of the state legislature. Political demands generated by these changes were as diverse as the economic conditions themselves, and the task of resolving those demands fell to the state representatives in Harrisburg.

Two methods were used to describe the diversity of antebellum Pennsylvania. The state was first divided into seven regions. Defining the boundaries of regions, however, is not always a simple task. Indeed, very little consensus exists among scholars as to what the precise definition of a region is. "Social scientists might all agree that a region is larger than a city and smaller than a nation;" lamented historian Burton Folsom,

> but there the agreement ends. Some have used _region_ to signify a multistate area nearly resembling a section, while others have used a mere county for regional analysis. Market areas and exports seem to be important in classifying a region, but different cities within a region sometimes have different market areas for different products; furthermore, these market areas, and sometimes the exports, change over time. So the complexity of economic activity in America prevents perfection in any regional analysis. But the development of industrial society in contexts broader than that of the individual city means we must try some sort of regional analysis.[1]

The fact remains, however, that distinct regional patterns of development do exist. The shared experiences of those living within the region create common interests that frequently lead to a clear identification with, if not a fierce loyalty to that specific geographical locale. This attachment to a region can result in overt political expression as the area's representatives seek to promote and fulfill the region's specific, often unique needs.

Differences occur, however, within regions, especially with respect to levels of economic development. Some parts of a region are more involved in the emerging network of new economic relationships and others retain more traditional patterns of activity. The more developed areas of the region could well have similar outlooks and the same could be the case for the less developed areas. To focus on the potential economic bases of public policy, a "commercial-economic continuum" has been created which orders all counties in terms of their levels of development.

With these two measures of economic context in mind, one based on regional areas and the other on levels of economic development, one can pose the key question of the study: did Pennsylvania representatives tend to vote on the basis of regional identity, or did they ally with fellow members from counties with similar levels of commercial-economic development?

II

Antebellum Pennsylvania was a prototype of a society undergoing the first stages of industrialization; hence the more dramatic advances in the mining and manufacturing sectors generally attract attention. Yet throughout the four decades under examination, Pennsylvania remained first and foremost an agricultural state. Agriculture changed steadily from self- or semi-subsistence farming to commercial agriculture with an increasing emphasis on regional crop specialization. In 1820, the typical Pennsylvania farmer practiced "general farming." Although wheat was the principal cash crop, it was usually planted in a well-established rotation of corn, oats, winter wheat or rye, clover, and hay.[2] In addition, livestock was an important mainstay of the family farm.

The significance of Pennsylvania as an agricultural state cannot be overemphasized. The state led the country in wheat production until 1839 when it relinquished the title to Ohio. Once again in 1849, Pennsylvania ranked as number one, but had lost its preeminence by 1859. In addition, the commonwealth was the largest corn producer in the nation until 1830, and produced over one-third of the country's rye crop in 1839.[3] The long-term national trend was thus apparent by 1840: the western states of the Ohio valley and beyond would become the major grain-producing section. Pennsylvania farmers increasingly abandoned the practice of all-grain or "general farming" and concentrated more and more on crop or livestock specialization for local and regional markets depending on climactic and soil considerations.[4] While the patterns of regional specialization which emerged are not as sharp in other states[5], trends distinguished one area of Pennsylvania from another.

The continued importance of agriculture to the state's economy was reflected in its manufacturing activities as well. Flour milling, for example, was still the most important single manufacture in Pennsylvania until after the Civil War. While small-scale milling for the local community remained common, larger commercial milling centers emerged.[6] The importance of milling notwithstanding, the dynamic of Pennsylvania's economic growth during the antebellum decades was in the rapid growth of the dominant nineteenth century industries, most notably metals, machinery, and textiles.

The story of Pennsylvania's rise to industrial supremacy centers around the development of Philadelphia and Pittsburgh as major manufacturing metropolises. Philadelphia's ascent as a leading textile, metals, and machinery center was closely linked, if not dependent upon, the exploitation of the anthracite region in the city's northwestern hinterland. Similarly, Pittsburgh's emergence as the "Iron City," industrial provider of the Ohio Valley and points west, depended on ready access to abundant supplies of iron ore and bituminous coal. While it is tempting to overconcentrate on the importance of Philadelphia and Pittsburgh in the state's industrial development, other areas of the state contributed to and shared in this economic expansion.

The iron industry had been an important mainstay of the Pennsylvania economy since the colonial period, and many, if not the majority of Pennsylvania counties could boast of the existence of several forges and furnaces. New fuel sources led to a concentration of iron production in the two urban centers, yet the older iron areas continued to contribute an important share of the state's total output. The conversion to large corporate iron manufactories, as Paul Paskoff recently asserted, was not as rapid as once assumed. Older forms of iron production and industrial organization continued to co-exist side by side with the new well into the 19th century.[7]

By 1860, Pennsylvania had established a substantial national lead in the production of metals. But by that time, the state also ranked number two in the production of machinery, food products, stone, clay and glass, and printing and publishing. In addition, the commonwealth registered a close third in the production of textiles and leather products.[8] Clearly, the foundations for Pennsylvania's industrial revolution had been securely planted during the 1820-1860 decades.

Exploitation of the state's natural resources was closely tied to its industrial expansion. While the importance of both anthracite and bituminous coal is the most obvious example, Pennsylvania's lumber also had a marked effect upon economic expansion. "Penn's Woods," was originally a forest which contained a wealth of different species, including an abundant supply of valuable white pines and other conifers. Lumbering was initially engaged in not for the money it would bring on the market, but to clear the land for settlement and agriculture. Production for local construction, and the manufacture of charcoal iron and tanned goods then followed. Slowly but surely, the lumbering industry began to assume a larger importance. Spurred by improved transportation and growing urban markets, Pennsylvania was surpassed in the value of lumber produced only by New York in 1850, and by 1860 had become the number one state in the nation.[9]

These major economic trends--the shift to more

commercial, specialized agriculture, the development of major manufacturing industries and the accompanying emergence of manufacturing centers, and the exploitation of the state's mineral and lumber resources--were closely linked to an improved transportation network. The story of Pennsylvania's "transportation revolution," to use George Rogers Taylor's term, has been more than adequately told by Taylor and others.[10] Only those developments that have a direct bearing on the commonwealth's regional economic patterns are emphasized here.

Pennsylvania enjoyed a superior system of rivers which, would provide the basis for the state's transportation system for many decades to come. The north-south arteries included the Delaware, Lehigh, Schuylkill, Susquehanna, Youghiogheny, Allegheny, Monongahela, and Beaver rivers. Those running in a more east-west direction were the Juniata, Clarion, Red Bank, Kiskiminetas, and Conemaugh Rivers, as well as the West and North Branches of the Susquehanna. (See Figure 1.)

River traffic, however, was confined to a down-river direction, and even this flow was frequently halted during winter months. To supplement river traffic, Pennsylvanians constructed a fairly well-developed system of turnpike roads during the latter part of the 18th and early 19th centuries. By the 1820s, roads extended into virtually every part of the state. The larger roads, such as the Lancaster Turnpike, were well-constructed, well-maintained turnpikes, but many of the smaller country routes were kept in barely passable condition especially during periods of inclement weather.[11]

During the 1820s and 1830s, Pennsylanians engaged in a period of unprecedented and unsurpassed canal construction. The state completed a series of canals and slack-water improvements on the main rivers in the eastern and central portions of the state. The Pennsylvania Main Line, a combination of canals and railroads, opened east-west traffic between Philadelphia annd Pittsburgh in 1834. The canal between Erie and Beaver in the northwest was completed in the 1830s. The Monongahela Slackwater was completed to Brownsville by 1844, but did not reach New Geneva near the Maryland line until 1856. Finally, improvements of the Allegheny River were frequently discussed, but never implemented.[12]

Many of these canals were constructed with commonwealth funds and came to be known collectively as the public works. Historians have been quick to point to the engineering failures and financial mismanagement of the Pennsylvania canals. Once the state had authorized the building of the Main Line, plans arose to construct lines in all of the various sections of the state. "Instead of first completing her Main Line route to the west," criticized Taylor,

> Pennsylvania, because of sectional political pressures, constructed a whole system of canals simultaneously with the Main Line. The total canal mileage built by 1834, the date of completion of the Main Line, was nearly twice that necessary to complete the through route to

FIGURE 1

THE PRINCIPAL RIVERS OF PENNSYLVANIA

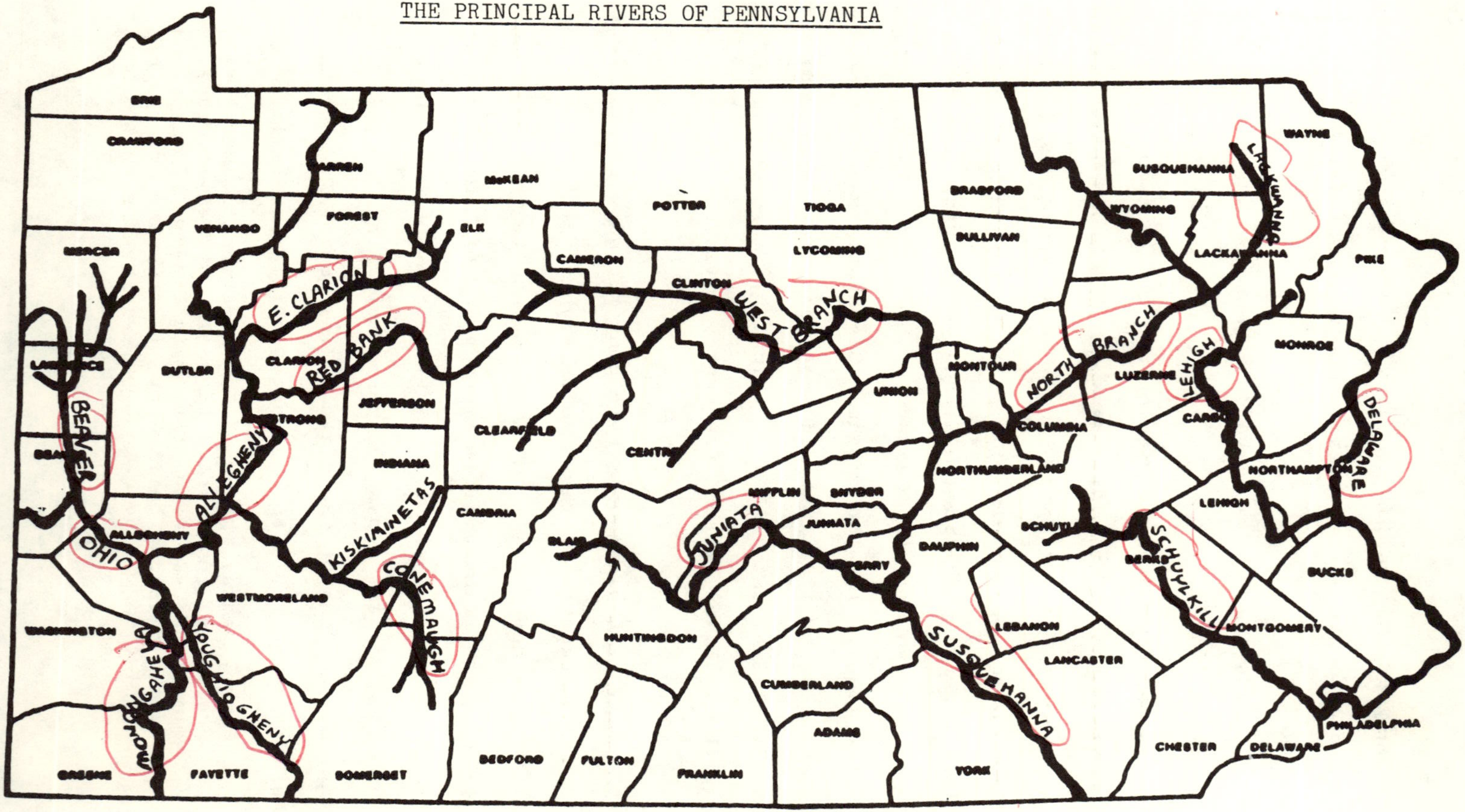

> Pittsburgh. Yet many sections of the state were still unsatisfied, and canal building on a considerable scale continued with some interruptions to 1842. By that date about 772 miles of canal had been constructed, and 162 miles were in various stages of completion. . . . Of all the states, Pennsylania was topographically the least suited to canal building. This meant excessively high original cost, expensive operation, and relatively slow movement of traffic.[13]

While it is tempting to dwell on the ultimate demise of the public works, both the public and private canals made an important contribution to Pennsylvania's economic development. They did much to promote and define intra- and inter-state patterns of regional economic growth. Indeed, it could be argued that external pressure from out-of-state competing markets influenced the canal mania as much as internal political pressures. The driving incentive behind the building of the ill-fated Main Line was an attempt to compete with the Erie Canal, and thus preserve Philadelphia's commercial position in competition with New York City.

Philadelphia also felt pressure from its nearest southern competitor, Baltimore. The impetus behind the construction of many of the early turnpikes, canals, and railroads in the eastern half of the state sprang directly from the ever-present fear of losing valuable trade to Baltimore. The southern city's tentacles reached far into the Susquehanna valley, and until Philadelphia could develop adequate, low-cost routes between the Susquehanna and the Schuylkill Rivers, the competition between these two metropolises for control of the Susquehanna trade remained a persistent theme.[14]

The decade of the 1850s belonged to the railroad. In the ten year period between 1850 and 1860, railroad mileage within Pennsylvania increased from 822.34 miles to 2,542.49 miles, over a 200% increase.[15] Many of the early railroads were constructed as short-distance "feeder" lines, designed primarily to connect the main canal networks or, in the anthracite region, to bring the coal from the mine to the canal. The longer railroads built before the Civil War closely paralleled the canal routes. Constructed to overcome the capriciousness of canal travel, these lines greatly contributed to the financial disaster of the canal system.[16]

Before 1860, railroads tended to enhance existing marketing and commercial patterns rather than carve out new ones. Built over time-worn and well-tried routes of trade, they reinforced existing networks. Moreover, the railroad construction boom was largely confined to the eastern half of the state. "The rivers served the region and Pittsburgh so well," noted Thomas Pavick in his study of the economy of southwestern Pennsylvania in the 1850s, "that comparatively little attention was given to the development of railroad lines until the 1840's, . . . As a result, there was not a single mile of railroad line in operation in southwestern Pennsylvania in 1850."[17] The same generalization can be extended to the northwestern part of the state. In contrast, Schuylkill county in the heart of the anthracite district was laced by over 800 miles of track by the early 1860s, the densest system of railroads in the world.[18]

These agricultural, industrial, and commercial trends encouraged and reinforced regional differences in antebellum Pennsylvania and have served as the major criteria for defining the boundaries of the seven regions. Topography, terrain, agricultural or crop specialization, manufacturing or extractive activity, exports, transportation networks, and market orientation have all been taken into consideration in determining each region's geographical limits.[19] The regional boundaries had to conform with county boundaries as legislative districts used the county as the basic geographical unit. As a result, new counties were occasionally an analytical problem. In 1820, Pennsylvania consisted of 51 counties. By 1860, this number had increased to 65. While most new counties were created from areas within a single region, in five instances a newly-created county belonged in another region different from the one in which it had been previously. In these cases the parent county was treated as a single entity for the earlier decade, and the new county was not placed in the other region until political separation actually occurred. Figure 2 indicates the boundaries of the seven regions, and Table 1 lists the counties in each area for 1820/30 (no new counties were created during this decade), 1840, 1850, and 1860.

Each of the seven regions was marked by distinguishing physiographic characteristics, and each developed a unique economy, shaped by the convergence of various agricultural, industrial and commercial experiences, that set it apart from the other areas of the commonwealth. These are described below in order.

III

Southeastern Pennsylvania, which contained the original land of the proprietary colony, had developed a more sophisticated and complex economy by the middle of the nineteenth century than other regions in the state. Although its population growth rate between 1820 and 1860 was only 134.89%, well below the state rate of 177.44%, the region remained the most populous area in the commonwealth. Over fifty percent the state's population resided in these 13 counties in 1820; by 1860, that figure still remained at forty percent.[20]

Lying within the Older Appalachian or Piedmont chain, the region is particularly famed for its rolling, gentle hills, good, limestone-rich soils, long summers, and short, mild winters.[21] It retained a strong agricultural focus throughout the antebellum years, characterized by growing concentration on cash crops and perishable products for the Philadelphia market.

In 1850 and 1860 the region ranked second of the seven, in terms of percapita farm value, but in terms of absolute

FIGURE 2

THE GEOGRAPHICAL REGIONS OF PENNSYLVANIA

1820/30

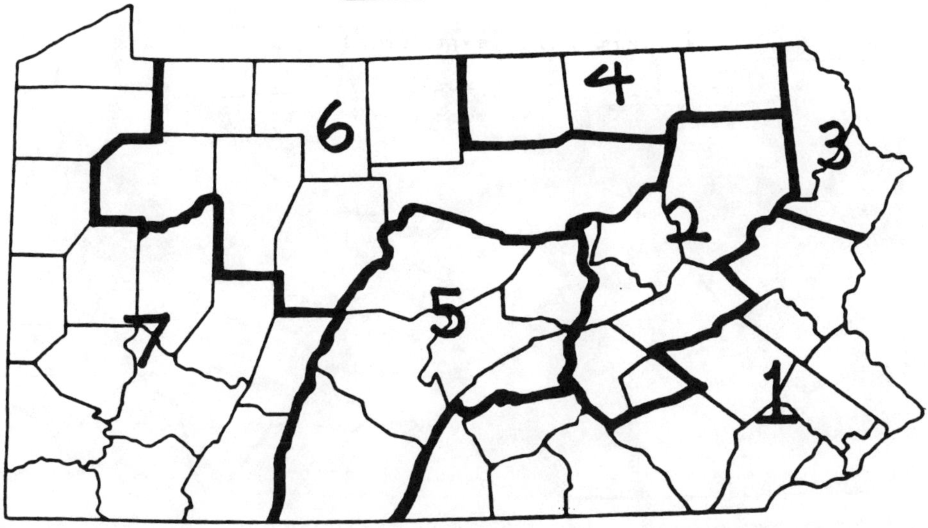

1840

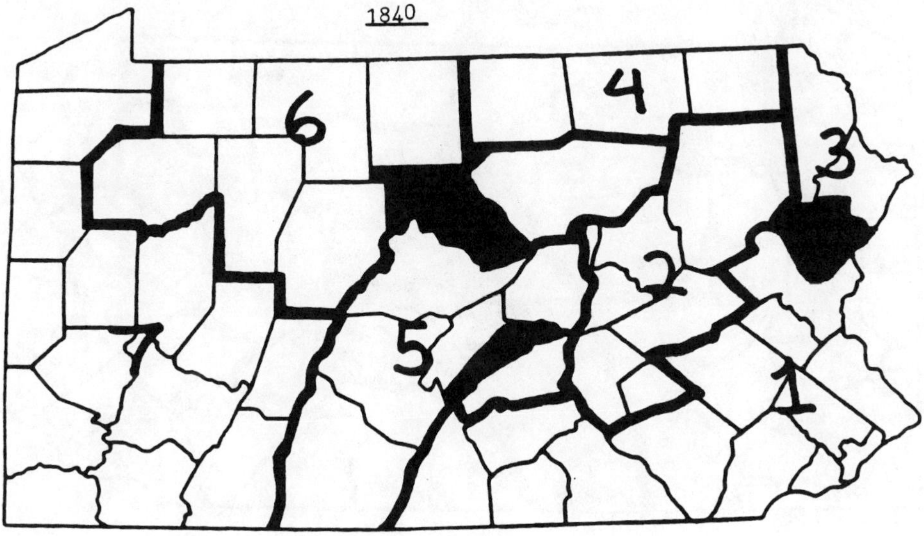

1850

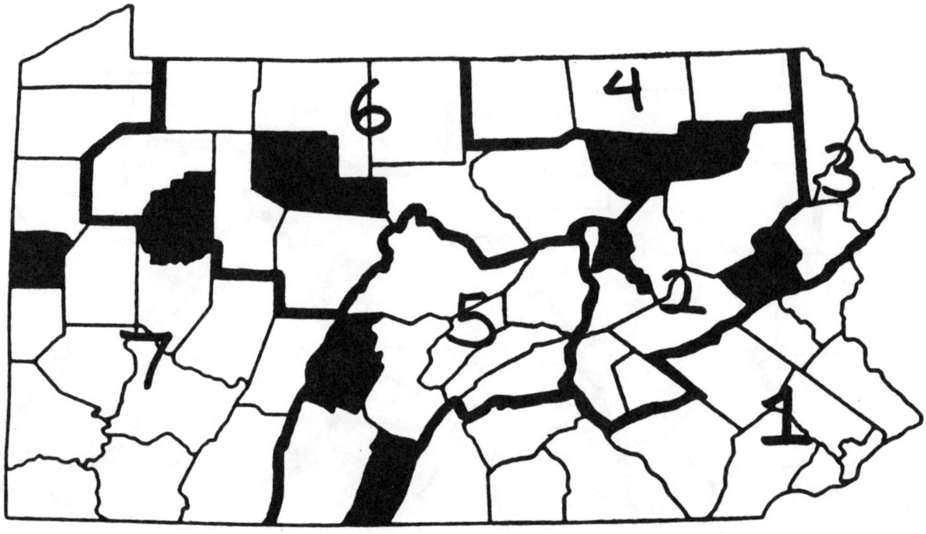

1860

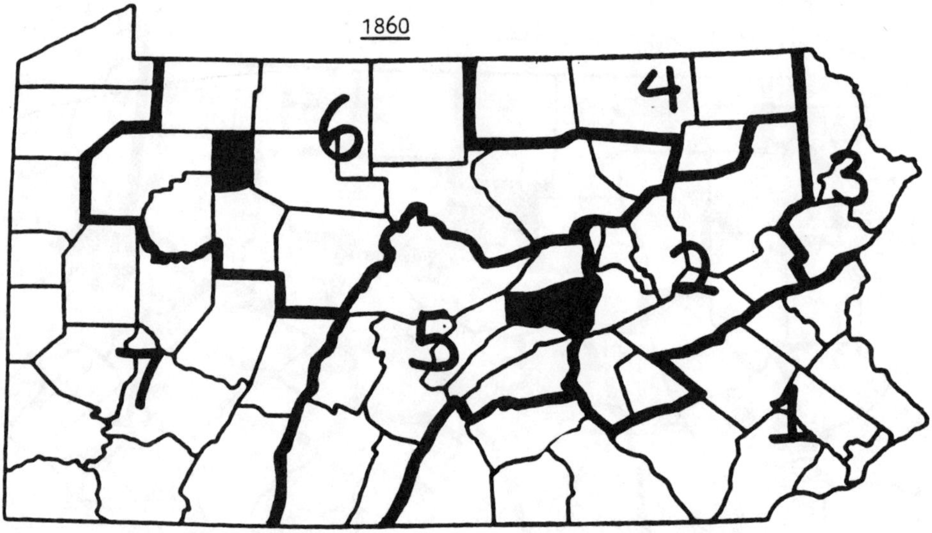

Note: New counties are shaded.

Table 1

THE REGIONS OF ANTEBELLUM PENNSYLVANIA

1820/30	1840	1850	1860
Region 1: Southeastern Region			
Philadelphia	Philadelphia	Philadelphia	Philadelphia
Delaware	Delaware	Delaware	Delaware
Chester	Chester	Chester	Chester
Montgomery	Montgomery	Montgomery	Montgomery
Bucks	Bucks	Bucks	Bucks
Northampton[1]	Northampton[2]	Northampton	Northamptn
Lehigh	Lehigh	Lehigh	Lehigh
Berks	Berks	Berks	Berks
Lancaster	Lancaster	Lancaster	Lancaster
York	York	York	York
Adams	Adams	Adams	Adams
Cumberland	Cumberland	Cumberland	Cumberland
Franklin	Franklin	Franklin	Franklin
Region 2: Anthracite Region			
Dauphin	Dauphin	Dauphin	Dauphin
Lebanon	Lebanon	Lebanon	Lebanon
Northumberland	Northumbrlnd	Northumbrlnd	Northumbrlnd
Schuylkill	Schuylkill	Schuylkill	Schuylkill
Columbia	Columbia	Columbia	Columbia
Luzerne[3]	Luzerne[3]	Luzerne	Luzerne
		Carbon	Carbon
		Montour	Montour
Region 3: Pocono Region			
Wayne	Wayne	Wayne	Wayne
Pike	Pike	Pike	Pike
	Monroe[4]	Monroe	Monroe

oriented to the Lehigh Valley

Region 4: Northeastern Region

Tioga	Tioga	Tioga	Tioga
Bradford	Bradford	Bradford	Bradford
Susquehanna	Susquehanna	Susquehanna	Susquehanna
		Wyoming	Wyoming

Region 5: Ridge and Valley Region

Centre[a]	Centre	Centre	Centre
Bedford	Bedford	Bedford	Bedford
Huntingdon	Huntingdon	Huntingdon	Huntingdon
Mifflin	Mifflin	Mifflin	Mifflin
Perry	Juniata	Juniata	Juniata
Union	Perry	Perry	Perry
	Union	Union	Union
		Blair	Blair
		Fulton	Fulton
			Snyder

Region 6: Allegheny Forest Region

Warren	Warren	Warren	Warren
McKean	McKean	Mckean	McKean
Potter	Potter	Potter	Potter
Venango	Venango	Venango	Venango
Jefferson	Jefferson	Jefferson	Jefferson
Clearfield	Clearfield	Clearfield	Clearfield
Lycoming	Lycoming	Lycoming	Lycoming
	Clinton	Clinton	Clinton
		Clarion	Clarion
		Elk	Elk
		Sullivan	Sullivan
			Forest

Region 7: Western Region

Erie	Erie	Erie	Erie
Crawford	Crawford	Crawford	Crawford
Mercer	Mercer	Mercer	Mercer
Beaver	Beaver	Beaver	Beaver
Washington	Washington	Washington	Washington
Greene	Greene	Greene	Greene
Butler	Butler	Butler	Butler
Allegheny	Allegheny	Allegheny	Allegheny
Fayette	Fayette	Fayette	Fayette
Armstrong[6]	Armstrong[6]	Armstrong	Armstrong
Westmoreland	Westmoreland	Westmoreland	Westmoreland
Indiana	Indiana	Indiana	Indiana
Cambria	Cambria	Cambria	Cambria
Somerset	Somerset	Somerset	Somerset
		Lawrence	Lawrence

[1]Includes future Carbon county and part of future Monroe county
[2]Includes part of future Carbon county
[3]Includes future Wyoming county
[4]Includes part of future Carbon county
[5]Includes part of future Clinton county
[6]Includes part of future Clarion county

values it was the wealthiest area of the state. In 1850, it contained 7 of the 10 wealthiest counties and by 1860, this number had increased to 8. By 1860, 8 of the 10 top wheat producing counties and 9 of the top corn producing counties were here. Six of the region's counties consistently ranked among the top 10 in hay and oats production.[22] While the counties in the southern tier, and particularly Lancaster county, were generally considered to contain the best agricultural land, those to the northeast of Philadelphia were reputed for their high grain yields. Easton, the county seat of Northampton county, had become "the centre of the great grain trade of that part of the valley" by the early 1830s, and the entire area from Northampton county to Lancaster was frequently referred to as "the garden of the state."[23]

The patterns of agricultural specialization within the region became more marked during the first several decades of the nineteenth century. As Diane Lindstrom noted in her study, Economic Development in the Philadelphia Region, by 1840, "the entire greater Philadelphia region engaged in extensive agricultural specialization, . . . The variance among counties in crop mix indicates that general farming (semi-subsistence production with some wheat for export) no longer characterized the region."[24] The counties closest to the urban core shifted toward dairy goods and livestock fattening; the number of pounds of butter and cheese increased by 30% during the 1850s alone and percapita dairy output was much higher than the state average.[25] Chester and Delaware counties' concentration on livestock fattening was commented upon as early as 1825, and Chester County in particular consistently had percapita cattle values well above the regional and state averages.[26]

The region also tended to concentrate on the more lucrative cash crops of the day. In York and Lancaster counties tobacco production expanded, York county dominating in 1840, but Lancaster assuming the lead it would hold throughout the rest of the 19th century.[27] While many other areas of the state were moving out of wheat production as a result of competition from the West, the Southeastern Region increased its production by nearly 62% between 1840 and 1860.[28]

While the Southeastern Region retained a strong, increasingly commerical agricultural orientation throughout the antebellum decades, the most impressive structural shifts in the region's economy occurred in manufacturing. By 1840, Philadelphia and much of the surrounding hinterland, had shifted from commerce to manufacturing.[29]

This shift, as Diane Lindstrom points out, occurred at a relatively early date. Contrary to traditional views, Philadelphia did not necessarily cling to its commercial orientation longer than other Eastern seaboard cities. Indeed, the city's emphasis on manufacturing is readily apparent as early as 1822. The list of articles manufactured in Philadelphia county in that year far surpassed that for any other county in the region or the state. Furthermore, the mix of manufacturing was fairly diverse. Articles which brought an annual market value of $50,000 or better, included boots and shoes, leather products, books, textiles, and iron and brass ware. Production of textiles, boots and shoes, and iron products can be noted in those counties nearest the urban core: Delaware, Montgomery, and Chester. Flour milling, however, remained the single largest manufacturing endeavor in both Montgomery and Chester counties.[30]

By 1850, the entire Southeastern Region had established manufacturing supremacy in the commonwealth. In both the 1850 and 1860 censuses, the region ranked first in percapita value of manufactured goods. In 1850, the value of product for the region was almost 63% of the total for the entire state and by 1860, had risen slightly to 65%. Philadelphia county's percentage of the commonwealth total is even more impressive. This so-called "Manchester of America" accounted for almost 40% of the state's annual value of product in 1850, a figure that approached 47% by 1860![31]

This remarkable industrial concentration in the Southeastern Region owed much to the development of the anthracite resources which facilitated the growth of iron production and iron products. Flour milling remained an important regional activity accounting for 67% of all barrels produced in 1840 and 54% of the total state value in 1860.[32] Textiles, particularly cotton goods, continued to be a regional mainstay. But iron production and machinery grew most dramatically.[33] In 1840, only 3 of the top 10 iron counties were located in the Southeastern Region. By 1860, that number had increased to 6 and the regional annual value of product amounted to nearly 45% of the state total.[34]

Major manufacturing centers emerged in the region outside of Philadelphia. Lancaster county, for example, not only excelled in agricultural produce, but also developed a substantial industrial foundation. In 1839, the county boasted a total of 102 furnaces, forges, and rolling mills within fifty miles of the city of Lancaster.[35] The county, moreover, was able to retain its position among the top ten iron producing counties (based on total dollars invested) between 1840 and 1860 by converting to anthracite furnaces.[36] In addition, Lancaster expanded its manufacturing base to include not only agricultural processing industries such as flour milling and distilling, but textiles, cigars, paper, and rifles.[37]

The iron industry also registered impressive gains in Berks, Lehigh, Northampton, and Montgomery counties. Again, benefiting from the close proximity of the anthracite fields, the manufacture of iron and iron products had become the mainstay of these counties' industrial economies by 1860. Reading had become a major iron center by the late 1840s, and Berks county as a whole claimed a larger number of iron works than any other county in Pennsylvania by 1851.[38]

The four counties to the west of the Susquehanna River, York, Cumberland, Franklin, and Adams, in general did not share in the region's industrial diversity. York county, for example, developed a substantial iron district along the river during the earlier decades of the century. Unlike neighboring Lancaster County, York failed to shift to anthracite fuel, and the iron industry had markedly declined by 1860.[39] Although iron production remained important in these four counties, particularly for the manufacture of agricultural implements, and while York, Adams, and Cumberland counties had become the centers of a substantial coach-making industry as early as the 1830s, this area for the most part drew its economic livelihood from the agricultural processing industries of milling and distilling.[40]

The Southeastern Region's increased agricultural specialization and industrial diversity were promoted by the development of a more efficient transportation system that facilitated movement between the hinterland and Philadelphia as well as between various points of the region itself; tapped the resources of the anthracite country, and secured Philadelphia's position in the larger Mid-Atlantic economy. The Southeastern Region owed its agricultural and industrial superiority in no small part to its rivers. And it was toward the improvement of the Schuylkill, Susquehanna,

Delaware, and Lehigh Rivers that Philadelphia and the region devoted their attention.

Traffic along the Schuylkill, Delaware, and Lehigh Rivers, both before and after canal or slack-water improvements had been made, suited the needs of the region quite well, but the system became even more efficient with the construction of railroads, such as the Philadelphia and Reading. Much more troublesome was the Susquehanna River. Philadelphia and Baltimore engaged in a concerted struggle for control of the trade throughout the Susquehanna valley during the first half of the nineteenth century. At issue was the valuable agricultural trade of the southern tier counties whose turnpike routes as well as the Susquehanna, looked toward Baltimore. Philadelphia, therefore, sought to improve connections between the Susquehanna and the Schuylkill Rivers. While the four counties to the west of the Susquehanna River retained closer connections with Baltimore than most Philadelphians would have liked, transportation improvements by the 1850s had assured that Philadelphia would get at least a respectable share of the trade it had so eagerly sought.[41]

By the eve of the Civil War, the Southeastern Region had developed the most complex, industrially-diversified economy in the state. Although there was a good deal of differentiation within the region as well as some competition for markets, these thirteen counties shared a common economic outlook and similar patterns of development.

That economy, moreover, was closely tied to the increasing availability of coal in the neighboring Anthracite Region.

IV

Although anthracite coal had been used as a fuel on a purely local basis for quite some time, it was not until the War of 1812 that the potential of the fuel became widely known, and therein lies the history of the economic development of the Anthracite Region. Indeed, it is doubtful that large sections of the region would have prospered at all without the exploitation of this valuable mineral base. The terrain of the region is among the most mountainous and rugged in the commonwealth, making both settlement and cultivation difficult. In fact, portions of Schuylkill, Luzerne, Northumberland and Columbia counties were not settled until the 1820s, and a large area of northeastern Carbon county, the so-called "Switzerland of America", was not settled until the following decade.[42] Once the future of anthracite seemed secure, the region's population increased rapidly. The region showed an impressive 236.29% growth rate between 1820 and 1860, with the 1840s registering the greatest increase, an increase that paralleled the marked expansion and application of anthracite to various industrial pursuits.[43]

Although portions of Columbia, Dauphin, Lebanon, and Northumberland counties noted for their agricultural fertility did utilize the Susquehanna River to market some crops, mostly wheat and flour, to Philadelphia and Baltimore,[44] the region as a whole does not measure up well agriculturally. In fact, the number of bushels of wheat percapita as well as the percapita number of sheep and cattle fell steadily. While the region ranked fourth of the seven in terms of percapita farm value in 1850, by 1860, it had the lowest percapita farm value in the state.[45] The energies of the residents of the Anthracite Region were directed toward the most lucrative staple product: anthracite coal.

There were four main fields of anthracite coal: (1) the Northern Field (also known as the Wyoming or Lackawanna Field) in the western portion of Luzerne county; (2) the Western Middle Field (or Lehigh Field) which included parts of Schuylkill, Columbia, and Northumberland counties; (3) the Eastern Middle Field (also sometimes referred to as the Lehigh Field) in the southern portion of Luzerne county and the northern part of Carbon county; and (4) the Southern Field (or Schuylkill Field) which included portions of Schuylkill, Dauphin, and Northumberland counties.[46] The story of the development of the Anthracite Region and these respective coal fields necessarily involves the history of transportation not only within the region, but between the coal fields and the major market centers as well. The Susquehanna River was the logical avenue of transport; howver, the rugged terrain of the region surrounded and shut off the basins of coal from the major rivers.[47] Consequently, a complex network of canals and railroads were constructed to facilitate movement of the coal to market.

During the 1820s and 1830s, six major canals were constructed, two owned and operated by the state. The earliest canals were privately owned, and two, the Lehigh Coal and Navigation Company, and the Delaware and Hudson Canal Company (a joint New York-Pennsylvania venture), were also given the power to own coal estates, rail facilities, and coal boats in order to have more control over the mining, transporting, and marketing of their own coal. Of the other two private canals, the Schuylkill Navigation Company which fed directly into the Southern Field was denied these vast corporate powers and legally allowed only to transport the coal from the mines to the market. The fourth privately-owned canal, the Union Canal, was not built strictly as an anthracite canal. In fact, the canal represents the first attempt to link the Schuylkill and Susquehanna Rivers. Yet by the early 1830s, the Union Canal had constructed feeders into both the Southern and Western fields, and anthracite coal made up the largest amount of its tonnage.[48] The state-owned Delaware Division Canal was designed, in part, to supplement the improvements made by the Lehigh Company, and the route had been completed between Easton and Bristol by 1832.[49] Finally, the canal which ran along the North Branch of the Susquehanna, again financed and built by the state, was intended to tap the Northern Field. Completed as far as Pittston by 1834, it was an engineering nightmare, only partially offset by the fact that the anthracite trade along the route eventually exceeded the original estimates.[30]

While these six canals acted as the major trade arteries for the region, the construction of several smaller canals and numerous railroads served as feeders, facilitating the movement of the coal from the mine to the main shipping points. By 1847, 315 miles of canals and 503 miles of railroad track had been built. Thus, long distance coal traffic throughout the antebellum decades remained largely dependent upon canal traffic. The main exception was the Philadelphia and Reading Railroad. Paralleling the route of the Schuylkill Navigation Company, the Philadelphia & Reading was completed by 1842 and actively demonstrated the enormous superiority of railroad over canal shipment. Although the other canals were equally susceptible to flooding during spring freshets, only the Southern Field gained long-haul railroad access before the late 1850s. The Lehigh Coal and Navigation Company, for example, retained its monopolistic hold over the trade of the middle fields until the very eve of the Civil War. Similarly, the Delaware, Lackawanna & Western Railroad, which provided access to the Northern Field, although chartered earlier than the Lehigh route, was also not fully completed until the late 1850s.[31]

There was little order or systematization to the growth of the railroad feeder lines in the Anthracite Region. The heaviest activity during the four antebellum decades was in the Southern Field. Of the 503 miles of railroad track in the entire region by 1847, 357 (including 94 miles of the Philadelphia & Reading Railroad) were built in this southern area.[52] And by the early 1860s over 800 miles of track traversed Schuylkill county alone.[53] Not surprisingly, the Southern Fields dominated the anthracite trade and provided roughly fifty percent of the supply of coal between 1820 and 1860.[54] Mining towns seemed to spring up overnight. "Here, half a dozen summers since, there was not more than one shabby log hut standing," wrote a Hazard's Register reader from Pottsville, Schuylkill county in 1830,

> . . . The road to Sunbury [Northumberland county] over the broad mountain ran through it, and the weekly stage, in all its courses from Philadelhia to the place of its destination, did not witness a wilder or more desolate scene. . . . But now what a contrast! . . . The town of Pottsville--for under that name we shall include Mount Carbon and Port Carbon, as they are three in one, if not one in three--contains upwards of four thousand people, besides the hordes of Tartar looking people hovering on its skirts. . . . Pottsville has every requisite for becoming a great city--an uninterrupted navigation by canal to Philadelphia, coal enouth to supply the world of thousands of years; . . . Pottsville, bold as the assertion may seem, will rival the large cities of the sea-board in population and wealth.[55]

Although this unbridled optimism in the future of Pottsville was never fulfilled, the town and the region it represented, played an important role in the economic development of antebellum Pennsylvania.

The iron industry of the Southeastern Region benefited greatly from the technological advances made by the application of anthracite to the process of iron production. Although experimentation with the fuel had begun in the 1820s, the first successful anthracite furnace was put into blast in Pottsville in 1839. "The discovery of the process of smelting iron ore with anthracite coal," wrote the author of a nineteenth century Schuylkill county history, "was an event of transcendent importance in the manufacture of iron in Pennsylvania, and, as a resulting consequence in the production of anthracite coal. The impulse it gave to the trade in both commodities diffused inestimable benefits upon commerce, navigation, manufactures, and every industrial pursuit."[36] The Anthracite Region itself shared in the expansion of the iron industry, and to a large degree, was the first area to experiment with new forms of industrial organization.

In 1840, the Anthracite Region accounted for 7.5% of the state's total capital invested in iron production. Twenty years later, this figure had more than doubled to 16%. This increase was primarily located in Lebanon, Montour, Dauphin and Columbia counties.[37] Lebanon county, for example, had easy access to the iron ore deposits in the Cornwall fields and had concentrated on iron production since the colonial period. Once the application of anthracite had been established, Lebanon capitalized on its highly favorable proximity to the Southern Field and soon became one of the top ten percapita producers of iron in the state.[58] Even more impressive was the meteoric rise of Danville, Montour county, as a major iron center. Montour county itself was formed in 1850 after the residents of Danville, angry at losing their place as the county seat of Columbia county, agitated for the creation of a new county. By the end of the decade, the construction of the behemoth iron works at Danville had secured a prominent place for the town and the county within the industry. The county led the state in percapita value of iron production in 1860, registering a whopping $166.77 percapita as compared to the state average of $12.07, and it ranked fifth in the commonwealth in terms of annual value of product.[59]

The development, exploitation, and application of anthracite coal dominated the direction of economic growth in the Anthracite Region between 1820 and 1860. Those counties which contained deposits of the mineral devoted their energies to mining and marketing. Those counties on the fringes of the coal fields engaged in iron production. In either case, anthracite coal served as the common denominator which bound these counties together into a distinctive Anthracite Region.

V

The Pocono Region and the Northeastern Region were the two smallest regions in antebellum Pennsylvania. While each shared certain characteristics with the neighboring

Anthracite and Allegheny Forest Regions, neither was an extension of these larger geographical entities.

The Pocono Region contained some of the most undeveloped territory in the commonwealth between 1820 and 1860. Portions of Monroe county, like neighboring Carbon county were not settled until the late 1820s and 1830s.[60] Indeed, much of the region, with the exception of parts of Wayne county, long remained little more than a wilderness. Even though the region demonstrated relatively strong population growth rates between 1820 and 1860, this was due more to the fact that so few people lived there in 1820 rather than to impressive levels of economic development. Less than one percent of the total state population resided in the Pocono Region in 1820. By 1860, this proportion had not yet reached two percent.[61]

Little commercial activity save lumbering took place in Pike and Monroe counties. The area was heavily wooded, and even when cleared, yielded poor soils. This fact coupled with a short growing season made the region particularly unsuited for grain growing.[62] Percapita measures of bushels of wheat, number of sheep, and number of cattle actually dropped between 1840 and 1850, giving the region the lowest percapita farm value of the seven. Agricultural activity increased during the 1850s, for by 1860, the region registered slight gains in percapita wheat and livestock output, and improved its position to the third lowest region as measured by percapita farm value.[63] Still, very few of these agricultral goods found their way to market.

The lumber industry fared somewhat better. Pike county, for example, ranked in the top ten lumbering counties both in terms of absolute value of product and percapita output in 1840. Twenty years later, Pike's position had slipped considerably, while neighboring Wayne county had secured a place in the top ten. The region did not compare well, however, in manufacturing output or diversity. In both 1850 and 1860, its percapita annual value of product fell below the state average.[64]

One cannot escape the impression that Monroe and Pike counties were considered by contemporary Pennsylvanians as a veritable no-man's land. In Trego's 1843 <u>Geography of Pennsylvania</u>, for example, Monroe county was described as "this hitherto almost inaccessible region . . . so solitary and unfrequented as to be called 'the shades of death.'" Although Trego generously wrote of the county's forest productions as a "lively industry," the rest of his account did little to enhance the image of the county's economy.[65] Similarly, Trego described a large portion of Pike county as "neglected wilderness," and dismissed Milford, the county seat, as "not a place of much importance."[66] While the unruly terrain may have made a thriving economy an antebellum impossibility, the Pocono Region was nevertheless already developing a reputation as a resort area. Indeed, as early as 1832, <u>Hazard's Register</u> described Nagleville in southern Wayne as "a fashionable resort for fishermen, sportsmen, and love-sick dames, and their lovers, who seek a romantic retirement in the Beechwoods."[67]

Wayne county possessed a much more highly developed and diversified economy than its southern neighbors. Although the terrain of Wayne was similar to that of Pike and Monroe, the Delaware and Hudson canal through Honesdale, the county seat, made it more accessible. As a result of this connection, Wayne developed primarily as a satellite of New York City. One year after the completion of the canal in 1829, the county could boast of a number of woolen manufactures and carding machines, a glass factory, and numerous grist and saw mills.[68] By 1860, Wayne county had clearly benefited from its New York City orientation. The metropolis' markets had continued to stimulate the county's textile industry in particular, and had given impetus to other manufacturing concerns.[69] By 1860, Wayne's percapita annual value of all manufactured goods had passed the state average by a respectable margin.[70]

VI

Like the Pocono Region, the Northeastern Region failed to develop a substantial manufacturing base. Unlike the Pocono Region, however, well-defined, commercial agriculture emerged here. Devoting its energies and resources toward livestock raising between 1820 and 1860, this region was more dependent upon agriculture than any other area of the state.[71] Once the land was cleared of dense forests, the terrain and climate proved remarkably well-suited to grazing.[72] The percentage of the total state population increased from 2.44% in 1820 to 4.42% by 1860.[73]

Manufacturing activity remained remarkably minimal between 1820 and 1860. Although the region actually ranked first in terms of percapita annual value of lumber in 1840, and continued to register above the state average in 1860, lumbering appears to have been nothing more than a necessary preliminary step to the more important business of livestock raising. Indeed, in both 1850 and 1860, of all the seven regions, the Northeastern Region had the lowest percapita value of manufactures.[74]

In contrast, the percapita farm value measures were consistently close to the commonwealth average. The regional averages were $184.33 in 1850 and $235.14 in 1860 compared to the respective state averages of $182.80 and $235.04. While the region ranked below the state percapita levels in bushels of wheat produced, the percapita values for cattle and dairy products were roughly double the state averages from 1840 to 1860. There had been a greater emphasis on sheep raising in 1840 than in 1860. The number of sheep percapita in 1840 was almost 2 1/2 times that of the state, but by 1860 the percapita number of sheep had dropped to .87, a figure much closer to the state percapita measure of .79.[75]

The region was hampered in its economic development by a lack of adequate transportation. The major markets for livestock and dairy products lay to the north, across the New York state line and the transportation routes that were eventually built facilitated this avenue of trade. The main transportation improvements, however, were not completed until the 1850s. The North Branch Extension Canal which connected with the North Branch Canal at Pittston was begun in 1836, but work on the canal was suspended between 1841 and 1849 and the route did not reach the New York state line until 1856. Similarly, the Tioga Railroad and the Williamsport and Elmira Railroad were not availble for use until 1853 and 1854 respectively. All three of these routes had a distinct northerly orientation, and each of the three were designed to hook into New York's Chemung Canal feeder network.[74] Despite the comparatively late construction of transportation improvements, the Northeastern Region had developed into a thriving livestock area by the eve of the Civil War, widely renowned for the quality of its cattle and dairy products.

VII

The Ridge and Valley Region, as the name implies, is one of the most topographically complex areas of the state. Indeed, the barriers created by the region's physiography caused antebellum engineers countless headaches in their quest to construct east-west transportation corridors. The region was, nevertheless, well-settled by 1820 and contained approximately 11% of the state's population. During the next four decades, however, the region had the slowest rate of population growth of any of the seven, barely doubling its population by 1860. By the eve of the Civil War, its proportion of the commonwealth's population had slipped to less than 8%.[77] Despite this comparatively small population increase, the region continued to support a healthy agricultural and manufacturing base throughout the antebellum period.

The Ridge and Valley Region, in fact, ranked number one in terms of percapita farm value in both 1850 and 1860. As one of the principal grain-growing districts of the commonwealth, the region also ranked number one in terms of bushels of wheat produced percapita in 1840, 1850, and 1860.[78] The degree of agricultural fertililty, however, varied markedly from county to county, or in reality, from valley to valley. The mountainous ridges were punctuated with valleys of widely variable soil quality. Highly fertile limestone valleys in Mifflin and Centre counties were juxtaposed to the shale valleys of Juniata and Perry counties. The result was a somewhat checkered pattern of agricultural productivity.[79]

Mifflin county emerged as the foremost agricultural producing and processing county in the region. "Perhaps there is no county in the State," wrote county historian Israel D. Rupp in 1847, "in which better wheat is grown than in this. Many of the farms are highly improved and very productive. Upon the whole, this country can vie with any other in the state for its excellence of water, fertility of soil, in some parts, and for its picturesque scenery."[80] Indeed, Mifflin consistently outranked every other county in the region in terms of percapita wheat production, and it was the premier wheat producer in the state in 1840, a position which slipped slightly to second place in 1850 and fourth in 1860. Concomittant with these high wheat yields were the impressive amounts of flour milled between 1840 and 1860. While the region ranked third among the seven in percapita barrels of flour produced in 1840, by the latter date, the Ridge and Valley Region ranked number one in percapita annual value of flour milled, a position due in no small part to the concentration of the industry in Mifflin county. The state average percapita value of flour in 1860 was $10.28 and the region's average was $14.81. Mifflin's, on the other hand, was $40.83, by far the largest percapita average in the commonwealth.[81]

Agriculture continued to play an important role in the economy of the other counties in the Ridge and Valley Region. Their exports consisted primarily of grains and grain by-products, such as flour and whiskey, and these goods were sent down the well-traveled river routes of the Susquehanna and its tributaries, the Juniata and the West Branch. The region's agricultural exports found ready markets in both Philadelphia and Baltimore, as well as in some of the smaller-sized towns along the way. The fertile valleys of the Ridge and Valley Region became one of the major areas of interest in the Philadlphia-Baltimore rivalry for supremacy over the traffic of the Susquehanna River. The region's rivers were among the first to be improved in the 1830s.[82]

Although famed for its agricultural produce, it was for its high-quality charcoal iron that the region was most renowned. While iron was mined in every county of the region, the best red and brown hematite ores were located in Blair (which was part of Huntingdon and Bedford counties until 1846), Centre, and Huntingdon counties, and it was here that the iron industry was most concentrated. In addition to the rich deposits of this valuable mineral, these three counties also possessed more than adequate supplies of timber and limestone, both essential ingredients in the manufacture of Juniata charcoal iron.[83] In 1840, Centre, Huntingdon and Perry ranked among the top ten iron producing counties in the state, and the region ranked first in percapita dollars invested, accounting for 24.43% of all money invested in the iron industry within the commonwealth.[84] By 1860, the region's percent of the total iron investments had dropped to 10.21%, and to fourth place in terms of percapita value of iron production.[85] Older forms of iron production that were dependent upon charcoal and managed primarily by individuals or small partnerships were losing ground to the areas in the east and the west that were successfully experimenting with new mineral fuels and new forms of business organization.[86]

The pigs and bars of Juniata charcoal iron were shipped west to Pittsburgh's rolling mills. Before the completion of the Main Line, it was carried by horseback, an arduous and almost cost-prohibitive form of travel. The route of the Main Line followed the Juniata River, thus cutting through the heartland of the charcoal iron industry. In addition, the eastern terminus of the Allegheny Portage Railroad, the rail portion of the Main Line, was in Hollidaysburg (originally in Huntingdon and later in Blair county). This community remained a major transshipment point for Juniata iron until the Pennsylvania Railroad was completed in 1857. The new railroad passed slightly north of the old route shifting many of Hollidaysburg's economic activities to Altoona, the newly-created terminus of the Pennsylvania Railroad.[87]

The Ridge and Valley Region possessed yet another valuable mineral that deserves at least brief mention. A rich area of bituminous coal was located in the Broad Top Mountain region which included parts of Huntingdon, Bedford and Fulton counties. This 80-square mile bed of coal was discovered early in the nineteenth century, but mining was intermittent and small-scale until the 1840s. By that time, the importance of bituminous coal was becoming ever apparent, particularly in nearby Cambria county, a factor which undoubtedly contributed to the eventual building of the Broad Top Railroad. The route linked the coal fields with the Pennsylvania Railroad in 1856, thus adding a further dimension to the economy of the Ridge and Valley Region.[88]

As varied as the Ridge and Valley Region may appear on the surface, several recurring themes can be detected that served to bind the region together. The increasing specialization in wheat production and flour milling and the continuing concentration in the production of iron are the two most prominent antebellum regional economic trends. In addition, the West Branch, Juniata and Susquehanna rivers created natural regional boundaries. Although the limitations of these water networks were somewhat surmounted by, first, the canals, and later the Pennsylvania Railroad, the trading networks were not greatly affected; regional patterns of agricultural and industrial specialization continued to follow the trends established earlier.

VIII

The Allegheny Forest Region is a vast geographical area located in the northwestern and north-central portions of the state, characterized in the antebellum era, as the name suggests, by thickly wooded forests composed chiefly of valuable white pines and other conifers. This area, like the Ridge and Valley Region, presented almost insurmountable barriers to the construction of adequate transportation routes. Over three-fourths of the region was woodlands, and even when cleared, the soil and the terrain made farming difficult.[89] Large sections of present-day Potter, Mckean, Warren, Forest, and Elk counties were not settled until well into the 1830s.[90] In 1820, only 24,225 people, or 2.31% of the state population lived in the entire region. By 1860, this number had increased to close to 200,000, but still represented less than 7% of the total population of the commonwealth. Much of this region, moreover, remained very sparsely settled. Forest county , for example, was created in 1848, but by 1860, only 898 people lived within its borders![91]

The principal economic activity of the region between 1820 and 1860 involved forest products. First engaged in as a necessary prerequisite to agricultural cultivation, the lumbering industry quickly became an important economic endeavor in its own right. The Allegheny Forest Region is drained directly by the Susquehanna and the Allegheny, and these rivers and their tributaries provided the major avenues of transportation for the lumber industry. Elk, Clearfield, Clinton, Lycoming and Sullivan counties relied on the Susquehanna and its branches to get their timber to market, while Potter, Mckean, Warren, Forest, Venango, Clarion, and Jefferson counties depended on the Allegheny River to export products to Pittsburgh, the major lumber center west of the Alleghenies.

The lumber industry along both transportation routes long remained the domain of the farmer-raftsman. Lumbering offered a source of employment during the agricultural slack seasons as well as a means to market the region's small amount of agricultural surplus. The two types of river craft used, the ark and the raft, were broken up and sold for lumber at the end of the voyage. The ark was constructed to carry a small cargo, usually agricultural goods or furs and pelts, but the raft, had no other purpose than to get the lumber of which it was made to market.[92] Some of these rafts, particularly those along the Allegheny, reached enormous proportions. One, originating in Warren county, allegedly contained 1,500,000 feet of boards and covered an area approaching two acres.[93]

In 1840, the Allegheny Forest Region ranked second behind the Northeastern Region in percapita annual value of lumber produced, and in absolute terms, accounted for 27.81% of the total state value. By 1860, that percentage had increased to 38.91%, and the regional percapita value stood at $24.18 compared to a state average of only $4.15.[94]

Few centers of lumbering activity developed within the region itself between 1820 and 1860. The two most notable lumbering towns were Lock Haven and Williamsport, both located along the West Branch of the Susquehanna River. Lock Haven, Clinton county, stood at the fork of the various tributaries of the West Branch and emerged as a central location and temporary safe harbor for rafts descending the turbulent streams. Groups of six to eight professional rafters then undertook the responsibility of navigating the crafts down the main branch of the Susquehanna River to more centrally-located major market centers.[95] The entire organization of the industry, at least along the West Branch, began to change in the 1850s with the construction of a log boom at Williamsport. While the creation of the boom made Lycoming county the leading lumber area of the 1860s, 1870s, and 1880s, its initial construction met with vehement opposition from the lumber-raftsmen as it seriously threatened the existing patterns of forest exploitation and the transportation of lumber. The tension between the old and new forms of lumbering thus became a consistent theme in the Williamsport area, eventually resulting in open battle in 1857. While the advocates of the boom ultimately emerged victorious, the lumbering practices of the more independent raftsmen remained important on the West Branch, as well as on the Allegheny, throughout the antebellum era.[96]

Although lumbering was clearly the economic mainstay of the Allegheny Forest, some counties did develop more diversified economies. Lycoming County, profiting from its favorable location along the West Branch, was also a major iron producing county, and in fact, ranked among the top ten counties in terms of percapita and absolute investments in 1840. By 1860, however, this had declined to $3.63 compared to a state average of $12.07.[97] Some of the counties in the western half of the region likewise produced modest quantities of iron. The southern half of Clarion county, in particular, was a major iron producing area, transporting its pig metal down the Red Bank, Clarion, and Allegheny Rivers to Pittsburgh. Indeed, the percapita value of iron in Clarion county surpassed the state average by roughly one-third in 1860, a fact which led Clarion residents to refer proudly to their home as "the Iron County."[98] Finally, the counties of Warren and Venango were frequently held up as examples of the economic progress taking place in the forest region. Hazard's Register, often carried accounts of life in Northwestern Pennsylvania during the late 1820s and early 1830s, and the quantities of iron ore, livestock, and agricultural crops produced in Warren and Venango were invariably noted.[99]

The fact remains that for the majority of these counties, the physiography of the region coupled with the lack of adequate transportation throughout the 1820-1860 period meant that lumbering would remain the most lucrative, commercial mainstay of the economy. Although farming was carried on in all counties, it never became an important commercial consideration in any part of the Allegheny Forest Region, remaining instead at subsistence levels. The region was simply too isolated, too unpopulated, and too undeveloped as yet to achieve a more diversified economic base.

The lack of transportation improvements, with the exception of those along the West Branch of the Susquehanna, is especially striking. While the rest of the state was participating in the canal boom during the 1830s, residents of the Allegheny Forest Region bemoaned the lack of adequate turnpike roads. "The Allegheny river, so far as it extends in this county," wrote a Hazard's Register correspondent from McKean county in 1832,

> is navigable for descending craft; large quantities of lumber, such as boards, scantling, joists, timber, and shingles, are annually taken down this river, through this county to market at Pittsburg, Wheeling, and Cincinnati. . . . [Yet] this county has been for years nearly insulated from the surrounding country, and shut off from foreign communications by that insurmountable barrier, our rugged roads.[100]

Nor did the situation change much with the advent of new forms of transportation. Williamsport became the southern terminus of the Williamsport and Elmira Railroad in 1854, thereby providing Lycoming county with an important link to southern New York. The only other railroad worthy of mention, the Sunbury and Erie, reached Warren from Erie in 1859, while the remainder of the proposed route which would have diagonally traversed the entire region was never completed. The Allegheny Forest Region remained, for the most part, unaffected by the monumental transportation advances in the rest of the state.[101]

IX

The region designated as the Western Region may, at first glance, appear much too large and diverse to be considered a single geographical entity. During the antebellum years, however, these counties were linked by three important factors: (1) the region's superior system of navigable rivers and the location of Pittsburgh, the commercial and manufacturing center, at the confluence of the three major water routes; (2) the similarity, with the exception of the coastal plain along Lake Erie, of climate and topography which proved particularly conducive to grain growing and livestock raising; and (3) an abundance of the valuable mineral resources, bituminous coal and iron ore, which could be found in varying degrees in virtually every county of the region.

Pittsburgh's place as the metropolis of western Pennsylvania and the upper Ohio Valley was definitely established by 1800.[102] Due to favorable river location and to the abundant mineral resources which could be transported to the city with relative ease, Pittsburgh, wrote Catherine Reiser in her study of the city's antebellum commercial development,

> was a natural depot for the products of the entire region of Western Pennsylvania, and the rivers flowing from the north and south were the principal arteries of travel and communication. . . By means of the Allegheny River, Pittsburgh was thus able to tap the trade of the northwest area of the State. This river was the principal connecting link between northern and southern

> Pennsylvania prior to 1850. . . . The Monongahela River, on the other hand, tapped the trade of northern Virginia and the extreme southern areas of Pennsylvania in much the same way in which the Allegheny did in northern Pennsylvania. . . . Pittsburgh's geographic importance was further emphasized because the Allegheny Mountains separated eastern and western Pennsylvania and seriously retarded transportation and communication between the two sections.[103]

In many ways, therefore, Pittsburgh dominated the economic life and patterns of development in the Western Region.

Most portions of the region had been explored and settled by 1820. Containing a population of almost 226,000 in 1820, or 21.57% of the state's total, the area's population grew by roughly 200% in the next forty years and the proportion of the total remained approximately the same.[104] Throughout the antebellum period, the majority of the Western Region's residents were dependent on agriculture for their livelihood, concentrating primarily on grains and livestock. In 1850, the region ranked fourth of the seven in terms of percapita farm value, and by 1860, had advanced to third ranked. Although the area showed an overwhelming concentration on livestock raising throughout the 1820-1860 decades, considerable acreage had been devoted to wheat cultivation in the earlier part of the century, particularly in Allegheny, Washington, and Westmoreland counties. Between 1840 and 1860 percapita production fell from 7.66 bushels in 1840, to 6.75 in 1850, to a low of 1.57 in 1860. In contrast, the area had become the leading sheep region by 1850. The Western Region also contained more cattle than any other region in both 1850 and 1860, and ranked a close second behind the Northeastern Region in number of cattle percapita.[105]

The transportation routes for these agricultural products followed several well-established paths. At first, most grain produce was shipped down the Ohio River to New Orleans. With the opening of the Main Line in 1834, farmers gained easier access to eastern markets. While the amount of agricultural produce shipped over the Pennsylvania system never approached the levels transported by its rival, the Erie Canal, the Main Line nevertheless was an important carrier of agricultural products and provisions. Despite its financial and engineering difficulties, the Pennsylvania Canal served as a great boon to the agricultural economy of the Western Region, further enhancing Pittsburgh's position as a depot for western products gathered from surrounding agricultural areas.[106]

Livestock farmers, on the other hand, had always sought their primary markets in the east. Unlike grain growers, the livestock breeders could simply walk their produce to market. The three major cattle driving routes were described in <u>Hazard's Register</u> in 1832: the first followed the National Road through Cumberland, Maryland and then eastward to Baltimore; the second followed the southern Pennsylvania course to Philadelphia; and the third, the northern road through Ebensburg and Huntingdon county to eastern Pennsylvania.[107] The cattle were then fattened in areas, such as Chester county, and ultimately sold in the urban markets. Cattle droving remained an important method of transporting livestock to market throughout the antebellum decades.

Industrial development in the Western Region was relatively uneven before the Civil War, centering almost solely in Allegheny county, and in Pittsburgh, in particular. Indeed, the percapita average of annual value of product for the region as a whole fell well below the commonwealth's average in both 1850 and 1860.[108] Pittsburgh, on the other hand, experienced remarkable growth during the antebellum decades. The city's rise as a manufacturing center has been referred to by Pennsylvania historian, Sylvester K. Stevens, as "the most important single aspect of Pennsylvania's industrial expansion, in terms of its nature and distribution prior to 1860."[109] During these years, Pittsburgh developed a diversified manufacturing base and became a major center of the Pennsylvania iron industry.

The future of the city was apparent as early as 1822, when Pittsburgh manufacturers reported respectable annual market values for a variety of products, including "hoop and slit iron, nails, spikes, &c.," the clear leader with an annual value of $67,500, followed by glass, paper, ale, beer, and porter, hats, and ploughs, harrows, wagons, and carts.[110] By 1840, Allegheny county ranked second only to Philadelphia in terms of percapita capital invested. At mid-century, the county ranked third in percapita value of product behind Philadelphia and Delaware counties, and by 1860 had slipped to a close fourth behind Montour, Delaware and Philadelphia.[111] Renowned for its iron products, Pittsburgh was referred to as the "Birmingham of America" as early as 1829.[112] By 1860, the city had secured its postion as the major western supplier of manufactured goods, including steam engines, agricultural tools and implements, machinery, glass, and woolen textiles.[113]

The counties in the immediate vicinity of Allegheny played an important role in the rise of Pittsburgh as a major manufacturing center. These areas fulfilled a critical function as suppliers of iron pigs to the Pittsburgh foundries and rolling mills. Fayette and Westmoreland counties, for example, were important iron centers during the 1820s, 30s, and 40s. Although the iron output from these two counties diminished significantly in the 1850s, other counties in the region stepped in to provide Pittsburgh with a steady supply of iron. By 1860, Indiana, Armstrong, Butler, Mercer, and Lawrence were all producing iron for the Pittsburgh mills.[114]

Equally important to the economy of the Western Region was the development of the bituminous coal industry, especially in the southwestern corner of the state along the Monongahela River. In 1840, the top five bituminous producing counties were Allegheny, Fayette, Washington, Armstrong, and Westmoreland. By 1860, Fayette and Armstrong reported no bituminous coal production, while Allegheny,

Washington, Westmoreland, and Cambria accounted for 89.6% of the total value of bituminous coal produced in that year.[115] This ready supply of bituminous coal not only fueled the industries of Pittsburgh, but in large part, was responsible for the rise of Johnstown, Cambria county, as a major iron center by the eve of the Civil War. "This town is surrounded by coal, which may be dug from the hills on every side," reported Hazard's Register in 1835."

> No spot in the United States, not even Pittsburg, possesses greater facilities, or offers superior advantages to the enterprising manufacturer than this place. Iron ore, pigs, and blooms, are to be procured in the greatest abundance, in the neighboring counties,and the means of transportation are so cheap and convenient as to dispel every doubt on the subject.[116]

Despite this optimistic pronouncement, Cambria's industrial revolution did not really "take-off" until the 1850s. As late as 1850, the county registered percapita manufacturing values well below the state average. By 1860, this figure had surpassed the state average, and Cambria showed a percapita value of iron products second only to Montour, the great iron-producing county of the Anthracite Region.[117] Allegheny county, then, along with Cambria, represented the two major centers of industrial growth in the antebellum Western Region. Although the counties bordering Ohio, notably Beaver, Lawrence, Crawford and Erie, showed signs of developing a broader manufacturing base, all registered percapita manufacturing values well below the state and regional averages in both 1850 and 1860.[118] These counties would become more important industrial areas in the post-Civil War era, but their economies retained a dominant agricultural orientation from 1820 to 1860.

Transportation patterns for both agricultural and manufactured products tended to follow the well-established river and canal routes. Railroad construction came comparatively late to western Pennsylvania, in part a testimony to the serviceability of the river and canal traffic. Although the opening of the Pennsylvania Railroad in the early 1850s facilitated certain types of trade, the rivers and canals continued to play an important role since many of the items produced in the Western Region--coal, lumber, bar and sheet iron, and steam engines--were simply too bulky to be handled by these early railroads.[119] As a result, antebellum residents of the Western Region continued to rely on the rivers and the canals as their major transportation network. Indeed, coal traffic along the Monongahela slack-water navigation registered a three-fold increase during the 1850s alone. The entire Western Region continued to be shaped both geographically and economically by the patterns of river and canal traffic established early in the antebellum era.

X

The dominant economic trends toward agricultural specialization, industrialization, and the exploitation of mineral and natural resources, then, were played out in different ways in the seven regions of antebellum Pennsylvania. Each geographical area developed a unique economy shaped by physiographic conditions that either encouraged the cultivation of wider commercial contacts, or restricted the residents to more locally-oriented activities. Some sections moved quickly into manufacturing; others continued to devote the majority of their time to various agricultural pursuits. The growing demand for timber and coal led those areas naturally endowed with these resources to concentrate on extractive industries.

Yet each region was far from homogeneous. Considerable internal economic variability, and in some cases, tension existed within these regions. The following chapter will direct more attention to the differentiation between the counties and emphasize the complex patterns within each of Pennsylvania's seven regions between 1820 and 1860.

FOOTNOTES

[1]Burton W. Folsom, Jr. Urban Capitalists: Entrepreneurs and City Growth in Pennsylvania's Lackawanna and Lehigh Regions, 1800-1920 (Baltimore and London: Johns Hopkikns Press, 1981), p. 9.

[2]Stevenson Whitcomb Fletcher, Pennsylvania Agricultural and Country Life, 1840-1940 (Harrisburg: Pennsylvania Historical and Museum Commission, 1955), p. 128; Percy W. Bidwell and John I. Falconer, History of Agriculture in the Northern United States, 1620-1860 (Washington: Carnegie Institution of Washington, 1925), p. 327.

[3]Fletcher, pp. 121-27.

[4]Willard W. Cochrane, The Development of American Agriculture: A Historical Anaylsis (Minneapolis: University of Minnesota Press, 1979), pp. 71-72; Fletcher, pp. 1-2, 98-99.

[5]In his forthcoming study of the political economy of Virginia, for example, Van Beck Hall was able to isolate distinct regions in early nineteenth century Virginia based in part upon the distinct crop systems of the various regions.

[6]Sylvester K. Stevens, Pennsylvania: Titan of Industry, 3 vols. (New York: Lewis Historical Publishing Co., 1948), 1:256-57.

[7]Paul F. Paskoff, Industrial Evolution: Organization, Structure, and Growth of the Pennsylvania Iron Industry, 1750-1860 (Baltimore and London: Johns Hopkins University Press, 1983).

[8]These rankings are based on the value added by manufacturing data for 1860 as adjusted to the 1963 SIC categories. See Albert Niemi, Jr., State and Regional Patterns in American Manufacturing, 1860-1900 (Westport, Conn.: Greenwood Press, 1974), pp. 114-167.

[9]James Elliott Defebaugh, History of the Lumber Industry of America (Chicago: The American Lumbreman, 1906-09), vol. 2, pp. 517, 530; Fletcher, pp. 330-32.

[10] See, for example, George Rogers Taylor, The Transportation Revolution, 1815-1860 (New York: Holt, Rinehart, & Winston, 1951; reprint ed. Armonk, N.Y.: M.E. Sharpe, Inc., 1977); Louis Hartz, Economic Policy and Democratic Thought: Pennsylvania, 1776-1860 (Cambridge:

Harvard University Press, 1948; reprint ed., Chicago: Quadrangle Paperback Books, Inc., 1968); Julius Rubin, Canal or Railroad? Imitation and Innovation in the Response to the Erie Canal in Philadelphia, Baltimore, and Boston (Transactions of the American Philosophical Society, New Series, Vo. 51, Part 7, 1961).

[11]Taylor, pp. 17-18; Charles A. Williams, "The History and Operations of the Pennsylvania Turnpike System" (Ph.D. dissertation, University of Pittsburgh, 1954), p. 38.

[12]See Christopher T. Baer, Canals and Railroads of the Mid-Atlantic States, 1800-1860 (Greenville, Wilmington, Delaware: Regional Economic History Research Center, Elelutherian Mills-Hagley Foundation, 1981), for the dates of organization and completion of the various canals and railroads in Pennsylvania.

[13]Taylor, pp. 44-45.

[14]James W. Livingood, The Philadelphia-Baltimore Trade Rivalry, 1780-1860 (Harrisburg: Pennsylvania Historical and Museum Commission, 1947); Richmond E. Meyers, "The Development of Transportation in the Susquehanna Valley: A Geographical Study, 1700-1900 (Ph.D.dissertation, The Pennsylvania State College, 1951).

[15]United States. Executive Documents. House of Representatives. Second Session of the 37th Congress, 1861-62. Table No. 38: "Railroads of the United States" (Washington: Government Printing Office, 1862).

[16]Baer, Canals and Railroads; Taylor, p. 45.

[17]Thomas Peter Pavick, "An Economic History of Southwestern Pennsylvania, 1850-1860" (Ph.D. dissertation, West Virginia University, 1973), pp. 54-56.

[18]C. K. Yearley, Jr. Enterprise and Anthracite: Economics and Democracy in Schuylkill County, 1820-1875 (Baltimore: Johns Hopkins Press, 1961), p. 28.

[19] In 1937, Raymond and Marion Murphy devised sets of regions for Pennsylvania at various points in time. Their regional configurations which incorporated a variety of physical, social and economic attributes have stood the test of time remarkably well. The 1840 group of regions has particular relevance for the present study. This schema, which falls directly in the middle of the period under examination, seems to reflect and embody the patterns of economic differentiation extraordinarily well. Thus, after much consideration, further experimentation, and application of the above-mentioned criteria, the Murphy regions have served, to a large degree, as a primary guideline of the

seven regions outlined in this study. See Raymond E. Murphy and Marion Murphy, Pennsylvania: A Regional Geography (Harrisburg: The Pennsylvania Book Service, 1937), pp. 113-134.

The author is also indebted to geographer Wilbur Zelinsky whose article "What Are the Regions of Pennsylvania?," paper presented at the 78th Annual Meeting of the Pennsylvania Federation of Historical Societies, Bethlehem, Pennsylvania, April 12, 1985, helped immeasurably in determining the criteria to use when defining the regions of antebellum Pennsylvania.

[20]Ninth Census of the United States, 1870, Volume 1: Population (Washington, D.C.: Government Printing Office, 1871), p. 58. The 1870 census gives the corrected population figures for all previous censuses for Pennsylvania and its various counties. These populations have been used as the basis for all population statistics and resulting calculations throughout the remainder of this study.

[21]Raymond and Marion Murphy, Pennsylvania Landscapes: Geography of the Commonwealth (State College, PA: Penns Valley Publishers, 1951), p. 96.

[22]J. D. B. Debow, comp. Statistical View of the United States . . . Being a Compendium of the Seventh Census (Washington, 1854), pp. 296-301(herein after referred to as Census of 1850); Agriculture of the United States in 1860; Compiled from the Original Returns of the Eighth Census (Washington: Government Printing Office, 1865), pp. 122-25 (herein after referred to as the Agricltural Census of 1860).

[23]Hazard's Register of Pennsylvania, 23 March; 14 September 1833.

[24]Diane Lindstrom, Economic Development in the Philadelphia Region, 1810-1850 (New York: Columbia University Press, 1978), pp. 140-41.

[25]Sixth Census of the United States, 1840. Compendium of Enumeration of Inhabitants and Statistics of the United States (Washington: Thomas Allen, 1841) (herein after referred to as the Census of 1840); Census of 1850 and Agricultural Census of 1860. The dairy statistics in 1840 were recorded in terms of value of products of the dairy, while the 1850 and 1860 censuses reported in terms of pounds of butter and cheese produced.

[26]Bidwell and Falconer, p. 234-5; Censuses of 1850 and 1840; Agricultural Census of 1860. The cattle data for 1840 and 1850 includes all neat cattle, and for 1860 includes milch cowns, working oxen, and other cattle.

[27]Fletcher, p. 154-5.

[28]Censuses of 1840 and 1850, Agricultural Census of 1860.

[29]Fletcher, p. 164; Lindstrom, passim.

[30] Fourth Census of the United States, 1820. Book II: Digest of the Accounts of Manufacturing Establishments in the United States and of their Manufactures (Washington: Gales & Seaton, 1823) (herein after referred to as the Manufacturing Census of 1822).

While there are problems and limitations in using the 1822 manufacturing census, it can nevertheless be used to demonstrate a county's general degree of economic diversification.

Flour was listed as a manufactured article in Delaware county, but no value was given.

[31]Census of 1850, Manufactures of the United States in 1860; Compiled from the Original Returns of the Eighth Census (Washington: Government Printing Office, 1865), pp. 493-544 (herein after referred to as the Manufacturing Census of 1860); Stevens, p. 163.

[32]Census of 1840; Agricultural Census of 1860.

[33]Lindstromm, pp. 254, 157.

[34]Census of 1840; Manufacturing Census of 1860. The 1840 iron data includes all cast iron plus bar iron produced. The 1860 iron figures include all iron and iron products listed under manufactures of each county.

[35]Klein, Harry Martin John, Lancaster County, Pennsylvania: A History (New York: Lewis Historical Publishing Co.,1924), pp. 656-57.

[36]Frederick Moore Binder, Coal Age Empire: Pennsylvania Coal and Its Utilization to 1860 (Harrisburg: Pennsylvania Historical and Museum Commission, 1974), pp. 66-69; Census of 1840, Manufacturing Çensus of 1860.

[37]Klein, p. 670; Hazard's Register 16 July 1831; Stevens, pp. 165-8; Carlton O. Wittlinger, "Early Manufacturing in Lancaster County, Pennsylvania, 1710-1840" (Ph.D. dissertation, University of Pennsylvania, 1953), passim.

[38]Morton L. Montgomery, History of Berks County in Pennsylvania (Philadelphia: Everts, Peck & Richards, 1886), pp. 98, 692.

[39]Meyers, p. 101; Stevens, pp. 165-68; Census of 1840; Manufacturing Census of 1860.

[40]History of Cumberland and Adams Counties, Pennsylvania (Chicago: Warner, Beers, & Co., 1886), p. 256; Stevens, pp. 165-8; 210-11; Hazard's Register 5 February 1831.

[41]Livingood, Philadelphia-Baltimore Trade Rivalry.

[42]John William Florin, The Advance of Frontier Settlement in Pennsylvania, 1638-1850: A Geograhic Interpretation (University Park, PA: Department of Geography, Pennsylvania State University, 1977), pp. 81-82, 85-86; Alfred Mathews and Austin N. Hungerford, History of the Counties of Lehigh and Carbon in the Commonwealth of Pennsylvania (Philadelphia: Everts & Richards, 1884),p. 650.

[43]Census of 1870, Population volume.

[44] Israel D. Rupp, History and Topography of Northumberland, Huntingdon, Mifflin, Center, Union, Columbia, Juniata, and Clinton Counties, Pennsylvania (Lancaster, PA: G. Hills, 1847), p. 315; George H. Morgan, Centennial: The Settlement Formation and Progress of Dauphin County, Pennsylvania from 1785 to 1876 (Harrisburg: Telegraph Steam Book and Job Printing House, 1877), p. 109; Frederic K. Miller, "The Rise of an Iron County: An Economic History of Lebanon County from 1740-1865" (Ph.D. dissertation, University of Pennsylvania, 1948), pp. 65-7, 193-95.

[45]Censuses of 1840 and 1850; Agricultural Census of 1860.

[46]Robert D. Billinger, Pennsylvania's Coal Industry (1954), p.17; J. Bogen, The Anthracite Railroads (New York: Ronald Press, 1927), pp. 4-5; Donald F. Schaefer, "A Quantitative Description and Analysis of the Growth of the Pennsylvania Anthracite Coal Industry, 1820 to 1865" (Ph.D. dissertation, University of North Carolina, 1967), pp. 4-9.

[47]Meyers, p. 106.

[48]H. Benjamin Powell, "The Pennsylvania Anthracite Industry, 1769-1976," Pennsylvania History 47(January 1980): 6-8.

[49]Chester Lloyd Jones, The Economic History of the Anthracite-Tidewater Canals (Phildelphia: University of Pennsylania Press, 1908), pp. 60-61.

[50]H. Benjamin Powell, Philadelphia's First Fuel Crisis: Jacob Cist and the Developing Market for Pennsylvania Anthracite (University Park, PA: Pennsylvania State University Press, 1979), pp. 137-38.

[51]Bogen, pp. 14-15, 22-23, 82-84.

[52]Ibid., pp.14-15.

[53]Yearley, p. 28.

[54]History of Schuylkill County, Pennsylvania (New York: W. W. Munsell, 1881), p. 62.

[55]Hazard's Register, 27 November 1830.

[56]History of Schuylkill County, pp. 50-51.

[57]J. H. Battle, History of Columbia and Montour Counties (Chicago: A. Warner & Co., 1887), pp. 32-34; George P. Donehoo, Harrisburg and Dauphin County: A Sketch of the History for the Past Twenty-five years, 1900-1925 (Dayton, Ohio: The National Historical Association, 1925), vol 1., pp. 158-59; Miller, Lebanon County, pp. 200-03; Stevens, pp. 214-17.

[58]Miller, Lebanon County; pp. 200-03; Census of 1840, Manufacturing Census of 1860. These figures are based upon the percapita capital invested.

[59]Battle, pp. 22-23; Manufacturing Census of 1860.

[60]Florin, pp. 81-82; 84-85.

[61]Census of 1870, Population volume.

[62]Murphy and Murphy, Landscapes, p. 173.

[63]Censuses of 1840 and 1850; Agricultural Census of 1860.

[64]Censuses of 1840 and 1850; Manufacturing Census of 1860. The lumbering data for 1860 includes both lumber, sawed and lumber, planed.

[65]Charles B. Trego, A Geography of Pennsylvania (Philadelphia: E. C. Biddle, 1843), pp. 298-301.

[66]Ibid., pp. 340-41.

[67]Hazard's Register, 28 July 1832.

[68]Hazard's Register, 8 August 1829.

[69]Linda Pritchard, "Religious Change in a Developing Region: The Social Contexts of Evangelicalism in Western New York and the Upper Ohio Valley during the Mid-Nineteenth Century" (Ph.D. dissertation, University of Pittsburgh, 1980), pp. 99-100.

[70]Manufacturing Census of 1860.

[71]Murphy and Murphy, *Landscapes*, pp. 184-93; Henry C. Bradsby, *History of Bradford County, Pennsylvania* (Chicago: S. B. Nelson & Co., 1891), p. 2; *History of Tioga County, Pennsylvania* (New York: W. W. Munsell & Co., 1883), pp. 57-60; *Hazard's Register*, 4 February 1832.

[72]*Hazard's Register*, 16 July 1831.

[73]Census of 1870, Population volume.

[74]Censuses of 1840 and 1850; Manufacturing Census of 1860.

[75]Censuses of 1840 and 1850; Agricultural Census of 1860.

[76]Baer, *Canals and Railroads*.

[77]Census of 1870, Population volume.

[78]Censuses of 1840 and 1850; Agricultural Census of 1860.

[79]Murphy and Murphy,*Landscapes*, pp. 136-54.

[80]Rupp, *History and Topography of Northumberland . . . and Clinton Counties*, p. 229.

[81]Censuses of 1840 and 1850; Agricultural Census of 1860.

[82]Blair County Historical Society, *Blair County's First Hundred Years, 1846-1946* (Altoona, PA: The Mirror Press, 1945), pp. 353-58; Ellis, Franklin and A.N. Hungerford, *History of that Part of the Susquehanna and Juniata Valleys embraced in the Counties of Mifflin, Juniata, Perry, Union and Snyder in the Commonwealth of Pennsylvania* (Philadelphia: Everts, Peck & Richards, 1886), pp. 2-3, 20; *A History of the Juniata Valley*, 3 vols. (Harrisburg: Telegraph Press, 1936), 2: 41-62; *Hazard's Register*, 19 January 1828; Livingood, passim.

[83]Stevens, pp. 60-61.

[84]Census of 1840.

[85]Manufacturing Census of 1860.

[86]Paskoff, pp. 91-132.

[87]J. Simpson Africa, History of Huntingdon and Blair Counties, Pennsylvania (Philadelphia: L. H. Everts, 1883), pp. 4-5; Blair County's First Hundred Years, pp. 381-84; Tarring S. Davis, ed., A History of Blair County, Pennsylania, 2 vols. (Harrisburg: National Historical Association, 1931) 1: 255-56; Paul Kurtz, Blair, Main Line: A History of the Tuckahoe Valley (Bellwood, PA: Bicentennial of the Bellwood Antis Area, 1976), pp. 104-6; 113, 129, 137.

[88]Blair County's First Hundred Years, pp. 381-4; History of the Juniata Valley, 2:515-21; Milton Scott Lytle, History of Huntingdon County, in the State of Pennsylvania (Lancaster: William H. Roy,1876), p. 163; Israel D. Rupp, The History and Topography of Dauphin, Cumberland, Franklin, Bedford, Adams, Perry, Somerset, Cambria, and Indiana Counties (Lancaster: Gilbert Hills, 1848), p. 492.

[89]Murphy and Murphy, Landscapes, pp. 194-223.

[90]Florin, p. 86.

[91]Census of 1870, Population volume; Florin, pp. 82-83, 84-85.

[92]Thomas R. Cox, "Transition in the Woods: Log Drivers, Raftsmen, and the Emergence of Modern Lumbering in Pennsylvania," Pennsylvania Magazine of History and Biography 104(January 1980): 346-49; Meyers, pp. 112-13, 122.

[93]Defebaugh, p. 623.

[94]Census of 1840; Manufacturing Census of 1860.

[95]Defebaugh, pp. 602-03.

[96]Cox, pp. 345-46.

[97]Census of 1840; Manufactuing Census of 1860; Hazard's Register, 4 October 1834, 22 August 1835.

[98]Aaron J. Davis, History of Clarion County, Pennsylvania (Syracuse: D. Mason & Co., 1887), p. 114; Manufacturing Census of 1860.

[99]See, for example, Hazard's Register, 22 August 1829; 5 July 1834.

[100]Ibid., 14 July 1832.

[101]Baer, Canals and Railroads.

[102]Solon J. Buck and Elizabeth Hawthorne Buck, The Planting of Civilization in Western Pennsylvania (Pittsburgh: University of Pittsburgh Press, 1939), pp. 217-8; Binder, p. 42; Stevens, p. 168.

[103]Catherine Elizabeth Reiser,Pittsburgh's Commerical Development, 1800-1850 (Harrisburg: Pennsylvania Historical and Museum Commission, 1951), pp. 1-2.

[104]Census of 1870, Population volume.

[105]Censuses of 1840 and 1850; Agricultural Census of 1860.

[106]Reiser, pp. 43-44, 100-101.

[107]Hazard's Register, 1 September 1832.

[108]Census of 1850; Manufacturing Census of 1860.

[109]Stevens, p. 168.

[110]Manufacturing Census of 1822.

[111]Censuses of 1840 and 1850; Manufacturing Census of 1860.

[112]Hazard's Register, 3 October 1829.

[113]Thomas Cushing, et al., History of Allegheny County, Pennsylvania (Chicago: A. Warner & Co., 1889), pp. 550-56, 597-602; Hazard's Register, 11 August 1832; Reiser, pp. 191-3.

[114]Hazard's Register, 10 December 1831; Stevens, pp. 213-14.

[115]Census of 1840; Manufacturing Census of 1860.

[116]Hazard's Register, 25 July 1835.

[117]Censuses of 1840 and 1850; Manufacturing Census of 1860.

[118]Census of 1850, Manufacturing Census of 1860.

[119]Pavick, pp. 60-63.

CHAPTER THREE

THE COMMERCIAL-ECONOMIC CONTINUA

Not all Pennsylvania counties developed at the same rate or in the same way during the antebellum years. The counties within a given region did share common patterns of economic involvement. But some counties developed more quickly than others; some grasped new economic opportunities before their neighbors; some were favored with more abundant natural resources, and some, because of a strategic transportation location, became tied into a broader commercial network sooner than adjacent counties.

To explore these variations, an index has been created which ranks each county according to its level of economic development and the degree to which it was integrated into larger commercial and financial networks. An awareness of the comparative advantages and disadvantages of one's community coupled with the extent of its commercial involvement helped to create a perception of the county's economic future; this, in turn, was reflected in the behavior of the district's representatives on the floor of the state assembly. Counties with well-established multi-state or even multi-regional economic and commercial contacts placed very different types of demands upon the state government than those from counties with more localized economies.

Representatives may have had their region's interests in mind when they went to Harrisburg, yet those from the more economically and commercially developed counties in the region envisioned a future for their area that was significantly different from that envisioned by those from the less developed counties. These varying perceptions had a profound impact on legislative debates, policy outcomes, and the general role of the state in economic affairs.

II

Five major measures have been used to construct the commercial-economic continuum for each of the four decades: (1) agricultural magnitude; (2) manufacturing magnitude; (3) percapita postal receipts; (4) percapita bills discounted by the county's banks; and (5) real and personal property assessments. The concept of magnitude, which is used in the first two measures and as the basis of the final continua, was developed by E. Willard Miller who used the method extensively in the final section of <u>An Economic Atlas of Pennsylvania</u>.[1] Van Beck Hall, likewise, employed a similar logic in constructing a commercial-cosmopolitan continuum in his study of late-eighteenth century Massachusetts, <u>Politics Without Parties</u>.[2] Magnitude, to use Miller's definition, "refers to the relative significance or importance of a selected economic or cultural aspect in a county. The magnitude formula may be expressed as $M = \frac{\Sigma X}{n}$ where M is the magnitude, X is the individual rank of the county in the series of data, Σ is the summation of all the values of X and n is the number of criteria used."[3] Use of multiple criteria helps to give a more reliable picture of each county's relative development by reducing the effect of peculiarities in individual variables such as inaccurately recorded data or abnormally skewed population distribution. Magnitude combines a number of related measures into a single index number which can be used to describe a county's position vis a vis the other counties in the state.

The concept of magnitude is first used to construct more manageable agricultural and manufacturing profiles. The data come primarily from the Censuses of 1840, 1850, and 1860, which recorded the agricultural and manufacturing statistics from the preceding years. The postal and banking data are taken from the midpoints of each decade, or 1826, 1835, 1845 and 1855; and property values from 1829-31, 1845, and 1855.[4] Due to the paucity of data, 1820-1830 has been treated as a single period. These other continua are drawn from the final four years of each of the remaining decades, 1835-39, 1845-49, and 1855-59. The commercial-economic continua assign a single index number to each county; this number in turn expresses the county's relative level of commercial-economic development for each of the four decades.

With the exception of property valuation data, the ranks are based on percapita figures.[5] The use of absolute values would give overwhelming preponderance to counties like Philadelphia and Allegheny at the expense of smaller counties whose inhabitants might be just as industrially or commercially oriented as those in the metropolitan areas. Percapita figures, on the other hand, help to uncover how a particular county's residents might perceive the larger economic world by indicating how affected or dependent they were on various financial and economic developments. They indicate how crucial agriculture, manufacturing, or mining was for each county's inhabitants and, through the postal and banking measures, how much they were tied to broader financial and commercial networks.

The index numbers which serve as the basis for the four continua are not strictly comparable from one decade to the next. For one thing, the range of each scale changes due to the addition of fourteen counties between 1820 and 1860. Thus, an index number or rank of 25 in 1820 would not be the same as a similar rank forty years later. Dividing each magnitude into five groups of an approxmiately equal number of counties, however, does permit some degree of comparison between years. A county's pace and relative level of commercial-economic development can be traced over the years through its movement, or lack thereof, in and out of the five groups along the four continua.

These four continua, then, help to clarify the degree of complexity which characterized commercial and economic development in antebellum Pennsylvania. All counties in the state experienced economic growth and commercial expansion between 1820 and 1860. While some counties remained in one of the five groups throughout the four decades, most counties' relative positions or rankings shifted considerably. Agricultural and manufacturing specialization coupled with improved transportation produced a trend toward increasing commercial, industrial, and financial concentration in several key counties, and more particularly, in several key regions.

III

The agricultural data reveal the process of specialization occurring in most sections of Pennsylvania. The variables used in the calculation shifted from decade to decade depending upon the availability of data. The Census of 1820, for example, listed only the number employed in agriculture. By 1840, census statistics on a wide variety of agricultural products had been added. The 1850 and 1860 census reports began to record more precise data, such as the value of farms and the number of improved acres. While the agricultural magnitudes of 1849 and 1859 are undoubtedly the most sophisticated scales, they can be compared with data from earlier decades.

The four agricultural scales included: (1) 1820: number employed in agriculture as a percentage of county population; (2) 1839: number employed in agriculture as a percentage of county population, and percapita crop statistics for wheat, corn, cereal grains (a combination of rye, oats, and buckwheat), hay, cattle, sheep, and value of dairy products; (3) 1849 and 1859: percapita value of farms and implements, average value of farms and implements, number of acres of improved farmland as a percentage of total county area, and percapita crop statistics for the same products analyzed for 1839.[6] The agricultural magnitudes for 1839, 1849 and 1859 were calculated by constructing county rankings for percapita production of each crop and for other available measures. These ranks were then added together and divided by the number of categories of data used. For comparative and mapping purposes, the final agricultural index numbers were divided into five equal groups. The resulting patterns can be seen in Figures 3-6. Those counties in the highest ranked group are considered to be the most dependent on agriculture for their livelihood, while those in the lower groups engaged in other types of economic activity as well.

Because the 1820 map is based only upon employment data, the top ranked counties turn out to be those in some of the most undeveloped areas of the commonwealth, such as the Allegheny Forest Region and the Pocono Region. This is largely a result of the population structure of frontier societies which have a disproportionate number of young men and women of working ages. Those counties with rocky terrain, such as Schuylkill and Luzerne, on the other hand, rank appropriately at the bottom of the scale, and those with more highly diversified economies, most notably

Allegheny, Philadelphia, and Delaware, also register rather low levels of agricultural dependency. The top ranked counties, therefore, were the most agriculturally dependent ones and not necessarily the wealthiest agricultural areas.

Crop statistics and employment data give a good indication of the areas of agricultural concentration in 1839 and foreshadow patterns that become stronger in the final two decades. Counties in southwestern Pennsylvania, northwestern Pennsylvania, and along the Susquehanna and Juniata Rivers all emerged as fourth or fifth ranked counties by 1839. In the Southeastern Region, Lancaster, Chester, and Bucks were already among the top ranked counties, while the southern tier counties of Franklin, Adams and York moved into the middle rank. In contrast, the Anthracite Region counties remained solidly in the bottom two groups, along with counties from the other regions that were becoming increasingly dependent upon the extractive resources.

The farm value and improved acreage data used in the calculations for 1849 and 1859 indicate the degree of agricultural specialization that had occurred by the eve of the Civil War. The most obvious trend is the increasing concentration of top ranked counties in the Southeastern Region. Although some of the northeastern and southwestern counties as well as Mifflin county in the Juniata Valley continued to hold their own with an increase in livestock raising and grain-growing, respectively, the southeastern

FIGURE 3

AGRICULTURAL MAGNITUDE, 1820

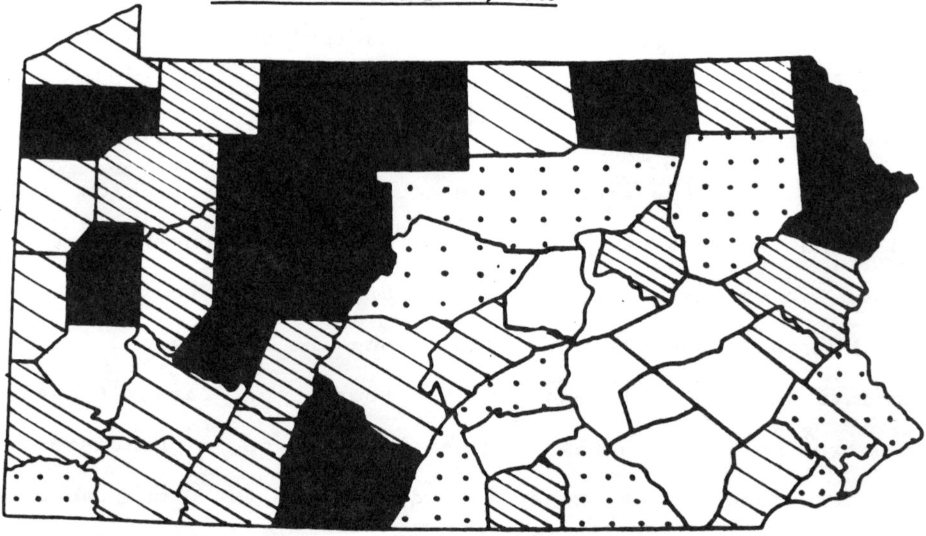

Criteria Used: Agricultural employment as percentage of county population.

Lowest Rank: Philadelphia, Union, Northumberland, Cumberland, Lancaster, Schuylkill, Dauphin, Berks, Lebanon, Allegheny

Second Rank: Montgomery, Centre, Perry, Bucks, Franklin, Delaware, Greene, York, Lycoming, Luzerne

Third Rank: Westmoreland, Mifflin, Lehigh, Chester, Huntingdon, Fayette, Mercer, Beaver, Tioga, Erie

Fourth Rank: Adams, Northampton, Washington, Columbia, Cambria, Susquehanna, Venango, Warren, Somerset, Armstrong

Highest Rank: Crawford, Bedford, Indiana, Jefferson, Potter, Bradford, Wayne, McKean, Butler, Clearfield, Pike

FIGURE 4

AGRICULTURAL MAGNITUDE, 1839

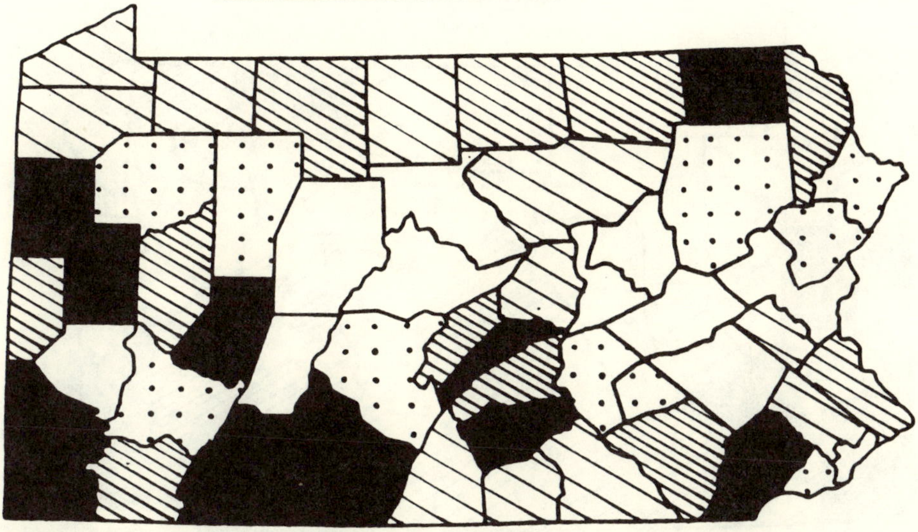

Criteria Used: Agricultural employment as percentage of county population*; Percapita crop production for wheat, corn, cereal grains, hay, cattle, sheep, value of dairy products

- Lowest rank: Philadelphia, Schuylkill, Allegheny, Cambria, Clearfield, Berks, Northampton, Northumberland, Centre, Clinton, Columbia, Carbon
- Second rank: Monroe, Dauphin, Lebanon, Huntingdon, Luzerne, Venango, Jefferson, Westmoreland, Pike, Delaware
- Third rank: Adams, York, Crawford, Lehigh, Montgomery, Union, Lycoming, Erie, Franklin, Potter, Warren
- Fourth rank: Wayne, Beaver, Lancaster, Fayette, McKean, Mifflin, Bradford, Tioga, Bucks, Perry, Armstrong
- Highest rank: Susquehanna, Bedford, Cumberland, Mercer, Indiana, Somerset, Washington, Chester, Butler, Greene, Juniata

*Employment data missing for Berks, Clearfield and Wayne

FIGURE 5

AGRICULTURAL MAGNITUDE, 1849

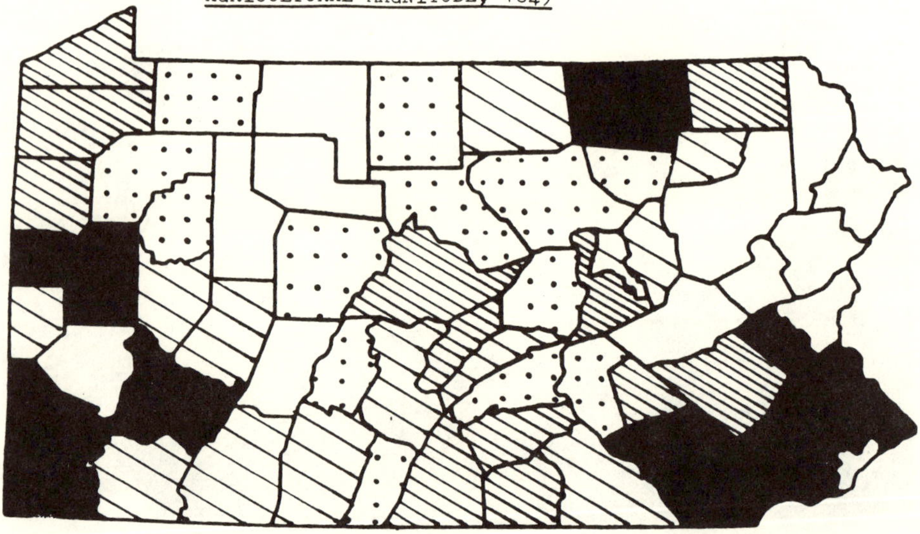

Criteria Used: Percapita farm value; Average value per farm; Improved acres as percent of total county area; Percapita crop production for wheat, corn, cereal grains, hay, cattle, sheep, pounds butter and cheese

Lowest Rank: Carbon, Northampton, Schuylkill, McKean, Philadelphia, Luzerne, Elk, Cambria, Wayne, Allegheny, Pike, Jefferson, Monroe

Second Rank: Lycoming, Clearfield, Blair, Fulton, Clinton, Clarion, Perry, Potter, Sullivan, Dauphin, Warren, Union, Venango

Third Rank: Armstrong, Bedford, Columbia, Indiana, Fayette, Huntingdon, Tioga, Beaver, Wyoming, Montour, Juniata, Somerset, York

Fourth Rank: Northumberland, Crawford, Lebanon, Mercer, Erie, Franklin, Centre, Mifflin, Adams, Cumberland, Berks, Susquehanna

Highest Rank: Greene, Butler, Bradford, Lehigh, Lawrence, Delaware, Montgomery, Lancaster, Bucks, Washington, Chester, Westmoreland

FIGURE 6

AGRICULTURAL MAGNITUDE, 1859

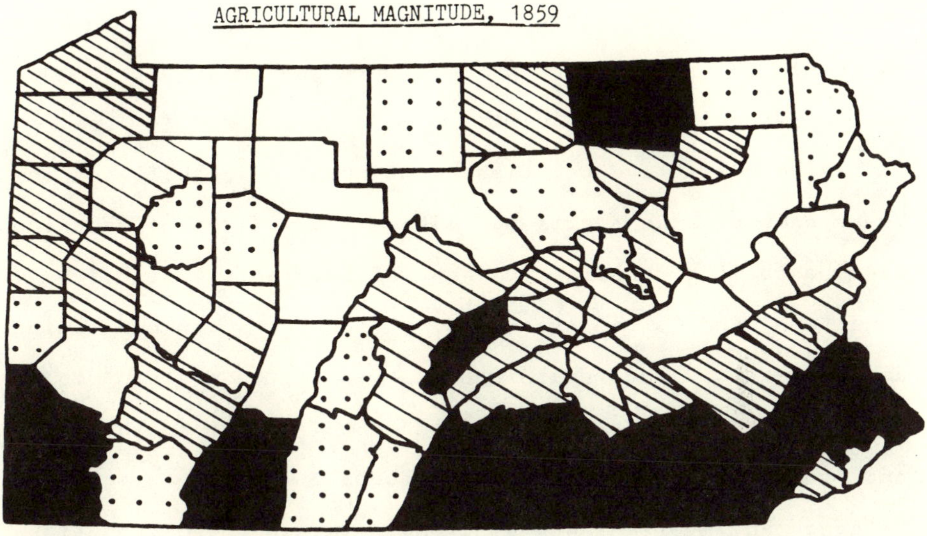

Criteria Used: Percapita farm value; Average value per farm; Improved acres as percent of total county area; Percapita crop production for wheat, corn, cereal grains, hay, cattle, sheep, pounds of butter and cheese

Lowest Rank: Carbon, Schuylkill, Elk, Philadelphia, Cambria, Luzerne, Allegheny, Forest, Monroe, Clinton, McKean, Warren, Clearfield

Second Rank: Fulton, Blair, Pike, Jefferson, Potter, Lycoming, Montour, Wayne, Susquehanna, Beaver, Clarion, Fayette, Bedford

Third Rank: Armstrong, Juniata, Dauphin, Sullivan, Columbia, Centre, Snyder, Northumberland, Huntingdon, Perry, Indiana, Northampton, Venango

Fourth Rank: Berks, Tioga, Crawford, Lehigh, Erie, Delaware, Westmoreland, Wyoming, Butler, Lawrence, Union, Lebanon, Mercer

Highest Rank: Franklin, Montgomery, Cumberland, York, Greene, Lancaster, Bradford, Adams, Mifflin, Somerset, Washington, Bucks, Chester corner had become the "Garden of Pennsylvania," the wealthiest agricultural area in the commonwealth. Clearly, the continued emphasis on wheat-growing coupled with the favorable proximity to both Baltimore and Philadelphia had profound and lasting results.

The extractive counties continued their shift to the lower ends of the spectrum. This relatively poor showing was due to the comparative lack of favorable agricultural conditions and to an ever-growing concentration on mining and lumbering. The remaining counties in the Western Region and the Ridge and Valley area tended to cluster in the third and fourth ranked agricultural groups. While agriculture remained an important economic mainstay in these counties, they lacked the close proximity to markets, and the overall fertility of the land that made the Southeastern Region such a wealthy agricultural area.

IV

The manufacturing data also reflected increasing specialization and industrial concentration. The manufacturing census conducted in the early 1820s is too incomplete and inconsistent to use in systematic, multi-county analysis. Consequently, the only reliable data available for the 1820s are, once again, manufacturing employment figures, which exist for each of the four time periods. In addition, percapita capital investment data were used for 1839, 1849 and 1859, and percapita annual value of product figures for 1849 and 1859.[7]

As Figures 7-10 demonstrate, the manufacturing trends between 1820 and 1860 were much sharper and more distinct than for agriculture. The 1820 map shows very definite areas of concentration of manufacturing employment. The overwhelming majority of the top ranked counties clustered in the Southeastern Region. As the longest settled area of the state, these counties had developed larger scale milling establishments, and a more thriving artisan-craft sector; they were also among the first to support extensive iron production. At the other end of the state, Allegheny county and its most important early supplier of iron, Fayette county, stand out as important manufacturing centers. Somewhat perplexing is Pike county's appearance in the top ranked group. Since the county also scored high on the agricultural scale in 1820, Pike's peculiar population structure must have meant that the majority of the residents were employed in agriculture or in lumbering as a necessary preliminary to farming. There is no way to determine how the census enumerator made the distinction between agriculture and manufacturing.

The counties at the lower end of the spectrum in 1820 were located in the sparsely inhabited northern tier. Warren county, however, emerged as a fourth level county in this early decade, a position it would retain. Warren's relatively high regional rank came from its favorable location on the Allegheny River which has its headwaters in northern Potter county, meanders through southwestern New York, then reenters Pennsylvania in Warren. The town of Warren benefited from its location at the fork of several main tributaries and became the site of considerable saw milling and other manufacturing concerns.

By 1839, this pattern of manufacturing concentration had changed considerably. A temporary shift of concentration began from the Southeastern Region into the extractive areas of the Anthracite Region and the Juniata Iron counties. Wayne county also emerged as a top ranked manufacturing county, due in part to the initial growth of its textile industry along with Honesdale's favorable location as the terminus of the Delaware and Hudson Canal. The counties at the lower end of the manufacturing continuum were clustered for the most part in predominantly agricultural areas: the Western Region (with the notable exception of Allegheny county), and the Northeastern Region. Many of the Allegheny Forest counties, on the other hand, had moved into the middle ranks, and those with easier access to the West Branch of the Susquehanna River, Lycoming and Clinton, registered a relatively high rank.

By 1849, the commonwealth's manufacturing configuration had shifted again. The concentration of industry in the counties immediately surrounding and including Philadelphia became more apparent as well as the emergence of the Anthracite Region and the small iron-producing county of

FIGURE 7

MANUFACTURING MAGNITUDE, 1820

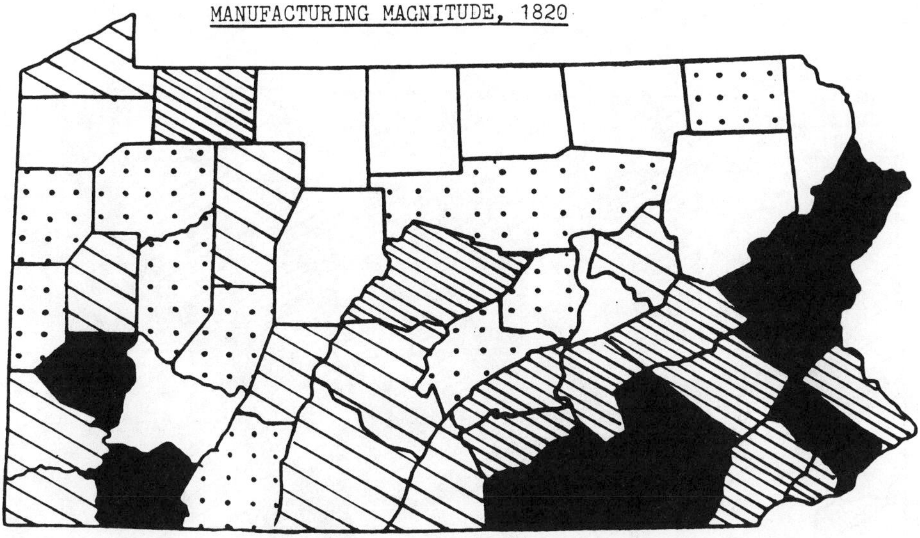

Criteria Used: Manufacturing employment as percentage of county population

Lowest Rank: Bradford, Clearfield, Northumberland, Tioga, Wayne, Westmoreland, Potter, Luzerne, McKean, Crawford

Second Rank: Union, Mercer, Susquehanna, Venanto, Beaver, Armstrong, Indiana, Mifflin, Somerset, Lycoming

Third Rank: Butler, Cambria, Erie, Huntingdon, Bedford, Greene, Washington, Franklin, Columbia, Jefferson

Fourth Rank: Delaware, Perry, Bucks, Schuylkill, Cumberland, Chester, Warren, Berks, Centre, Dauphin

Highest Rank: Lehigh, Allegheny, Montgomery, Fayette, York, Northampton, Lancaster, Lebanon, Adams, Philadelphia, Pike

FIGURE 8

MANUFACTURING MAGNITUDE, 1839

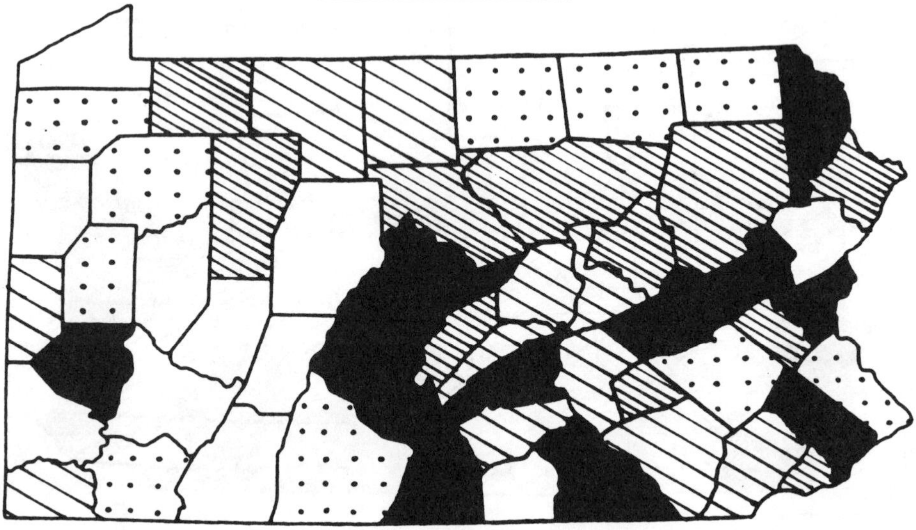

Criteria Used: Manufacturing employment as percentage of county population*; Percapita dollars invested in manufacturing, coal and iron; Percapita value of lumber

Lowest Rank: Clearfield, Mercer, Westmoreland, Armstrong, Adams, Indiana, Somerset, Cambria, Monroe, Erie, Washington

Second Rank: Susquehanna, Crawford, Bedford, Butler, Bucks, Venango, Fayette, Tioga, Bradford, Berks

Third Rank: Greene, Union, Chester, Potter, Beaver, Juniata, McKean, Cumberland, Dauphin, Northumberland, Lancaster

Fourth Rank: Lycoming, Warren, Columbia, Mifflin, Pike, Jefferson, Luzerne, Lebanon, Clinton, Delaware, Lehigh

Highest Rank: Centre, Schuylkill, Perry, Huntingdon, Wayne, York, Franklin, Montgomery, Allegheny, Northampton, Philadelphia

*Employment data missing for Berks, Clearfield and Wayne counties.

FIGURE 9

MANUFACTURING MAGNITUDE, 1849

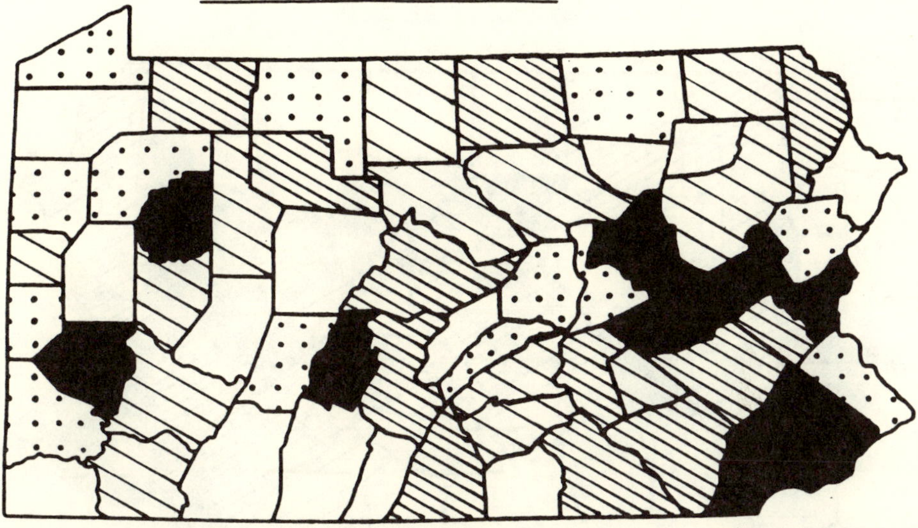

Criteria Used: Manufacturing employment as percentage of county population; Percapita dollars invested in manufacturing; Percapita annual value of manufactured products

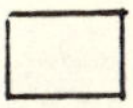

Lowest Rank: Indiana, Greene, Wyoming, Sullivan, Somerset, Crawford, Mifflin, Butler, Fulton, Bedford, Adams, Pike, Clearfield

Second Rank: Washington, Mercer, Bradford, McKean, Monroe, Northumberland, Union, Juniata, Venango, Erie, Beaver, Bucks, Cambria

Third Rank: Westmoreland, Lawrence, Susquehanna, Potter, Perry, Fayette, Clinton, Armstrong, Jefferson, Cumberland, Lebanon, Luzerne, Lycoming

Fourth Rank: York, Wayne, Tioga, Elk, Dauphin, Franklin, Warren, Centre, Lehigh, Berks, Lancaster, Huntingdon

Highest Rank: Columbia, Northampton, Chester, Blair, Clarion, Carbon, Montour, Montgomery, Allegheny, Schuylkill, Delaware, Philadelphia

FIGURE 10

MANUFACTURING MAGNITUDE, 1859

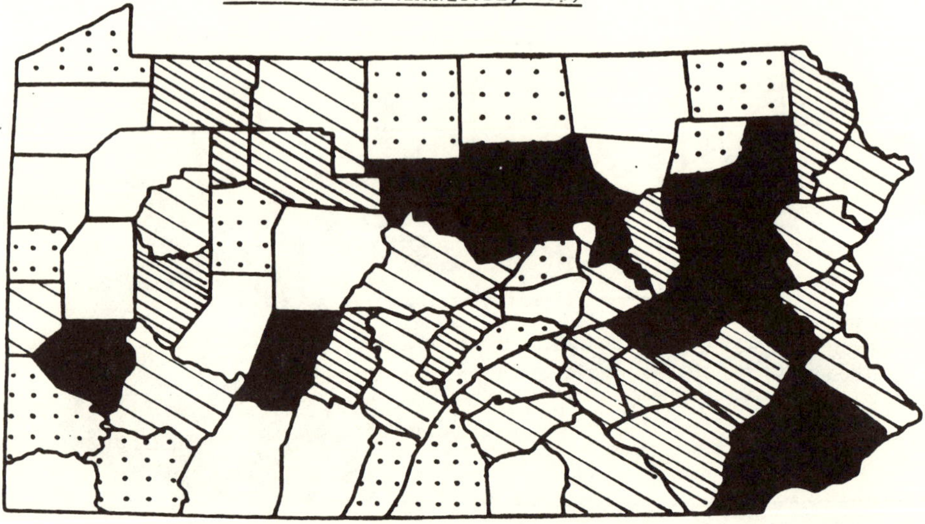

Criteria Used: Manufacturing employment as percentage of county population; Percapita dollars invested in manufacturing; Percapita annual value of manufactured products

(blank)	Lowest Rank:	Sullivan, Mercer, Indiana, Butler, Greene, Clearfield, Somerset, Crawford, Snyder, Adams, Venango, Bedford, Bradford
(dotted)	Second Rank:	Potter, Lawrence, Washington, Fulton, Juniata, Fayette, Wyoming, Union, Jefferson, Susquehanna, Tioga, Erie, Franklin
(wide hatching)	Third Rank:	Bucks, Huntingdon, Beaver, Westmoreland, McKean, Monroe, York, Centre, Cumberland, Perry, Pike, Clarion, Northumberland
(dense hatching)	Fourth Rank:	Warren, Elk, Lebanon, Blair, Forest, Mifflin, Dauphin, Lancaster, Wayne, Columbia, Armstrong, Northampton, Berks
(solid black)	Highest Rank:	Chester, Clinton, Lycoming, Montgomery, Luzerne, Cambria, Lehigh, Carbon, Allegheny, Schuylkill, Delaware, Montour, Philadelphia

Montour. Top rank counties in other areas stand out like regional beacons. Blair county, for example, retained its position as the center of the Juniata Iron district. Although the other iron counties in the Ridge and Valley region had slipped a notch by 1850, Blair's position was more secure due to its propitious position on the Pennsylvania Main Line. In the Western Region, Allegheny county stood out as the manufacturing center. Of more interest is Clarion county's high rank. Clarion, it will be recalled, had a brief period of major iron production in the 1840s and early 1850s, a fact that is clearly demonstrated in the 1849 manufacturing census.

The 1859 data resembles that of 1849 with a few important changes. The number of top ranked counties in the Anthracite Region expanded to include the northern coal fields, or Luzerne county. While the Southeastern Region continued to contain a disproportionate share of the fourth and fifth ranks, this concentration was increasingly confined to those counties east of the Susquehanna River, as the relative position of Cumberland, York, Adams and Franklin counties had slipped considerably. A similar decline can be noted in the Ridge and Valley counties. While Blair, which had become the home of a major Pennsylvania Railroad center, Altoona, in the early 1850s, still ranked in the fourth level along with the flour milling center, Mifflin, the remainder of the region's counties fell into the lower groups. The lumber industry led to the sharp rise of Clinton and Lycoming counties by 1859 and the growth of iron production in Johnstown made Cambria county a dominant manufacturing area in the Western Region. The lowest ranked manufacturing counties continued to be those in heavily agricultural areas: the northern part of the Western Region, and the Northeastern Region.

Although the Southeastern Region and Allegheny county are most often perceived as the primary industrial centers of antebellum Pennsylvania, their relative position between 1820 and 1860 was not always as dominant as one might think. Even though the southeastern counties were indisputably the wealthiest in absolute terms, other major manufacturing centers had developed as well. Manufacturing concerns were relatively just as important to the inhabitants of these smaller-scale centers as to the residents of Allegheny county and Philadelphia. This, in turn, contributed to a common outlook among state legislators from these counties.

V

While agricultural and manufacturing statistics identify important economic trends, annual postal receipts tell us much more about commercial patterns and help to isolate the major marketing centers. Collected by the United States Postal Service each year, these records list the annual net amount of receipts passing through each post office. Although some of this mail was purely personal, most, argues geographer Alan Pred, "was accounted for by shipping merchants, commission merchants, brokers, factors, retailers, and other commercial agents."[8] These records provide a reasonably accurate gauge of the degree of commercial involvement of a given county or community. For the purposes of the present study, the Pennsylvania postal returns for the years ending March 31, 1826 and 1836, and for the years ending June 30, 1845 and 1855 were used.[9]

The number of post offices in the commonwealth increased dramatically between 1826 and 1855. The 580 offices in 1826, had increased to 2081 by 1855. Comparison over time of total or percapita changes in postal receipts is difficult due to reductions in postal rates.[10] More and more Pennsylvanians utilized the postal service as the antebellum years wore on. The average number of post offices per county rose from 11.3 in 1826 to 32.5 in 1855. Yet, commercial activity as measured by postal volume concentrated disproportionately in the highly commercial areas of Pennsylvania.

In constructing the four commercial-economic continua, the aggregate percapita postal receipts for each county, and their respective rankings were used. But the percentage of post offices and of postal receipts compared to the percent of the total population by region more dramatically highlights the enormous concentration of commercial activity in a few selected regions and counties. (See Table 2.) Counties in the Southeastern Region accumulated a masively disproportionate share of the postal receipts despite the fact that the percentage of post offices consistently fell below the population percentage.

In contrast, the percentage of post offices in the more undeveloped areas--the Pocono, Northeastern, and Allegheny Forest Regions--consistently surpassed the percentage of population, testimony to the increasing effort on the part of the federal government to improve access to the postal system. Although the percentage of postal receipts in these areas gradually increased, they consistently fell below the comparable population percentage. Post offices more nearly matched population in the Anthracite, Ridge and Valley, and Western regions, but only in the Anthracite counties did net receipts approach these same levels. In the Western counties, receipts were roughly one-half the population, although a slight gain can be detected by 1855. In the Ridge and Valley Region, on the other hand, overall increase in receipts was remarkably minimal, and these figures ranged from within only one-third to one-half of the population. Clearly, residents in the Southeastern Region, and to a lesser degree, those in the Anthracite counties, made the greatest use of postal facilities.

The location and yearly receipt totals of the post offices that registered in the ninety-ninth percentile in terms of annual volume are even more striking. (See Table 3.) In 1826, for example, the six post offices in the top one percent accounted for 73.54% of all receipts registered in Pennsylvania. Of those six, four were located in the

TABLE 2

PERCENTAGE OF POST OFFICES AND POSTAL RECEIPTS BY REGION, 1826-1855

Region	% state population	% number post offices	% postal receipts
Southeastern			
1826	50.47	37.41	77.42
1835	47.27	36.67	66.92
1845	44.55	32.59	71.41
1855	44.10	30.13	63.82
Anthracite			
1826	9.81	10.34	6.49
1835	9.81	11.40	10.49
1845	10.54	10.70	8.93
1855	11.38	10.81	11.57
Pocono			
1826	0.81	2.41	.24
1835	1.08	2.21	.55
1845	1.57	3.73	.62
1855	1.86	3.94	1.03
Northeastern			
1826	2.97	8.28	1.07
1835	3.74	8.34	1.46
1845	4.64	8.97	1.53
1855	4.49	8.79	2.05
Ridge and Valley			
1826	9.52	14.14	3.57
1835	9.14	11.57	4.83
1845	8.06	10.41	3.62
1855	7.43	9.47	3.89

Allegheny Forest			
1826	2.74	5.00	.83
1835	3.80	8.85	1.88
1845	5.54	10.48	1.77
1855	6.36	12.83	2.62
Western			
1826	23.68	21.55	10.38
1835	25.16	20.60	13.89
1845	25.09	23.12	12.14
1855	24.38	24.03	15.01

Source: See footnote 8.

Southeastern Region, one in the Western Region, and one, the state capital, Harrisburg, in the southern part of the Anthracite Region. By 1835, the total percentage of receipts accrued by the twelve post offices in the ninety-ninth percentile had slipped slightly to 68 percent. Again, the Southeastern Region had by far the greatest number of post offices in this group, while the Anthracite Region had acquired a second top level post office, and Lewistown (Mifflin county) had emerged as a commercial center in the Ridge and Valley Region. In 1845, the percentage of total receipts passing through the post offices in the top one percent, had climbed again to 74.07%, while the spatial distribution of these facilities remained roughly similar to that of 1835.

By 1855, all of the regions, with the exception of the Northeastern Region, were represented in the 20 top percentile post offices which accounted for 70.76% of all postal activity in that year. The Southeastern Region had the most highly developed commercial network of the seven regions. With the two main post offices in Philadelphia county at the apex, seven other main commercial centers were rather evenly spaced throughout the region in the counties of Lancaster, Berks, Northampton, York, Chester, Cumberland and Montgomery. No other region in the commonwealth could even begin to match this level of postal activity. The Anthracite Region and the Western Region were, however, showing signs of more pervasive commercialization by 1855.

TABLE 3

NINETY-NINTH PERCENTILE POST OFFICES, 1826-1855

Post Office	County	Region	% postal receipts
1826			
Philadelphia	Philadelphia	Southeastern	62.37
Pittsburgh	Allegheny	Western	3.95
Harrisburg	Dauphin	Anthracite	3.46
Lancaster	Lancaster	Southeastern	1.54
Reading	Berks	Southeastern	1.11
Carlisle	Cumberland	Southeastern	1.11
		Total percentage	73.54
1835			
Philadelphia	Philadelphia	Southeastern	49.50
Pittsburgh	Allegheny	Western	6.73
Harrisburg	Dauphin	Anthracite	5.21
Lancaster	Lancaster	Southeastern	1.29
Reading	Berks	Southeastern	0.99
Pottsville	Schuylkill	Anthracite	0.89
Carlisle	Cumberland	Southeastern	0.79
Easton	Northampton	Southeastern	0.66
York	York	Southeastern	0.63
Chambersburg	Franklin	Southeastern	0.45
Lewistown	Mifflin	Ridge/Valley	0.44
Columbia	Lancaster	Southeastern	0.42
		Total percentage	68.00
1845			
Philadelphia	Philadelphia	Southeastern	58.75
Pittsburgh	Allegheny	Western	5.39
Harrisburg	Dauphin	Anthracite	4.31
Lancaster	Lancaster	Southeastern	0.82
Pottsville	Schuylkill	Anthracite	0.76
Easton	Northampton	Southeastern	0.66
Carlisle	Cumberland	Southeastern	0.56
Reading	Berks	Southeastern	0.46
Kensington	Philadelphia	Southeastern	0.45
York	York	Southeastern	0.43
Chambersburg	Franklin	Southeastern	0.41
Wilkes Barre	Luzerne	Anthracite	0.40
Hollidaysburg	Huntingdon	Ridge/Valley	0.34
Allegheny	Allegheny	Western	0.33
		Total percentage	74.07

1855

Philadelphia	Philadelphia	Southeastern	48.61
Pittsburgh	Allegheny	Western	6.42
Harrisburg	Dauphin	Anthracite	4.48
Lancaster	Lancaster	Southeastern	1.30
Pottsville	Schuylkill	Anthracite	1.14
Reading	Berks	Southeastern	1.10
Easton	Northampton	Southeastern	1.07
Kensington	Philadelphia	Southeastern	1.00
Allegheny	Allegheny	Western	0.65
York	York	Southeastern	0.63
West Chester	Chester	Southeastern	0.55
Carlisle	Cumberland	Southeastern	0.51
Norristown	Montgomery	Southeastern	0.46
Wilkes Barre	Luzerne	Anthracite	0.45
Hollidaysburg	Blair	Ridge/Valley	0.43
Honesdale	Wayne	Pocono	0.40
Hyde Park	Luzerne	Anthracite	0.39
Minersville	Schuylkill	Anthracite	0.38
Meadville	Crawford	Western	0.37
		Total percentage	70.70

Source: See footnote 8.

Top percentile post offices, for example, were strategically located in both the southern and northern anthracite coal fields. Similarly, while Pittsburgh and its "twin city," Allegheny, were the clear leaders in the Western Region, Meadville in Crawford county, squeaked into the top percentile ranks in 1855. The dominant commercial center in the Ridge and Valley Region was, not surprisingly, Hollidaysburg, the terminus of the Allegheny Portage Railroad. Although Altoona would usurp many of the city's commercial functions by the end of the decade due to its strategic position on the Pennsylvania Railroad, Hollidaysburg was still an important Juniata Iron community in the mid-1850s. Finally, even the least developed Pocono and Allegheny Forest Regions had developed major commercial centers by 1855. Honesdale in Warren county and Williamsport in Lycoming county were the obvious candidates for these positions due, in no small part, to their favorable location along important transportation routes.

There was very little fluctuation in the rank and identity of these high-volume post offices over the forty years. The six post offices in the top percentile in 1826 remained in this category throughout all four decades. Moreover, the top four post offices never lost or changed their position and consistently accounted for an outrageous share of the commonwealth's total postal activity. The fact that the majority of the top percentile post offices increasingly became linked together into a larger, more efficient transportation network lends credence to Pred's assertion that major commercial centers tended to perpetuate one another's growth through the constant interchange of information via frequently traversed trade and travel routes.[11]

VI

Banking activity, like postal volume, serves as an indicator of commercial development. Throughout the antebellum period, all incorporated banks were required to submit an annual report to the Auditor General of the Commonwealth of Pennsylvania. The level of financial activity in a given area, therefore, can be gauged by the amount of bills discounted by the various banks, a reflection of their loans outstanding.[12] Although incorporated banks were the most visible form of banking in antebellum Pennsylvania, there were other banks as well. Only the main banks, and not their branches, however, reported to the Auditor General. Moreover, there was considerable private banking, even though reliable data about the extent of their economic activity is unavailable.[13]

The mere ability of a community to support an incorporated bank is one indication of its level of commercial development, while analysis of the amount of bills discounted by these banks allows us to rank the counties in percapita as well as absolute terms. Both of these measures are built into the commercial-economic continuum. Although the percapita rank of the individual county serves as the primary indicator, the absence of a bank within a county was not treated as missing or unavailable data, but continued to be numbered as one of the criteria. Counties without banks in effect registered a rank of zero, a factor which affected their final position on the commercial-economic scale.

The number of incorporated banks in Pennsylvania increased about 200% between 1826 and 1855, or from 25 to 71. Table 4 again points to the astounding concentration of financial activity in the Southeastern Region. Although the region's percentage of the total number of banks declined by approximately one-third during the period, the percentage of bills discounted slipped by less than half that amount and still accounted for over three-fourths all bills discounted in the entire commonwealth in 1855. Indeed, only two other regions supported banking activity to any substantial degree: the Anthracite Region and the Western Region. The Anthracite Region gained considerably in its share of the state's total number of banks, and also registered respectable increases in the percentage of bills discounted. The Western Region, on the other hand, showed much more modest gains on both counts. Banking activity in the other regions remained, for the most part, minimal. Although all regions contained at least one bank in 1845, neither the Towanda Bank of Bradford county which had reported returns in 1835, nor the Bank of Susquehanna County which had been in existence in 1845 survived in 1855, which made the Northeastern Region the only region which lacked both a bank and a top percentile post office in 1855.

Like the concentration of postal receipts, financial business was confined primarily to several main centers. Philadelphia alone accounted for 60.81% of all bills discounted in the state in 1826, and for 69.20% of the regional total. By 1855, the county still accounted for close to 70% of the regional business, while its share of the state total had slipped somewhat to 51.22%. At the other end of the commonwealth, Pittsburgh registered a rather poor second with 9.13% of the state total in 1826, and only 8.29% in 1855. It was, however, the dominant regional financial center, accounting for 61.67% of the bills discounted in the Western Region in 1826, and an even more secure 75.30% thirty years later.

Other communities also served as loci for banking activity, albeit on a much smaller scale. Harrisburg, Dauphin county, is the most notable. As the state capital, Harrisburg was also an important commercial center favorably located on the banks of the Susquehanna River and within close proximity to the anthracite coal fields. The number of banks in the city had increased to four by 1855, and the bills discounted by these institutions represented 5.31% of the commonwealth's total. Already the hub of political activity in Pennsylvania, Harrisburg had become an important

TABLE 4

PERCENTAGE OF BANKS AND BILLS DISCOUNTED BY REGION, 1826-55

Region	% number banks	% bills disc.
Southeastern		
1826	84.00	87.88
1835	68.75	87.16
1845	64.71	76.74
1855	56.33	75.57
Anthracite		
1826	4.00	3.12
1835	14.58	3.69
1845	13.73	6.68
1855	16.90	11.26
Pocono		
1826		
1835		
1845	1.96	0.44
1855	1.41	0.58
Northeastern		
1826		
1835	2.08	0.76
1845	1.96	0.34
1855		
Ridge and Valley		
1826		
1835	2.08	0.25
1845	1.96	1.08
1855	1.41	0.31
Allegheny Forest		
1826		
1835	2.08	0.70
1845	1.96	0.36
1855	4.22	1.27

Western		
1826	12.00	9.00
1835	10.42	7.46
1845	13.73	14.35
1855	19.72	11.01

Source: See footnote 13.

financial center as well by the eve of the Civil War, a fact which led Dauphin county to surpass Philadelphia county with the highest percapita level of bills discounted by 1855.

Although Harrisburg is technically in the Anthracite Region, the real financial center for the coal industry was in Pottsville, Schuylkill county. Located in the heart of the southern coal field, Pottsville itself barely existed in the mid-1820s, and certainly did not have the wherewithall to support an incorporated bank. By 1835, the town had one bank. Thirty years later, three banks existed in Pottsville and they accounted for 18.65% of the bills discounted in the region, second only to Harrisburg.

Banking activity was more ephemeral in the Ridge and Valley Region. Mifflin county, not surprisingly, was the first county in the region to incorporate a bank, and it recorded a statement with the Auditor General in both 1835 and 1845. By 1855, however, the bank had met its demise, and the center of financial activity for the region had shifted to Union county possibly due to its more favorable location on the Susquehanna River and its closer proximity to the anthracite fields. The fact that no Juniata Iron county maintained a bank throughout the period likely indicates the independent and small-scale nature of iron production in this area.

In the Allegheny Forest Region, banks emerged in the three main centers of lumbering activity. Warren county was the first in the Allegheny Forest Region to support a bank which registered returns in 1835, but this institution did not survive the financial upheavals of the late 1830s. By 1855, however, Warren county, along with the dominant lumbering counties in the eastern part of the region, Clinton and Lycoming, each had one bank. Similarly, Wayne county, as the commercial center of the Pocono Region, was able to support an incorporated bank in both 1845 and 1855.

Evidence of increasingly diversified commercial activity can be detected in the Western Region. Fayette county, for example, was capable of supporting a bank throughout the antebellum decades, due most likely to its strategic position along the well-traveled National Road. Early Erie and Westmoreland banks, on the other hand, had a more difficult time of it, neither surviving into the 1840s. By 1845, four Western Region counties--Washington, Greene, Fayette and Allegheny--had incorporated banking institutions; and by 1855, Erie and Lawrence, in addition, reported the existence of at least one bank.

Although banking was becoming more widely dispersed in antebellum Pennsylvania, this type of financial transaction was the most highly concentrated form of commercial activity. While the extractive regions and the livestock-bitumnious coal area in southwestern Pennsylvania were the most tenacious in their attempt to gain a share of the banking business, the fact remains that over half of the counties, or 33 of the 65, were unable or unwilling to support an incorporated bank in 1855. Instead, these counties relied on the services of the small private banker at the local level, or turned to the larger banking institutions in the dominant financial centers.

VII

One final measure is used to create the commercial-economic continua: the assessed value of real and personal property. As early as 1815, the commonwealth began making county by county triennial assessments of real and personal property. Prior to the 1840s, however, these assessments did not always include all counties. For this reason, a combination of sources were relied upon to arrive at the valuation figures for the late 1820s.[14] No assessments were made between 1835 and 1840 and, thus, the 1835-39 commercial-economic continuum is based upon only four criteria. The data for 1845 and 1855 is more complete as a result of a more comprehensive system of taxation, enacted in 1831 and 1844 which gave rise to more effective bookkeeping.[15]

These property valuations must be used with some caution as much discretion was left to the individual tax assessor and to the legislature's judgment. Economic historian, Diane Lindstrom, for example, argues that personal property assessments generally escaped fair valuation, although real property was evaluated somewhat more uniformly.[16] Both types of property assessments have been used, however, as they were not listed separately in the legislative documents. These assessments represent the contemporary perception of the relative ranking of Pennsylvania's counties. For that reason, the real and personal property valuations are the only measures used in the calculation of the final continua which have not been converted to a percapita statistic. If we accept the premise that Pennsylvania representatives took a number of factors into consideration when they made the assessments, among them the number of taxable inhabitants, and the type and extent of wealth in the county, then these real and property valuations stand, in a loose sense, as already normed measures. Moreover, there is something to be said for using contemporary appraisals of the relative wealth of the various counties, as it is ultimately, the perceptions and judgments of nineteenth century Pennsylvanians which shaped the course of political action.

The property valuation patterns mapped in Figures 11-13 reveal what are now very familiar themes: the concentration of wealth in the Southeastern Region, the emergence of the Anthracite Region, the increasing importance of the iron counties in the Juniata Valley, the checker-board quality of economic growth in the agricultural counties in the Ridge and Valley Region, the rise of Lycoming county as the most developed, or commercial county, in the Allegheny Forest Region, the dominant position of the southern half of the

Western Region, and the relative underdevelopment of the counties in the Pocono and Northeastern Regions.

If anything, the patterns reflected in the property valuation maps are more static and less volatile than some of the other measures. Assessors and legislators alike may well have underestimated the velocity and degree of change that was occurring in these antebellum decades. While hindsight has given us the ability to pick up on long-term trends already in progress, these nineteenth century assessments did not always record contemporaneous developments. In 1855, for example, Cambria and Montour counties were already well on their way to becoming important centers of iron production, a fact not at all reflected in the property assessments. On the other hand, the decline in the relative position of Blair, Centre, and Huntingdon, Juniata iron counties, as well as Westmoreland and Fayette had not been detected, or were not judged important enough, to be reflected in the 1855 property valuations.

VIII

While each of the above measures--agriculture, manufacturing, postal receipts, banking assests, and property assessments--can be used to analyze and rank different aspects of the commonwealth's economy, combining these indicators into a single scale provides a gauge of the overall level of commercial-economic development. Within

FIGURE 11

REAL AND PERSONAL PROPERTY VALUATION, 1829-31

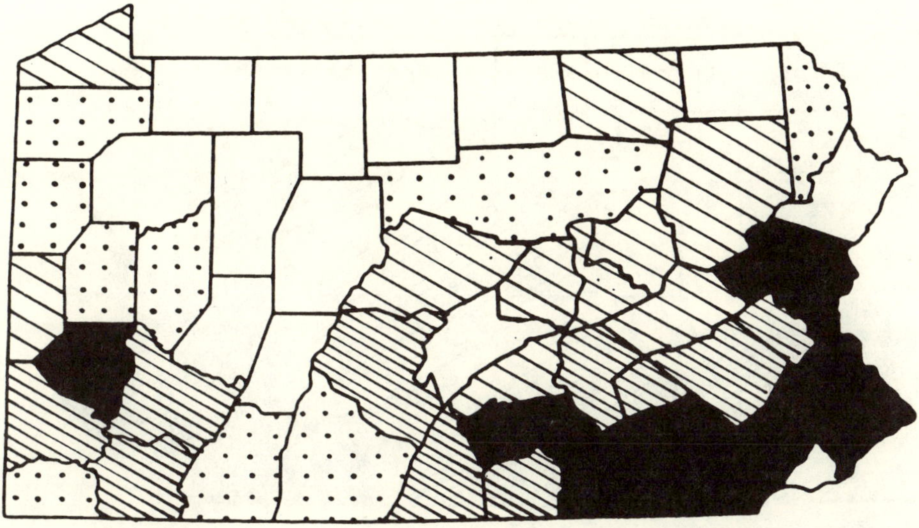

Source: See footnote 16.*

(blank)	Lowest Rank:	Cambria, Potter, Jefferson, McKean, Pike, Clearfield, Warren, Venango, Indiana, Susquehanna
(dots)	Second Rank:	Armstrong, Bedford, Greene, Somerset, Wayne, Butler, Lycoming, Crawford, Mercer
(hatched)	Third Rank:	Bradford, Luzerne, Schuylkill, Perry, Northumberland, Erie, Beaver, Columbia, Centre, Union
(dense hatched)	Fourth Rank:	Westmoreland, Huntingdon, Fayette, Lehigh, Washington, Dauphin, Adams, Lebanon, Franklin, Berks
(black)	Highest Rank:	Allegheny, York, Cumberland, Montgomery, Northampton, Chester, Bucks, Lancaster, Philadelphia

*Data missing for Delaware, Mifflin, and Tioga counties.

FIGURE 12

REAL AND PERSONAL PROPERTY VALUATION, 1845

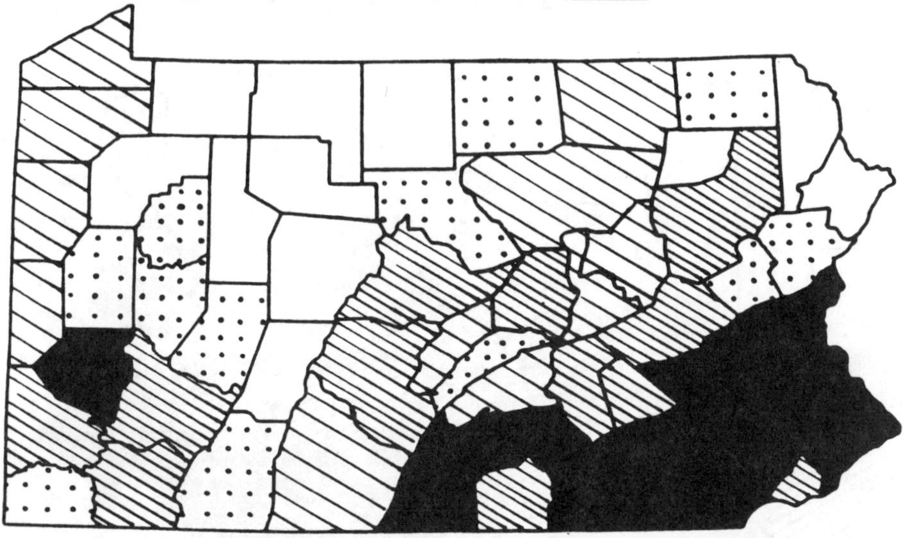

Source: See footnote 16.

☐	Lowest Rank:	Elk, McKean, Potter, Pike, Cambria, Clearfield Jefferson, Wyoming, Warren, Venango, Wayne
(dotted)	Second Rank:	Carbon, Clarion, Tioga, Monroe, Clinton, Armstrong, Susquehanna, Indiana, Greene, Butler, Somerset, Juniata
(hatched)	Third Rank:	Crawford, Perry, Bradford, Bedford, Erie, Mercer, Lycoming, Mifflin, Northumberland, Beaver, Columbia
(dense hatched)	Fourth Rank:	Fayette, Adams, Luzerne, Centre, Union, Westmoreland, Schuylkill, Washington, Lebanon, Delaware, Huntingdon, Dauphin
(solid)	Highest Rank:	Lehigh, Cumberland, York, Franklin, Northampton, Montgomery, Allegheny, Bucks, Chester, Berks, Lancaster, Philadelphia

FIGURE 13

REAL AND PERSONAL PROPERTY VALUATION, 1855

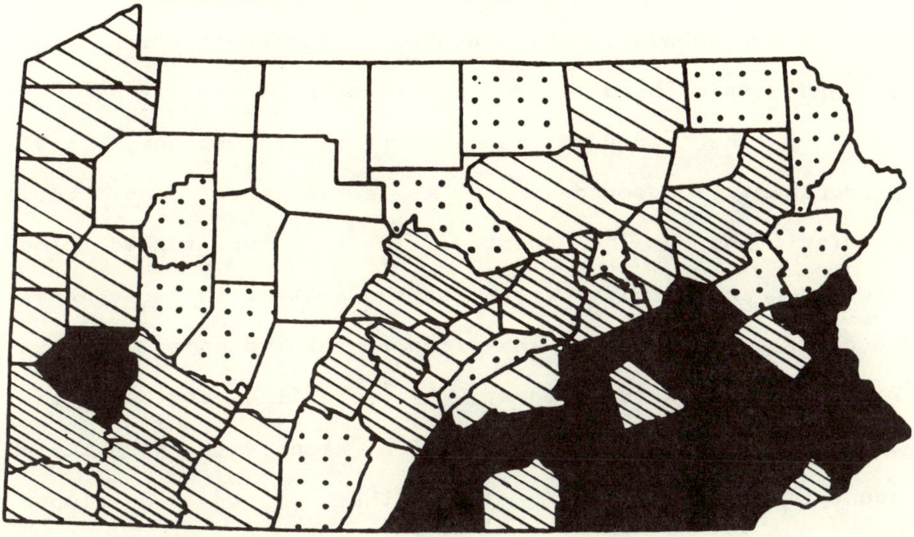

Source: See footnote 16.

Lowest Rank: Forest, Sullivan, McKean, Elk, Pike, Potter, Fulton, Wyoming, Jefferson, Clearfield, Warren, Cambria, Venango

Second Rank: Monroe, Wayne, Tioga, Clarion, Montour, Clinton, Carbon, Bedford, Armstrong, Indiana, Susquehanna, Juniata

Third Rank: Somerset, Greene, Butler, Columbia, Perry, Lawrence, Crawford, Mercer, Bradford, Beaver, Mifflin, Erie, Lycoming

Fourth Rank: Blair, Adams, Centre, Fayette, Northumberland, Huntingdon, Union, Luzerne, Westmoreland, Lebanon, Delaware, Lehigh, Washington

Highest Rank: Dauphin, Cumberland, York, Schuylkill, Franklin, Northampton, Montgomery, Bucks, Berks, Chester, Allegheny, Lancaster, Philadelphia the seven geographical areas, common patterns of development did indeed exist. (See Figures 14-17.) These continua also emphasize, however, the economic differentiation that emerged within these regions and throughout the state.

The 1820/30 map describes an economy still predominantly grounded in agriculture and rural manufacturing. The counties in the top ranked group clustered in the older areas of the state with good access to river transportation and close to the two major markets, Philadelphia and Baltimore. The fertile southern tier counties in the Southeastern Region, along with Northampton county, stand out as the most developed, commercially-oriented areas of the commonwealth. Pike county's position in the top group remains somewhat of an enigma. Since it ranked particularly high on agricultural and manufacturing employment measures of 1820, as well as moderately high on the percapita postal amounts in 1826, we can only conclude that the Pike's peculiar population structure and the early emphasis on lumbering combined to propel the county temporarily into the top ranked commercial-economic group. The other major area of commercial-economic concentration in the 1820s was in the southwestern corner of the state, in Allegheny and Fayette, and to a lesser degree, Washington counties. Noted for both livestock and wheat production in the early decades of the antebellum era, these counties also had favorable transportation access via the river network and the National

Road which cut diagonally across Fayette county and into Washington county. The counties in the northeastern corner of the state ranked relatively high in 1820, due no doubt to their emphasis on livestock and grains, and the Juniata iron counties were beginning to emerge as a top level area.

The counties in two lowest ranked groups were those still being settled in the 1820s, or not to be settled until the following decade.[17] They were in the Allegheny Forest, the Northeastern, and Western Regions in areas that did not have ready access to easily navigable river routes or to well-developed turnpikes.

The 1835-39 continuum map represents a Pennsylvania society in economic and commercial transition. It suggests the beginnings of regional patterns that would develop more fully in later decades, shaped by an urban-industrial rather than an agricultural society. Particularly striking is the emergence of dominant commercial centers. Not all of these centers retained their top level ranking in subsequent decades; yet in the 1830s, they experienced the first spurts of economic growth. Wayne, Mifflin, and Warren counties all ranked in the top group during the late 1830s, and each was to fulfill an important function as a commercial-economic center for their respective region. Schuylkill and Luzerne in the Anthracite Region, Huntingdon in the Ridge and Valley Region, and Bradford in the Northeastern Region, all ranked in the fourth group. Each of these would also play a significant role in the development of their region in the

FIGURE 14

COMMERCIAL-ECONOMIC CONTINUUM, 1820/30

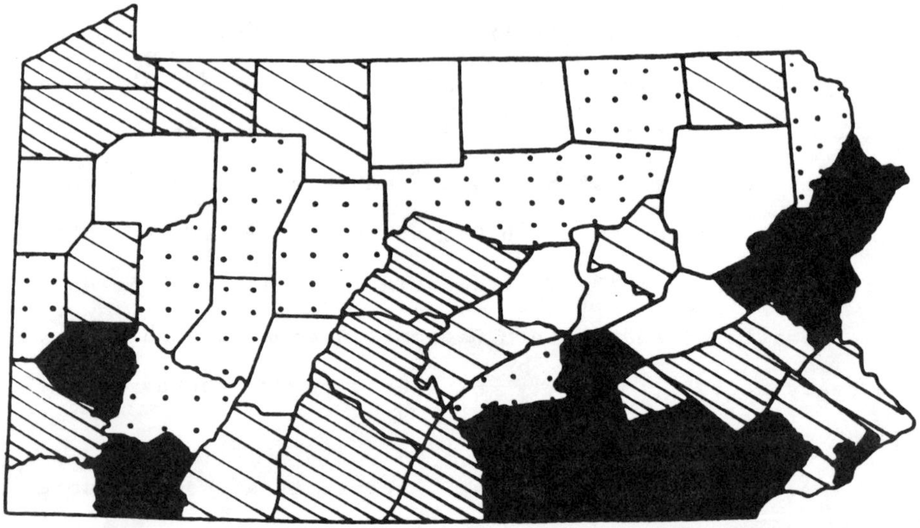

Criteria Used: Agricultural Magnitude, 1820; Manufacturing Magnitude, 1820; Percapita postal receipts, 1826; Percapita bills discounted by banks; Real and personal property valuations, 1829-31*

Lowest Rank: Union, Potter, Greene, Tioga, Cambria, Venango, Mercer, Schuylkill, Northumberland, Luzerne

Second Rank: Armstrong, Beaver, Jefferson, Clearfield, Westmoreland, Perry, Bradford, Wayne, Lycoming, Indiana

Third Rank: Somerset, Mifflin, McKean, Butler, Susquehanna, Lehigh, Bucks, Montgomery, Delaware, Columbia

Fourth Rank: Crawford, Huntingdon, Erie, Bedford, Berks, Centre, Franklin, Lebanon, Washington, Warren

Highest Rank: Pike, Chester, York, Cumberland, Dauphin, Fayette, Allegheny, Lancaster, Adams, Philadelphia, Northampton

*Data missing for Delaware, Mifflin and Tioga counties.

FIGURE 15

COMMERCIAL-ECONOMIC CONTINUUM, 1835-39

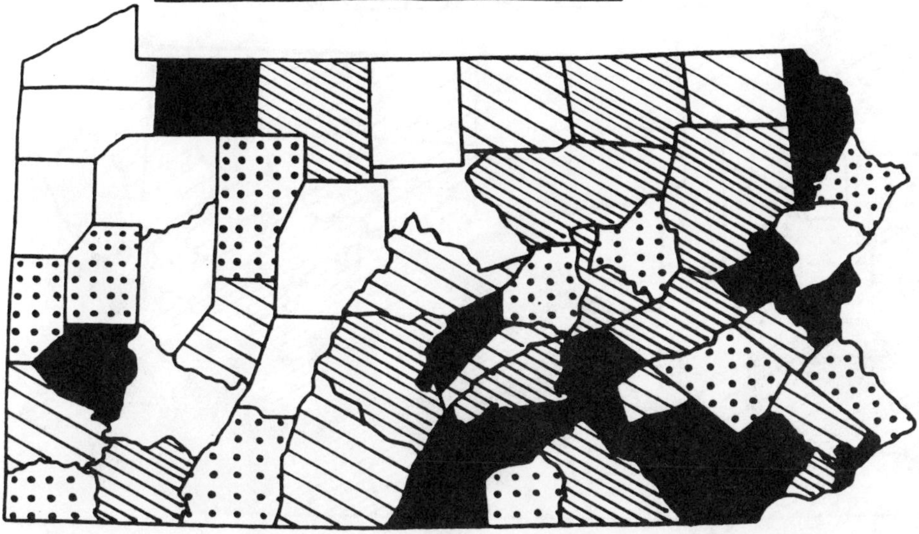

Criteria Used: Agricultural Magnitude, 1839; Manufacturing Magnitude, 1839; Percapita postal receipts, 1835*; Percapita amount of bills discounted by banks, 1835

Lowest Rank: Monroe, Clearfield, Westmoreland, Venango, Cambria, Mercer, Erie, Potter, Armstrong, Clinton, Crawford

Second Rank: Beaver, Columbia, Somerset, Butler, Jefferson, Pike, Union, Berks, Adams, Greene, Bucks

Third Rank: Indiana, Washington, Bedford, Juniata, Susquehanna, Montgomery, Lebanon, Centre, Tioga, Lehigh

Fourth Rank: Bradford, Luzerne, Schuylkill, Fayette, Delaware, Lycoming, Perry, York, Huntingdon, Northumberland, McKean

Highest Rank: Dauphin, Wayne, Northampton, Franklin, Chester, Lancaster, Allegheny, Mifflin, Warren, Philadelphia, Cumberland

*Postal data unavailable for Clinton and Monroe counties

FIGURE 16

COMMERCIAL-ECONOMIC CONTINUUM, 1845-49

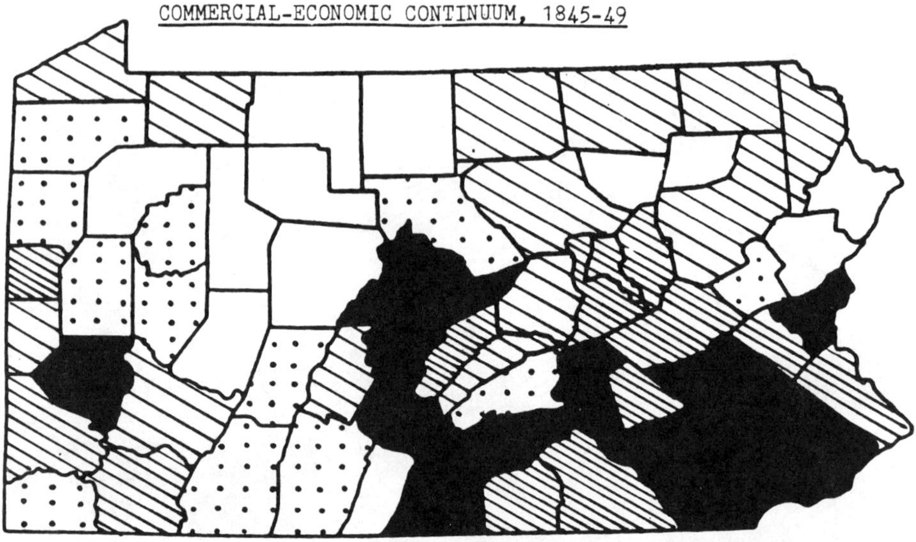

Criteria Used: Agricultural Magnitude, 1849; Manufacturing Magnitude, 1849; Percapita postal receipts, 1845*; Percapita amount of bills discounted by banks, 1845; Real and personal property valuation, 1845*

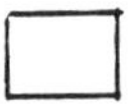

Lowest Rank: Sullivan, Fulton, Clearfield, Elk, Jefferson, Pike, Wyoming, Potter, McKean, Indiana, Monroe, Venango

Second Rank: Cambria, Somerset, Bedford, Clarion, Butler, Greene, Mercer, Crawford, Armstrong, Perry, Carbon, Clinton

Third Rank: Beaver, Juniata, Blair, Erie, Wayne, Tioga, Warren, Bradford, Union, Susquehanna, Westmoreland, Luzerne, Lycoming

Fourth Rank: Lawrence, Adams, Fayette, Montour, Northumberland, Lebanon, Columbia, Mifflin, York, Washington, Bucks, Lehigh, Schuylkill

Highest Rank: Berks, Centre, Huntingdon, Northampton, Montgomery, Cumberland, Franklin, Dauphin, Allegheny, Philadelphia, Delaware, Chester, Lancaster

*Postal and property data unavailable for Blair, Fulton, Lawrence, Montour, and Sullivan counties.

FIGURE 17

COMMERCIAL-ECONOMIC CONTINUUM, 1855-59

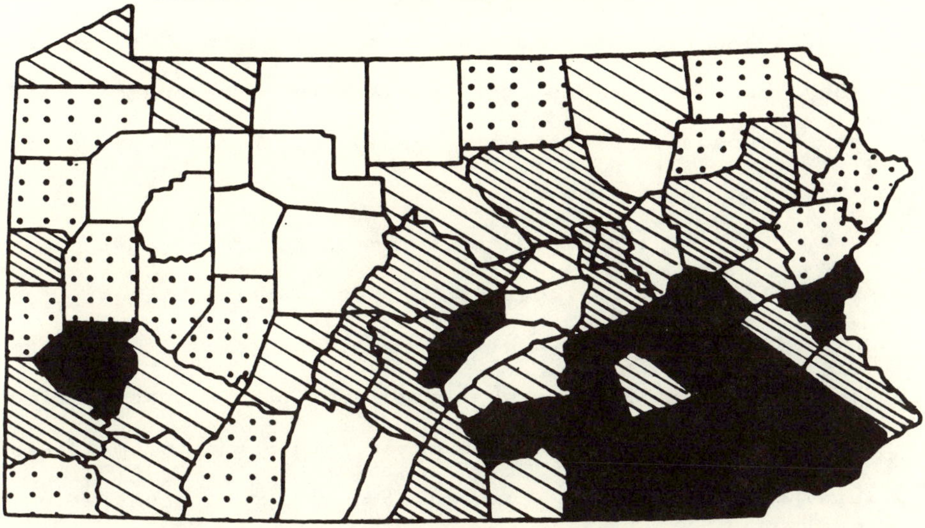

Criteria Used: Agricultural Magnitude, 1859; Manufacturing Magnitude, 1859; Percapita postal receipts, 1855*; Percapita amount of bills discounted by banks, 1855; Real and personal property valuation, 1855*

Lowest Rank: Sullivan, Clearfield, Fulton, Elk, Forest, Potter, Jefferson, Snyder, Venango, Bedford, McKean, Clarion, Juniata

Second Rank: Indiana, Butler, Pike, Monroe, Wyoming, Somerset, Greene, Mercer, Armstrong, Crawford, Susquehanna, Beaver, Tioga

Third Rank: Fayette, Perry, Cambria, Warren, Erie, Clinton, Bradford, Carbon, Westmoreland, Columbia, Union, Adams, Wayne

Fourth Rank: Centre, Lawrence, Huntingdon, Blair, Lehigh, Luzerne, Lycoming, Bucks, Lebanon, Northumberland, Montour, Washington, Franklin

Highest Rank: Schuylkill, Mifflin, York, Berks, Delaware, Cumberland, Allegheny, Montgomery, Dauphin, Philadelphia, Northampton, Chester, Lancaster

*Postal and property data unavailable for Snyder county.

antebellum years. Meanwhile, although the Southeastern Region remained the most developed area in the state, the top level counties were not as concentrated in this corner as they had been. The most impressive developments and rates of economic growth were happening in other parts of commonwealth during the 1830s.

By the late 1840s, the patterns of economic growth and commercialization characteristic of early stages of industrialization were beginning to solidify. Both the 1845-49 and 1855-59 maps highlight the overwhelming importance of proximity to the major rivers and turnpikes as a main determinant of commercial-economic concentration. Indeed, by the late 1850s, the top level counties clustered almost exclusively along the banks of the Susquehanna and Schuylkill Rivers.

Other river routes and avenues of transportation remained important. The iron counties in the Ridge and Valley Region as well as Mifflin county continued to benefit by their location on the banks of the Juniata River which, it will be recalled, had served as the basic route for both the Main Line and the Pennsylvania Railroad. Although the iron counties' importance had slipped a notch by the eve of the Civil War, a respectable degree of commercial-economic concentration remained in the central Ridge and Valley Region.

Similarly, the southwestern corner of the state continued to respresent a pocket of top level commercial-economic development throughout the 1840s and 1850s around the counties benefiting from the Monongahela and Beaver Rivers. Finally, Lycoming county as well as Luzerne county, emerged in the fourth rank by the late 1850s, a position attributable in no small part to the fact that the West Branch and the North Branch, respectively, traversed these counties and provided increasingly easy access to expanding markets.

At the other end of the spectrum, the counties in the lower ranks clustered overwhelmingly in the Allegheny Forest, and to a lesser degree, the Northeastern and the Pocono regions. Wayne, Bradford, Clinton, and Warren continued to stand out as regional centers, and each not coincidentally, benefited from its location along a major river or canal route. These counties and the regions they represented, however, continued to rank comparatively low. While they did indeed experience commercial and economic development, the disproportionate degree of commercial-economic concentration in the Southeastern and Anthracite regions made their progress pale in comparison.

IX

The preceding two chapters have examined the course of economic development in antebellum Pennsylvania in two related ways. The first method carved the commonwealth into seven geographical regions, each with a distinctive pattern of economic growth. Secondly, continua were created which ranked Pennsyvlania counties by their level of commercial and economic development at the end of each of the four antebellum decades, and each continua was divided into five comercial-economic groups. Comparison of these scales underscores the uneven pace of economic development among Pennsylvania counties during the early stages of industrialization and reveals the enormous commercial and economic variability that existed across the commonwealth and within individual regions.

These two ways of looking at economic growth will be used to analyze legislative behavior, policy development, and political party affiliation. Knowing where each county fits in both a geographical and developmental context helps to uncover the underlying influences in Pennsylvania politics and economic policy. Were legislators, for example, bound by allegiance to their geographical section, or did they join with those from counties with similar levels of commercial-economic development? Whereas the two are not mutually exclusive, using both helps to clarify the relationship between economic growth and political behavior in antebellum Pennsylvania.

FOOTNOTES

[1]E. Willard Miller, An Economic Atlas of Pennsylvania (Harrisburg: Commonwealth of Pennsylvania, State Planning Board, 1964), pp. 190-201.

[2]Van Beck Hall, Politics Without Parties: Massachusetts, 1789-1791 (Pittsburgh: University of Pittsburgh Press, 1972), pp. 3-9.

[3]Miller, p. 191.

[4]No property assessments were made by the state between 1835 and 1840. Consequently, the 1835-39 commercial-economic continuum is based on only 4 criteria, as opposed to five. See Leighton P. Stradley, Early Financial and Economic History of Pennsylvania (Chicago: Commerce Clearing House, Inc., 1942), p. 70.

[5]All of the population figures used in calculating percapita data in this chapter are taken from the adjusted populations in the Ninth Census of the United States, 1870, Vol. 1: Population (Washington: Government Printing Office, 1871). In order to calculate the mid-decade percapita data, an average of the census populations at either end of the decade was used. Population adjustments for the newly-created counties were based, where possible, on geographical area and population proportions at the next decennial census. The only exception to this is Forest county whose 1860 population of 898 was also used in computing the 1855 percapita data.

One word of caution about using percapita values as the basis for the various magnitudes is in order. Percapita figures for some of the more undeveloped, or frontier counties, particularly in the earlier decades of the antebellum period, occasionally result in some rather unpredictable ordinal positions. Some of these counties, for example, score extraordinarily high in the manufacturing or agricultural magnitudes, especially when employment data is used. For the most part, these scores can be explained by the structure of frontier demography which generally lacked a more balanced age and gender population pyramid. In other words, recently settled, frontier areas tended to be populated by an over-abundance of men and women of working ages. When this population is used as the basis of percapita economic measures, the result may give an overexaggerated sense of the relative level of economic development of the county. For the most part, the aberrations caused by these factors tend to diminish over time as the society matures. Even so, the influence of these abnormally high measures is counteracted within each commercial-economic magnitude by the weight of other criteria not as affected by population structure.

[6]Fourth Census of the United States, 1820 (Washington: Gales & Seaton, 1821); Sixth Census of the United States, 1840. Compendium of Enumeration of Inhabitants and Statistics of the United States (Washington: Thomas Allen, 1841); J. D. B. DeBow, comp. Statistical View of the United States . . . Being a Compendium of the Seventh Census (Washington, 1854); Agriculture of the United States in 1860; Complied from the Original Returns of the Eighth Census (Washington: Government Printing Office, 1864).

Dairy products in the latter two decades were reported in terms of pounds of butter and pounds of cheese rather than as a monetary value.

The county areas used in calculating the improved acreage as a percent of county area figure were taken primarily from the Sixteenth Census of the United States: Agriculture, Volume 1, Part 1 (Washington: Government Printing Office, 1942). The creation of new counties which involved more than one parent county made it impossible to use the 1940 data. These area statistics, while not always as accurate as those taken from the 1940 census, were taken from available gazetteers. The 1860 and 1850 areas for Elk, McKean, Potter,and Clinton counties was taken from Thomas Burrowes, A State-Book of Pennsylvania (Philadelphia, 1846). The areas for Jefferson and Venango counties for 1850 were taken from Thomas F. Gordon, A Gazetteer of the State of Pennsylvania (Philadelphia: T. Belknap, 1833), p. 215, 461.

[7]Census of 1820; Census of 1840; Census of 1850; Manufactures of the United States in 1860; Compiled from the Original Returns of the Eighth Census (Washington: Government Printing Office, 1865).

In an attempt to make the 1839 capital investment information as comparable as possible with the later data, the capital invested in both iron and coal was added to the manufacturing investment total. Unfortunately, lumber data, which are also listed under manufacturing in the later censuses, were only given in terms of value of finished product in 1839 and could not be included in the investment totals. A separate category for percapita value of lumber produced was thus included in the 1839 manufacturing calculations. As in the agricultural magnitude, all criteria were computed in percapita terms for each county, and then ordinally ranked. The ranks of each criteria were then added together, and divided by the number of criteria used.

[8]Alan Pred, Urban Growth and the Circulation of Information: The United States System of Cities, 1790-1840 (Cambridge, Mass.: Harvard University Press, 1973), pp. 81-82.

[9]U.S. Congress, House, Postage at Each Office in 1825 and 1826, H.Doc.35, 19th Congress, 2nd session; U.S. Congress, House, Postage accruing at Each Office, 1835, H.Doc. 262, 24th congress, 1st session; Register of All Officers and Agents, Civil, Military and Naval in the Service of the United States, 1845, 1855. The author is also indebted to Chester M. Smith, Jr. and John L. Kay whose book Pennsylvania Postal History (Lawrence, Mass.: Quarterman Publications, Inc., 1976) helped to locate the counties of many of the post offices listed in the above sources.

[10]Wayne E. Fuller, The American Mail: Enlarger of the Common Life (Chicago: University of Chicago Press, 1972), pp. 43, 65; Clyde Kelly, U.S. Postal Policy (New York: D. Appleton and Co., 1952), pp. 53, 57, 63.

[11]Pred, passim.

[12]Pennsylvania, House of Representatives, Legislative Journal, 1826, vol.2, Communication from the Auditor General, accompanied with a Statement of the Certain Banks, Read December 30, 1826, pp. 89-115; Pennsylvania, House of Representatives, Legislative Journal, 1835, vol. 2, Communication from the Auditor General, accompanied by a Statement of the Certain Banks, read January 5, 1836, pp. 144-193; Pennsylvania; House of Representatives, Legislative Journal, 1846, vol.2, Communication from the Auditor General transmitting Quarterly Statements of the Several Banks and Savings Institutions; Pennsylvania, House of Representatives, Legislative Journal, 1856, vol. 2, Communication from the Auditor General, transmitting the Returns of the Several Banks and Savings Institutions of this Commonwealth, p. 255.

See Joseph Van Fenstermaker, The Development of American Commercial Banking, 1782-1837 (Kent, Ohio: Kent State University Press, 1965), pp. 31-32, 43-49 for a discussion of discounts.

[13]Thomas Cushing, et al., History of Allegheny County, Pennsylvania (Chicago: A. Warner and Company, 1889), pp. 585-94; John Thomas Holdsworth, Financing an Empire: History of Banking in Pennsylvania, 4 vols. (Chicago: S. J. Clarke Publishing Co., 1928), 2:811-52.

[14]The property valuations, where possible, were taken from Gordon, Gazetteer of the State of Pennsylvania, and included both real and personal property for 1829. Bucks and Franklin data includes only real property. The figures for Armstrong, Clearfield, Crawford, Luzerne, Lycoming, Pike, Potter, Somerset, and Wayne counties include both seated and unseated lands.

In some cases, it was necessary to rely on the 1832 evaluations (which in reality, were citing assessments based on 1831 property holdings). Again, Gordon was used, where possible. The Dauphin county figure contains only 1832 real property valuations. The Lancaster figure includes both the 1832 real and personal property assessments; while the Montgomery assessment is based upon the 1832 real estate valuation, and the 1829 personal property assessment.

Finally, the property assessment figures for Beaver, Centre, Mercer, Northampton, Perry, Philadelphia, Union, and Warren counties are taken from Pennsylvania, House of Representatives, Legislative Journal, 1832-33, vol. 2, Returns of the County Commissioners. Increase of county rates and levies for the use of the commonwealth, per act of 25th March, 1831, pp. 189-231.

No property assessment data were available for Delaware, Mifflin, and Tioga counties.

[15]Pennsylvania, House of Representatives, Legislative Journal, 1846, vol.2, A Tabular Statement relating to the tax on real and personal estate, for State purposes, . . ., pp. 346-65; Pennsylvania, Legislative Documents, 1855, Report of the State Treasurer on the Finances of the State, pp. 40-41.

See also, Clyde I. Klechner, "Constitutional History of Pennsylvania with particular Reference to Taxation," (Ph.D. dissertation, Cornell University, 1939), pp. 149-50, 156-7, 178-9; Stradley, pp. 70, 75-79.

[16]Diane Lindstrom, Economic Development in the Philadelphia Region, 1810-1850 (New York: Columbia University Press, 1978), p. 27.

The real property valuations included land, houses, cattle, mills, distilleries, breweries, tanyards, furnaces, forges, foundries, machine shops, stores, and warehouses.

[17]John William Florin, The Advance of Frontier Settlement in Pennsylvania, 1638-1850: A Geographic Interpretation (University Park, PA: Department of Geography, Pennsylvania State University, 1977), pp. 81-82, 85-86.

CHAPTER FOUR

PATTERNS OF LEGISLATIVE COHESION: REGIONS, COMMERCIAL-ECONOMIC GROUPS AND CONTESTED ISSUES

Pennsylvania experienced an extraordinary expansion in governmental activity in the decades prior to the Civil War. State legislatures became the most important centers of policy formation as elected representatives were called upon to make decisions on countless economic and social issues that directly affected the daily lives of their constituents. Each state developed its own peculiar blend of legislation dictated by the social and economic exigencies of their society, and hammered out within the broad, frequently vague guidelines of a "decentralized federalism."[1]

The antebellum state legislatures had difficulty in keeping pace with the ever-increasing demands and duties placed upon them. Deluged by petitions and requests from non-members which required some type of response, legislators, by default, were forced to adopt a rather piecemeal approach to policy-making. Attempts to satisfy as quickly as possible the needs of a rapidly changing society led to a remarkable increase in the number of laws passed. The overwhelming majority of laws can be classified as "special" legislation--laws enacted for a specific purpose, such as charters of incorporation for individual companies. While most states eventually passed general incorporation laws which specified broad guidelines and delegated some authority to the courts, such acts, particularly in banking, insurance, transportation and manufacturing, came relatively late. Until that time, the legislators were constantly obliged to consider and debate the passage of countless individual charters and to review proposed alterations of the original act. This time-consuming task retarded the evolution of anything approaching a coherent legislative policy program.[2]

Policy-making entailed the distribution of the "'public largesse' to favored individuals, groups and localities."[3] As private constituent concerns throughout each state fought over the distribution of finite resources, the state legislatures became, in L. Ray Gunn's words, "essentially arena[s] where local and private interests contended for privileges and influence in a society in which 'public' and 'private' roles were virtually indistinguishable."[4] State legislatures were not engaged in making "policy" in any broad, over-arching sense of the word, but were responding to the multitude of individual demands arising from an increasingly complex society. Many of the tasks the legislature performed were largely administrative or judicial, such as overseeing the actual construction and administration of public transportation undertakings, granting divorces, processing claims against the states, and settling contested estates.[5]

This decision-making process, the lack of separation between legislative, administrative, and judicial functions, and the enormously high rates of turnover among legislators between sessions[6] have led some historians to criticize the ability of antebellum state legislatures to govern effectively. Gunn argues:

> The combination of social and economic changes with a tremendous expansion of [electoral] participation multiplied political demands and, at the same time, undermined the ability of existing political structures to satisfy those demands. Overwhelmed by the pressures of modernization, . . . the effectiveness of state governments [after 1840] was seriously undermined by decentralization, arrested administrative development, and a 'crisis of authority.'[7]

State representatives were wading in singularly uncharted waters as they sorted out and defined legislative, judicial, and administrative duties and their appropriate division of labor. The American people were demanding from their state assemblies financial and administrative assistance to create an economic and commercial infrastructure more suited to the needs of an increasingly modern society. State legislatures responded and played a critical role in formulating and promoting the nation's economic expansion during the first half of the nineteenth century. "It seems pointless and present-minded to blame nineteenth-century authorities for these 'failures,'" cautions Richard L. McCormick

> From everything we know, the American people got roughly the economic policies they wanted. Given a choice between governmental promotion and restraint, they clearly preferred the former. Except for the abolition of slavery, the distribution of economic

> benefits probably represents the outstanding achievement of nineteenth-century American government. Certainly it formed the most characteristic achievement.[8]

This incremental style of policy-making produced a rich record of the process of legislative decision-making in antebellum America. Indeed, the very lack of more general policies works to the historian's advantage as hundreds of roll-call votes were taken during each legislative session on countless numbers of laws. These roll-calls, taken in response to demands which frequently came directly from constituents, permit detailed analysis of how specific, often conflicting local needs were met and resolved at the state level. Legislative voting behavior, after all, to quote Joel Silbey, "is not the ritualistic recording of decisions made elsewhere. Rather, it is part of the battleground between contending forces in society. Congress and the state legislatures, in the way they behave, reflect these external forces battling for public policies."[9] The roll-calls, then, become indispensable tools in helping to unravel the relationship between the uneven pace of economic change and the policy-making process in antebellum Pennsylvania.

Four legislative sessions of the Pennsylvania House of Representatives have been selected for closer examination--the 1828-29, 1838-39, 1849, and 1859 sessions. The legislature's time continued to be dominated by economic and commercial issues, and the number of laws passed per session mounted steadily. The legislators arrived in

Harrisburg with a perception of Pennsylvania society formulated, at least in part, by their district's specific regional and community patterns of economic development. They responded both to the needs of their region, but increasingly, in terms of the level of commercial-economic development of their home county. Their roll-call voting was influenced by these regional and economic factors.

II

By 1820, the Pennsylvania General Assembly had evolved from the unicameral experiment of the Revolutionary era to a more typical two house legislature. Although the Senate had originally been conceived as an aristocratic counterpart to the House of Representatives, the two houses were, in reality, constitutionally equal in power. If anything, the rule that required all revenue bills to originate in the lower house made this body slightly more important, especially as the state stepped up its financial commitment to the publicly owned canal and rail system and in various other mixed enterprise experiments.[10]

The lower house was perceived as being "closer to the people" due to the fact that all one-hundred members were elected annually. In contrast, prior to the Constitution of 1838, only one-fourth of the thirty-three members of the Senate were elected each year to serve a term of four years. After the provisions of the new constitution were implemented, Senate terms were reduced to three years, one-third to be elected annually. Both the Senate and the House districts, which were apportioned every seven years in accordance with the number of taxables, used the county as the district of representation. While no county could be divided to form a district, the more sparsely settled counties were grouped with adjacent counties and the more populous counties such as Philadelphia and Allegheny frequently had more than one representative, and in Philadelphia county's case, more than one senator.[11]

Both legislative houses met annually for sessions lasting between four and five months. Occasionally, as in the 1838-39 legislature, the session was extended. Before the provisions of the Constitution of 1838 were put into effect, the legislature convened on the first Tuesday in December. As the legislators' responsibilities mounted, however, and as the commonwealth became more budget-conscious, this practice came under increasing attack. The legislators, it was charged, rarely accomplished much during the month of December and frequently were over-anxious to adjourn for Christmas, a vacation for which they were paid. In response, the opening day of each session was changed to early January, while adjournment remained set at some agreed-upon date in early April.[12]

Shortening the length of each session by several weeks merely compounded the difficulties the legislators faced in attempting to accommodate the growing demands placed upon them. The number of laws passed per session increased from 227 in 1828-29 to 753 in 1859.[13] The number of roll-calls per session did not grow nearly as much. Leaving aside the 1838-39 legislature which included a special session, the total number of roll-calls in the 1828-29, 1849, and 1859 sessions were 303, 470, and 403, respectively.[14] Various formal and informal mechanisms, therefore, were developed which allowed an increased amount of legislative business to be conducted within the same length of time.

Some attempts were made to make the legislative process less chaotic and more efficient. Some amounted to little more than calendar reorganization. Beginning in the 1833-34 session, petitions were presented only by county and on only two days each week.[15] Other changes, however, had much more lasting and far-reaching implications. The 1844 House of Representatives established a procedure which made special bills easier to pass. Following a practice used in Congress, each Tuesday morning was set aside for reading special or private bills. Those bills which were not objected to during the first reading, passed to a second reading and usually to enactment during the afternoon session. While this undoubtedly expedited the passage of countless bills, it was a marked departure from the previous policy of opening each bill to general debate.[16]

Prior to 1830, many of the committees called upon to review petitions and proposed legislation were select committees formed for a specific purpose. Slowly, standing committees replaced these more temporary ones in yet another attempt to deal with the flood of petitions descending upon the legislature. The committees were asked to gather information about each bill and to make a favorable or unfavorable recommendation. If favorable, the bill was then required to go through three readings before the whole House before it was enacted. If the report was unfavorable, the committee simply asked to be discharged from further consideration of the bill. Despite the resulting efficiency, these standing committees themselves soon felt that the time available to consider each bill was woefully inadequate.[17]

Attempts to streamline policy-making were only marginally successful. The increasing amount of business overwhelmed the representatives.[18] But those issues that were debated and voted upon reflected the most salient and divisive policy concerns, and the roll-calls reveal how members differed in their perception of the role of the state in economic development.

III

The roll-calls were classified by eleven major categories for analysis. Appendix A lists these categories and their subdivisions along with brief descriptions. A comparison of the types of laws passed with the percentage of roll-calls taken in each policy category during the four sessions is presented in Table 5. The Pennsylvania antebellum legislature was overwhelmingly preoccupied with economic development and transportation. Even though agriculture remained the most dominant and pervasive economic activity throughout the commonwealth, agricultural issues rarely required legislative enactment and even less frequently gave rise to debate or a roll-call vote. Instead, the representatives were more concerned with legislation that addressed the "newer," more rapidly-expanding sectors of the economy. Transportation, Banking and Business/Commerce laws accounted for one-third of the laws passed in 1829, 45% in 1839, and a little over 40% in both 1849 and 1859. The percentage of roll-calls generated by these issues was even greater than the percentage of laws. Forty-five percent of all roll-calls taken during the 1829 session, close to 50% in 1839 and 1849, and 43% in 1859 were in these three categories.

The state-owned system of canals and railways, was the single most important legislative topic in both the 1829 and 1839 sessions, when it accounted for 26.4% and 17.8% of all roll-calls respectively. By 1849, roll-calls concerning the public works still constituted 10% of all votes taken. The state had abandoned its experiment with government-subsidized transportation by the eve of the Civil War, but continued to play an active role by granting special charters. Nearly 21% of all roll-calls taken during the 1859 session involved railroad corporations, and especially a new form of transportation--the urban passenger railway.

The most dramatic increase in action during the antebellum decades, in terms of both roll-call and session law percentages was in business and commerce. The proportion of banking laws, on the other hand, remained remarkably consistent over the four legislative sessions, ranging from 1.57% to 3.67% of all laws passed. The fact that over one-fifth of all roll-calls taken in 1849 pertained to banking, however, demonstrates just how important and controversial this issue had become. Numerous banks petitioned for re-charter during this session in compliance with the provisions set forth in the Relief Act of 1841, and this gave the legislators ample opportunity to air their philosophical and political views on banks, while simultaneously shaping the future of Pennsylvania's banking system.

The average percent voting in the minority by policy sector reflects the degree of contention which surrounded the major issues. (See Table 6.) The closer the average number voting in the minority is to 50%, the more contentious was the issue, while conversely, policies with lower minority voting percentages were less controversial. Overall, the average percent voting in the minority for all roll-calls and for all policy categories did not vary greatly between the four sessions, ranging from a low of

TABLE 5

ROLL-CALL AND SESSION LAW PERCENTAGES BY POLICY CATEGORY

Policy Category	1829		1839*		1849		1859	
	%roll calls	%laws	%roll calls	%laws	%roll calls	%laws	%roll calls	%laws
1. Procedural	14.52	---	17.04	---	7.87	---	20.84	0.80
2. Private	9.90	33.04	2.96	14.51	6.38	14.45	5.21	9.16
3. Governmental	17.82	22.03	13.89	20.39	20.64	21.79	15.14	30.15
4. Transportation	39.27	29.07	39.07	30.20	17.66	27.29	26.05	27.76
5. Business/Commerce	2.64	2.20	7.22	13.33	9.79	10.32	9.68	11.69
6. Banking	2.64	2.20	2.78	1.57	21.06	3.67	7.69	2.26
7. Pub.Hlth/Welfare	7.26	2.20	4.81	6.27	6.60	6.88	5.21	7.57
8. Education	1.32	1.76	1.67	8.63	5.74	2.75	3.23	3.05
9. Religion	1.32	2.20	---	1.96	0.43	3.21	1.24	2.26
10. Agriculture	0.33	0.44	0.19	0.39	0.43	0.69	0.50	2.79
11. Miscellaneous	2.97	4.85	10.37**	2.74	4.04	8.94	5.21	2.52
	100.00	100.00	100.00	100.00	100.00	100.00	100.00	100.00

*Includes extra session. **Includes all roll-calls dealing with the Buckshot War. See Appendix A.

Total number roll-calls 1829 = 303
1839 = 540
1849 = 470
1859 = 403

Total number session laws 1829 = 227
1839 = 255
1849 = 436
1859 = 753

Source: Pennsylvania, House of Representatives, Legislative Journal, Vol. 1, 1828-29, 1838-39, 1849, 1859; Pennsylvania, Laws of the Commonwealth of Pennsylvania, 1828-29, 1838-39, 1849, 1859.

31.07% in 1859 to a high of 37.03% in 1839. But this obscures the variation among the policy categories.

Leaving aside the less substantive Procedural and Private categories, Banking was always among the top two most divisive issues during every session. Transportation, not surprisingly, registered above average percentages voting in the minority during 1838-39 and 1849 --the years when the mounting state debt called into question the administration of the public works as well as the continued expansion of the state transportation system. In contrast, by 1859 the minority percent on transportation issues, while still slightly above the total roll-call average, had slipped significantly. Roll-calls taken on Business and Commerce questions tended to arouse more divisiveness in the first two sessions than in the latter two, while Governmental issues displayed the reverse trend, becoming more contentious by 1849 and 1859. Finally, while issues such as Religion, and Public Health and Welfare occasionally registered above-average minority votes, these social policies produced less divisive voting patterns than did those relating to the economy or to government.

Although an attempt was made to retain as many roll-calls as possible, it was not always possible or desireable to keep every vote. Most of Procedural and Private roll-calls, for example, were eliminated unless they had broader policy implications. The lack of adequate information in the House Journal was the most serious

TABLE 6

AVERAGE PERCENT VOTING IN THE MINORITY BY POLICY CATEGORY AND LEGISLATIVE SESSION

Policy Category	1829	1839	1849	1859
1. Procedural	35.36	38.89	31.79	29.58
2. Private	39.71	34.13	37.23	31.39
3. Governmental	35.61	35.40	36.83	34.06
4. Transportation	35.07	38.57	36.90	31.30
5. Business/Commerce	39.48	36.09	32.05	30.00
6. Banking	39.67	36.45	38.00	37.17
7. Pub.Hlth/Welfare	32.74	32.86	39.86	14.35
8. Education	39.08	33.23	35.66	23.12
9. Religion	47.19	---	34.63	25.93
10.Agriculture	25.00	36.23	24.92	33.37
11.Miscellaneous	29.09	34.31	32.40	31.46
Session Average	35.70	37.03	35.97	31.07

Source: Pennsylvania, House of Representatives, Legislative Journal, Vol. 1, 1828-29, 1838-39, 1849, 1859.

limitation. All too often, the Journal simply noted that a roll-call was being taken on a specific section, and referred to the section by number without printing the text. Much the same procedure was followed when minor supplements or changes to already existing laws were presented. Unless the law was actually enacted, it was frequently impossible to determine the exact question on which the vote was taken. While an attempt was made to establish the precise nature of each roll-call by careful reading of the Journal, the newspaper accounts, and the session laws, it was still not always possible to ascertain the nature of the issue which generated the roll-call. Appendix B outlines in greater detail the procedure followed when making the final roll-call selection.

Approximately one-half of the original roll-calls, or 875 votes, survived the selection process. (See Table 7 for the distribution of these votes by policy category.) These roll-calls were then used to analyze the voting of representatives in terms of region and relative level of commercial and economic development of their districts.

IV

What influenced a representative's stand on the wide range of social and economic issues the legislature was called upon to consider during these antebellum decades? Did legislators strongly identify with their geographical regions? Were members motivated purely by a localized sense of self-interest? Or did the legislators' votes reflect a broader conception of the commonwealth's economic future and the role that the state should play in guiding that development even though that conception was modified by the unique economic and commercial characteristics of each legislative district?

To answer this question, Rice indexes of cohesion were computed on each of the selected roll-calls for the seven regions and the five commercial-economic groups. The Rice index of cohesion measures how cohesively the members of a specific group voted. Ranging from 0 to 100, with 100 representing total cohesion, the index subtracts the percent of a given group voting nay from the percent voting yea, and represents the result as a positive number.[19] By averaging the Rice indexes for all roll-calls by policy category, it is possible to get a sense of how consistently representatives from a given region, or from similar commercial-economic groups voted together on various issues.

In addition, the continuum ranks for each decade were averaged together to provide a single commercial-economic aggregate group score for each county, thus indicating which counties always remained among the most economically-developed, which among the least, and so on. Indexes of cohesion were computed for these aggregate groups as well. (Appendix C gives the number of representatives in each region, commercial-economic group, and

TABLE 7

SELECTED ROLL-CALL FREQUENCIES BY POLICY CATEGORY

Policy Category	1829		1839		1849		1859	
	#roll calls	per-cent	#roll calls	per-cent	#roll calls	per-cent	#roll calls	per-cent
1. Procedural	2	1.22	3	1.13	7	2.61	13	7.30
2. Private	---	---	---	---	---	---	---	---
3. Governmental	39	23.78	51	19.25	68	25.37	30	16.85
4. Transportation	81	49.39	133	50.19	51	19.03	57	32.02
5. Business/Commerce	3	1.83	30	11.32	33	12.31	21	11.80
6. Banking	8	4.88	11	4.15	67	25.00	24	13.48
7. Pub.Hlth/Welfare	21	12.80	18	6.79	19	7.09	14	7.87
8. Education	4	2.44	8	3.02	15	5.60	7	3.93
9. Religion	2	1.22	---	---	2	0.75	4	2.25
10. Agriculture	1	0.61	1	0.38	1	0.37	1	0.56
11. Miscellaneous	3	1.83	10	3.77	5	0.87	7	3.93
	164	100.00	265	100.00	268	100.00	178	100.00

Source: See Table 6.

commercial-economic aggregate group by session and discusses how the problem of multi-county districts was resolved.)

Average Rice indexes indicate whether a representative was influenced more by loyalty to geographic region, or by the specific economic experiences and commercial requirements of his district. To explore this problem, the seven regional cohesion indexes for each policy category were averaged together by legislative session. (See Table 8.) While the averages show a definite trend toward stronger regional cohesion, these figures become even more significant when compared to the random indexes of cohesion in Table 9. Random cohesion is computed from the yeas and nays of the total legislature and represents the level of cohesion one would expect to find regardless of region or commercial-economic group identification. As such, it operates as a yardstick by which to measure the relative importance of cohesion levels of the regions and the two sets of commercial-economic groups.[20]

The average regional indexes of cohesion for all roll-calls were significantly higher than the random indexes for every legislative session. Indeed, the regional indexes averaged almost twenty points higher than the random measures. While some minor fluctuations between the policy categories are evident, the overall pattern over the four legislative sessions was toward greater regional cohesion.

The average commercial-economic group indexes of cohesion demonstrate a similar trend. (See Table 10.)

Although the average measures for all roll-calls tend not to be as high as those of the regions, these indexes still averaged over eleven points higher than the random scores. With the exception of the Procedural and Education categories, the highest average indexes within each policy classification, as with the regional measures, were registered during the 1859 session.

The average cohesion measures for the commercial-economic aggregate groups present a much less convincing pattern. (See Table 11.) While still averaging over ten points higher than the random indexes for all roll-calls, the trends within the individual policy categories do not project the sense of increasing cohesion over time as the regional and commercial-economic group indexes do. This points to a fairly acute awareness of each district's <u>relative</u> commercial and economic position on the part of the representatives. In other words, views on various legislative issues, rather than remaining static over the four sessions, tended to fluctuate with the changing needs of the district.

Although the above tables indicate increasing levels of regional and commercial-economic cohesion, a great deal of variation occurred in the degree of cohesion among the regions and the two types of commercial-economic groups. Table 12 gives the four-session index average for the seven regions. Again, it is important to compare these results with the random averages. (See Table 13.) The regional

TABLE 8

AVERAGE REGIONAL RICE INDEXES OF COHESION BY POLICY CATEGORY AND SESSION*

Policy Category	1829	1839	1849	1859
1. Procedural	60.37	49.88	48.46	54.63
3. Governmental	45.85	47.46	48.30	50.89
4. Transportation	47.40	49.88	51.40	62.64
5. Business/Commerce	68.14	53.88	51.40	63.55
6. Banking	34.49	47.05	50.24	50.86
7. Pub.Hlth/Welfare	40.31	54.23	50.24	60.55
8. Education	21.10	51.82	45.84	50.55
9. Religion	24.13	---	41.36	49.96
10. Agriculture	51.33	42.76	45.80	47.42
11. Miscellaneous	58.70	57.01	46.52	72.47
All Roll-Calls	44.95	50.41	50.27	58.47

*The mean index of cohesion for each policy category was first computed by region. These regional means were then averaged to provide a single measure of regional cohesion by policy for each legislative session.

Source: See Table 6.

TABLE 9

RANDOM INDEXES OF COHESION BY POLICY CATEGORY AND SESSION*

Policy Category	1829	1839	1849	1859
1. Procedural	56.64	27.27	21.50	32.17
3. Governmental	31.31	29.38	28.27	27.69
4. Transportation	29.20	25.45	29.18	37.22
5. Business/Commerce	29.21	28.70	33.06	45.63
6. Banking	20.66	31.49	22.34	28.32
7. Pub.Hlth/Welfare	33.95	38.50	36.74	45.95
8. Education	16.63	29.26	26.26	36.00
9. Religion	7.41	---	30.75	51.19
10. Agriculture	23.80	27.54	14.28	5.88
11. Miscellaneous	56.51	71.06	31.14	54.00
All Roll-Calls	31.95	29.57	27.88	36.48

*The Random Index of Cohesion is computed from the yeas and nays cast by the total legislature.

Source: See Table 6.

TABLE 10

AVERAGE COMMERCIAL-ECONOMIC GROUP RICE INDEXES OF COHESION BY POLICY CATEGORY AND SESSION*

Policy Category	1829	1839	1849	1859
1. Procedural	53.26	40.06	58.23	50.69
3. Governmental	40.44	41.87	41.86	45.33
4. Transportation	40.99	37.24	41.99	53.20
5. Business/Commerce	30.14	34.79	45.20	49.33
6. Banking	33.17	39.75	34.77	41.65
7. Pub.Hlth/Welfare	41.45	47.83	47.54	58.23
8. Education	29.02	64.55	48.36	41.36
9. Religion	23.19	---	40.35	63.28
10. Agriculture	43.43	23.15	51.14	51.28
11. Miscellaneous	51.89	46.32	42.21	60.66
All roll-calls	40.16	39.14	41.42	50.65

*The mean index of cohesion for each policy category was first computed by commercial-economic group. These commercial-economic group means were then averaged to provide a single measure of commercial-economic group cohesion for each legislative session.

Source: See Table 6.

measures still registered above the random scores for all roll-calls and for most policy categories, yet there was enormous variation in the overall cohesion averages ranging from a low of 34.86 to a high of 83.15. In general, the more populous, economically-diverse regions like the Southeastern and Western regions rarely approached the more significant levels of cohesion found in the more sparsely inhabited areas like the Pocono, Northeastern, and Allegheny Forest Regions.

The indexes of cohesion for the commercial-economic groups reflect a complementary pattern. (See Table 14.) The cohesion scores for all roll-calls and, with few exceptions, for all policy categories are above the random index scores. The levels of cohesion in general, however, were lower than those of the regions. The less developed commercial-economic groups tended to vote with greater cohesion than the more developed groups. With the exception of the Business/Commerce and Agriculture policy categories, the most developed commercial-economic group (group 5) continually had the lowest levels of cohesion, while group 1, with the exception of Agriculture and Education, had the highest. The average indexes for the commercial-economic aggregate groups again reflect much less convincing patterns. The cohesion averages, as Table 15 indicates, were still slightly above the random indexes. Yet, with the exception of group 3, these average scores tended to be

TABLE 11

AVERAGE COMMERCIAL-ECONOMIC AGGREGATE GROUP RICE INDEXES OF COHESION BY POLICY CATEGORY AND SESSION*

Policy Category	1829	1839	1849	1859
1. Procedural	52.08	37.08	39.68	34.21
3. Governmental	38.23	39.92	40.86	33.84
4. Transportation	40.99	37.83	43.74	45.88
5. Business/Commerce	36.24	41.75	47.75	49.11
6. Banking	33.15	45.21	39.64	35.13
7. Pub.Hlth/Welfare	39.95	48.09	44.39	58.27
8. Education	31.05	40.72	34.38	43.24
9. Religion	11.20	---	33.63	50.28
10. Agriculture	48.74	40.60	33.81	63.81
11. Miscellaneous	52.07	48.86	39.82	58.61
All roll-calls	42.98	40.18	41.50	43.50

*The mean index of cohesion for each policy category was first computed by commercial-economic aggregate group. These commercial-economic aggregate group means were then averaged to provide a single measure of commercial-economic aggregate group cohesion for each legislative session.

Source: See Table 6.

TABLE 12

AVERAGE RICE INDEXES OF COHESION BY REGION AND POLICY CATEGORY FOR THE 1828-29, 1838-39, 1849 AND 1859 SESSIONS

Policy Category	Region 1	2	3*	4	5	6	7
1. Procedural	37.38	43.92	100.00	65.97	58.83	72.35	31.63
3. Governmental	32.22	41.42	80.00	65.98	45.48	63.83	37.57
4. Transportation	35.95	50.27	92.86	71.64	46.44	72.86	38.31
5. Business/Commerce	35.33	59.01	85.71	80.80	63.29	73.16	41.48
6. Banking	30.27	41.60	76.92	75.74	48.09	50.08	32.00
7. Pub.Hlt/Welfare	40.34	53.65	50.00	69.64	48.28	62.30	43.76
8. Education	28.12	43.07	66.67	56.87	47.74	44.93	38.17
9. Religion	27.53	32.38	0.00	36.25	71.76	36.61	47.16
10. Agriculture	17.12	67.86	---	100.00	51.11	33.33	27.62
11. Miscellaneous	47.13	59.44	83.33	75.87	56.90	64.65	49.65
ALL ROLL-CALLS	34.86	48.15	83.15	71.42	38.46	64.93	39.17

*Indexes of cohesion computed for Region 3 only during the 1859 session when the region was represented by more than one member.

Source: See Table 6 .

Table 13

AVERAGE RANDOM INDEXES OF COHESION BY POLICY CATEGORY FOR THE 1828-29. 1838-39, 1849 and 1859 LEGISLATIVE SESSIONS

Policy Category	Cohesion Index
1. Procedural	34.40
3. Governmental	29.16
4. Transportation	30.26
5. Business/Commerce	34.15
6. Banking	25.70
7. Public Health/Welfare	38.79
8. Education	27.04
9. Religion	29.78
10. Agriculture	17.88
11. Miscellaneous	53.18
ALL ROLL-CALLS	31.47

Source: See Table 6.

below those for the commercial-economic groups and for most regions.

Even though the regional indexes averaged higher than the commercial-economic or commercial-economic aggregate group scores, there was much greater variation among the regional indexes than among the two sets of commercial-economic measures. Those sparsely settled areas with less complex economies like the Pocono, Northeastern, and Allegheny Forest Regions and the less developed commercial-economic groups sent only a handful of legislators to the Assembly which made it much easier for them to agree on policies. Representatives from the regions and commercial-economic groups which sent the most members to Harrisburg had more sophisticated and varied demands and they, not surprisingly, had greater difficulty achieving the cohesion levels of these other regions and groups. In many ways, these patterns worked to the benefit of the less-developed areas by allowing them to counter the numerical advantage of the more populated regions with greater cohesion.

The fact remains, however, that the regional and two sets of commercial-economic cohesion scores all increased during the antebellum years. It may well be that these two trends were reinforcing one another. In other words, regional and economic development patterns tended to converge over time. As Table 16 indicates, the commercial-economic group distribution of the counties

TABLE 14

AVERAGE RICE INDEXES OF COHESION BY COMMERCIAL-ECONOMIC GROUP AND POLICY CATEGORY FOR THE 1828-29, 1838-39, 1849 AND 1859 SESSIONS

	Commercial-Economic Group				
Policy Category	1	2	3	4	5
1. Procedural	65.54	40.84	45.46	48.27	34.84
3. Governmental	51.75	41.67	43.88	39.71	34.85
4. Transportation	51.28	43.20	43.86	41.86	36.58
5. Business/Commerce	37.32	44.86	35.46	45.10	41.59
6. Banking	41.18	38.21	37.06	32.10	38.12
7. Pub.Hlth/Welfare	59.35	43.24	47.00	51.97	42.27
8. Education	42.95	39.97	49.88	39.64	28.01
9. Religion	63.49	45.20	28.79	46.06	27.83
10. Agriculture	40.00	53.38	30.50	46.32	38.23
11. Miscellaneous	61.67	47.73	47.36	45.51	49.10
ALL ROLL-CALLS	51.20	42.32	42.01	41.62	37.07

Source: See Table 6.

TABLE 15

AVERAGE RICE INDEXES OF COHESION BY COMMERCIAL-ECONOMIC AGGREGATE GROUP AND POLICY CATEGORY FOR THE 1828-29, 1838-39, 1849 AND 1859 SESSIONS

Policy Category	Commercial-Economic Aggregate Group			
	2	3	4	5
1. Procedural	30.02	46.72	45.05	41.26
3. Governmental	35.29	40.20	38.95	38.41
4. Transportation	39.03	49.47	41.35	38.59
5. Business/Commerce	42.90	48.20	39.13	44.61
6. Banking	36.28	37.82	34.83	44.21
7. Pub.Hlth/Welfare	56.82	49.01	50.89	43.38
8. Education	33.93	39.64	43.54	32.27
9. Religion	42.19	30.63	22.47	31.51
10. Agriculture	66.39	41.92	36.56	42.09
11. Miscellaneous	50.01	47.24	55.21	46.91
ALL ROLL-CALLS	38.85	48.14	40.20	40.98

Source: See Table 6.

Table 16

PERCENT OF COUNTIES IN EACH COMMERCIAL-ECONOMIC GROUP BY REGION AND SESSION

	Commercial-Economic Group				
Year	1	2	3	4	5
Region 1: Southeastern					
1829			30.77	15.38	53.85
1839		23.08	15.38	15.38	46.15
1849				30.77	69.23
1859			7.69	23.08	69.23
Region 2: Anthracite					
1829	50.00		16.67	16.67	16.67
1839		16.67	16.67	50.00	16.67
1849		12.50	12.50	62.50	12.50
1859			25.00	50.00	25.00
Region 3: Pocono					
1829		50.00			50.00
1839	33.33	33.33			33.33
1849	66.67		33.33		
1859		66.67	33.33		
Region 4: Northeastern					
1829	33.33	33.33	33.33		
1839			66.67	33.33	
1849	25.00		75.00		
1859		75.00	25.00		

Table 16 cont'd.

Year	Commercial-Economic Group 1	2	3	4	5
Region 5: Ridge and Valley					
1829	16.67	16.67	16.67	50.00	
1839		14.29	42.86	28.57	14.29
1849	11.11	22.22	33.33		33.33
1859	40.00		30.00	20.00	10.00
Region 6: Allegheny Forest					
1829	28.57	42.86	14.29	14.29	
1839	50.00	12.50		25.00	12.50
1849	63.64	18.18	18.18		
1859	75.00		16.67	8.33	
Region 7: Western					
1829	21.43	28.57	14.29	21.43	14.29
1839	42.86	28.57	14.29	7.14	7.14
1849	6.67	46.67	20.00	20.00	6.67
1859		53.33	26.67	13.33	6.67

Source: See Chapters 2 and 3.

within each region was much more diverse during the 1820s than it had become by the 1850s. Indeed, with the exception of the Ridge and Valley area, all regions tended to become more commercially and economically alike over the four decades. During the early decades, it was not uncommon for counties within each region to be spread all along the commercial-economic continuum. By the eve of the Civil War, however, the majority of the counties within each region clustered in one or two adjacent commercial-economic groups.

While a great deal of intra-regional diversity still remained, a growing commonality of economic and commercial needs bolstered and encouraged a more unified regional outlook. Representatives may have been motivated as much by the relative level of economic development of their districts as by an attachment to their specific region. A closer examination of the hotly contested banking, business, and transportation issues can help to sort out these distinctions.

FOOTNOTES

[1]Harry N. Scheiber, "Federalism and the American Economic Order, 1789-1910," Law and Society Review 10(Fall 1975): 83-84, 97-98. See also Ballard Campbell, Representative Democracy: Public Policy and Mid-Western Legislatures in the Late Nineteenth Century (Cambridge: Harvard University Press, 1980), pp. v-vi, 1-2; Ballard Campbell, "The State Legislature in American History: A Review Essay," Historical Methods Newsletter 9(September 1976): 185; L. Ray Gunn, "Crisis of Authority in the Antebellum States: New York, 1820-1860," The Review of Politics (April 1979): 276; Richard P. McCormick, "New Perspectives on Jacksonian Politics," American Historical Review 65(January 1960): 228-30.

[2]Douglas E. Bowers, "From Logrolling to Corruption: The Development of Lobbying in Pennsylvania, 1815-1861," Journal of the Early Republic 3(Winter 1983): 473-4; Douglas E. Bowers, "The Pennsylvania Legislature, 1815-1860: A Study of Democracy at Work" (Ph.D. dissertation, University of Chicago, 1974), pp. 128-29; Gunn, "Crisis of Authority," pp. 284-85; L. Ray Gunn, "Political Implications of General Incorporation Laws in New York to 1860," Mid-America 59(October 1977): passim.

[3]Scheiber, "Federalism," pp. 88-89. See also Gunn, "Crisis of Authority," pp. 284-85; L. Ray Gunn, "The New York State Legislature: A Developmental Perspective," Social Science History (August 1980): 271; Theodore J. Lowi, "Business, Public Policy, Case Studies, and Political Theories, " World Politics 16(July 1964): 677-715; Richard L. McCormick, "The Party Period and Public Policy: An Exploratory Hypothesis," Journal of American History 56(September 1979): 279-98.

[4]Gunn, "New York State Legislature," p.274.

[5]Ibid., pp.270-71; Gunn, "Crisis of Authority," p. 284; McCormick, "Party Period and Public Policy," pp. 283-85.

[6]Historians have found that turnover rates for state legislators increased rapidly during the antebellum decades. Southern states experienced turnover rates between 60-80% during the 1850s, 41.5% of those who sat in the New Jersey state legislature between 1829 and 1844 served for only one year while an additional 38.5% served for only two years. In New York, turnover reached its peak between 1845 and 1848 when 89% of the assembly had no prior legislative experience and no one had served for more than two terms. Membership

in the Pennsylvania House of Representatives was only slightly more stable. Between 1814 and 1823 close to 60% of all state legislators had previous experience. By the 1850s this figure had dropped to 40.4%.

See Bowers, "From Logrolling to Corruption," p. 443; Gunn, "New York Legislature," pp. 277-81; Peter D. Levine, The Behavior of State Legislative Parties in the Jacksonian Era: New Jersey, 1829-1844 (Rutherford-Teaneck, N.J.: Fairleigh Dickinson University Pres, 1977), pp. 76-78.

[7]Gunn, "Crisis of Authority," pp. 275-76. See also Bowers, "From Logrolling to Corruption," pp. 443-44; Bowers, "The Pennsylvania Legislature," pp. 5-8, 251-54.

[8]McCormick, "The Party Period and Public Policy," p. 285.

[9]Joel H. Silbey, The Partisan Imperative: The Dynamics of American Politics Before the Civil War (New York, Oxford: Oxford University Press, 1985), p. 13.

[10]Bowers, "The Pennsylvania Legislature," pp. 1-3, 94-95.

[11]Ibid.; Charles M. Snyder, The Jacksonian Heritage: Pennsylvania Politics, 1833-1848 (Harrisburg, PA: Pennsylvania Historical and Museum Commission, 1958), pp. 13-15.

[12]Bowers, "The Pennsylvania Legislature," pp. 251-53.

[13]Pennsylvania, Laws of the Commonwealth of Pennsylvania, 1828-29, 1859.

[14]Pennsylvania, House of Representatives, Legislative Journal, Vol. 1, 1828-29, 1838-39, 1849, 1859.

[15]Bowers, "The Pennsylvania Legislature," pp. 58-61.

[16]Ibid., pp. 62-63.

[17]Ibid., pp. 104-122.

[18]Prior to the 1838 Constitution, subjects of all descriptions were frequently united into a single bill. This practice was specifically outlawed by the new constitution in an attempt to keep legislators free from what was perceived to be the growing and pernicious influence of the lobbyists. See Bowers, "From Logrolling to Corruption."

[19]Lee F. Anderson, Meredith W. Watts, Jr., and Allen R. Wilcox, Legislative Roll-Call Analysis (Evanston: Northwestern University Press, 1966), pp. 29-43; Bowers, "The Pennsylvania Legislature," pp. 275-6; Stuart A. Rice, Quantitative Methods in Politics (New York: Alfred A. Knopf, 1928), pp. 207-27.

There appears to be no generally accepted level above which significant cohesion is reached. Random cohesion, or the index computed from the yeas and nays of the total legislature, must always be taken into account. Broadly speaking, cohesion below 40 is considered low, between 40 and 60, moderate, above 60, fairly high, and above 80, very high.

[20]Bowers, "The Pennsylvania Legislature," p. 275.

CHAPTER FIVE

AGENTS OF ECONOMIC AND POLITICAL CHANGE: BANKING AND BUSINESS CORPORATIONS

Throughout the first half of the nineteenth century, the Pennsylvania General Assembly grappled with the problems and challenges presented by a rapidly expanding economy. As demands from across the state flooded into the legislative chambers in Harrisburg, elected representatives struggled to strike some sort of balance between public and private interests and to develop adequate yet equitable ways of promoting and guiding the course of the commonwealth's economy. The institution which ultimately emerged as the most common form of economic enterprise was the corporation. Between 1800 and 1860, some 2,320 charters were granted incorporating companies for various financial, commercial, or manufacturing purposes by individual, special laws.[1] Most of these charters were enacted for turnpikes, bridges, canals, and later, railroads.[2] Questions concerning the powers the corporation should be allowed and the restrictions which should be placed upon it, however, were hammered out in debates over charters for banks, manufacturing, mining and other types of companies.

Only one corporation, the Philadelphia Contributionship for the Insuring of Houses from Loss by Fire, was created in Pennsylvania prior to the American Revolution.[3] During the Revolution both the newly-created Pennsylvania Assembly and

Congress began to experiment with chartered banks to help meet the financial exigencies of the war. In May, 1781, Robert Morris persuaded Congress to charter the Bank of North America as a national institution. The constitutionality of the charter had been in question during the debates and remained so even after the bank had begun business. As a result, the bank's board of directors applied to the Pennsylvania legislature for a state charter as well. Here, there was opposition to the provisions for a perpetual charter and to allow the bank to hold real estate. These objections were overcome and in 1782, the Bank of North America became the first bank to be chartered by the Pennsylvania General Assembly.[4]

The Bank of North America rendered invaluable service to both the commonwealth and the nation during the Revolution. But subsequent controversy over it continued into the 1790s and raised issues concerning the role of banks in general that would surface again and again well into the nineteenth century. The central questions revolved around its exclusive grant of power and the functions it should be expected to perform. In 1784, the Bank of North America quickly squelched an attempt to establish a competing bank. Yet the following year, it was bitterly attacked for its failure to support the state's paper money policy. Although the bank ultimately promoted the circulation of paper money, it was still charged with favoritism. The Assembly went so far as to appoint a committee "to inquire whether the bank established at Philadelphia was compatible with the public safety and that equality which ever ought to prevail between individuals and a republic."[5]

The state began to develop a variety of tactics to exert greater control over the institution it had incorporated. The new charter granted to the bank in 1787 was limited to fourteen years and prohibited it from owning real estate beyond that necessary to conduct business, or from trading in any merchandise other than bullion and bills of exchange. Embezzlement on the part of the bank's directors was punishable by death, a penalty that was relaxed somewhat the following year.[6]

Several years later, the state offered to purchase a portion of the bank's stock. When the board of directors rejected this scheme, the state chartered a rival institution, the Bank of Pennsylvania, in 1793. In addition to owning one million dollars worth of stock in the new bank, the state was authorized to appoint six of the twenty-five directors and was to use the bank as the official deposit agency for state funds, an arrangement that would continue until 1830. In turn, the bank was required to lend the commonwealth $500,000 on demand at interest not to exceed six percent. While the state had developed some official arrangements with the Bank of North America, its relationship with the Bank of Pennsylvania was much more specific and spelled out a much more intimate linkage of commonwealth and bank finances. It was a quasi-public institution.[7]

This type of close relationship between the state and the banks it chartered continued well into the 1840s. Like the Bank of North America, the Bank of Pennsylvania fought unsuccessfully to retain its privileged position by attempting to block the incorporation of additional banks. In 1803, the Bank of Philadelphia which had been operating as a partnership for a month or so, applied to the legislature for a state charter. Alarmed at the prospect of having a competing bank established within the same city, the Bank of Pennsylvania ultimately offered to pay the state $200,000 upon condition that no new bank be chartered. The commonwealth, however, was already feeling the woeful lack of adequate banking facilities and simultaneously recognized a way to improve the state's financial situation. In the end, the Bank of Philadelphia received its charter after agreeing to pay $135,000 to the state for the privilege. In addition, the commonwealth was authorized to subscribe up to one-half million dollars worth of stock in the new bank, while the bank had to promise to lend the state up to $100,000 at five percent upon demand.[8] The terms agreed upon in granting the Bank of Philadelphia's charter established precedents that would be followed for the next forty years. Through the bonus practice, state stock subscriptions, and the lending requirements, the commonwealth's finances were inextricably interwoven with the banks that it chartered. Eventually, the propriety of such a close relationship was called into question, and along with it the very nature of the banks themselves.

Pressure to charter new banks continued to mount during the first decade and a half of the nineteenth century. Despite the fact that the Bank of Pennsylvania had established several branch banks throughout the state, those living in the interior regions constantly complained about the inadequacy of banking facilities in their communities, claiming that the existing banks continually drained much-needed specie away from the country and toward the city. Implicit in these demands was the belief that the banks themselves were somehow responsible for creating prosperity. Desperately in need of a circulating medium, those living in less-developed areas without immediate access to financial institutions came to see banks as the certain path to economic progress. Those seeking new bank charters argued against the privileged position of earlier banks.[9]

Persuaded in part by these entreaties and in part lured by the financial perquisites that the state would accrue by granting additional charters, the legislature passed a very liberal banking act in 1814. The commonwealth undoubtedly profited from the bonuses, dividends and favorable loan terms it received from creating forty-one new banks in one fell swoop under the terms of the act. But the ensuing flood of paper money coupled with the economic dislocation caused by the termination of the War of 1812 led to a mass suspension of specie payments which continued into the early 1820s. Of the forty-one banks created by the act, only twenty-two remained as specie-paying banks ten years later. All this only confirmed the suspicions of the more cautious Governor Snyder who had twice vetoed the "omnibus" banking bill on the grounds that the existing banks served the needs of the commonwealth adequately.[10]

Despite this rather poor record and the financial distress caused by the Panic of 1819, the clamor for banking facilities in the interior areas continued. In response to these demands, the banking act of 1824 renewed the charters of the remaining 1814 banks under similar terms. Although the banks were now required to pay an eight percent, as opposed to a six percent, return on state dividends, the provision requiring the banks to make one-year loans for up to one-fifth of their capital to farmers, mechanics and manufacturers in their respective districts was retained and thus satisfied the need for a circulating medium and additional investment capital in areas removed from the larger financial centers.[11]

Demands for charters for other types of business endeavors were not as intense. Between 1800 and 1820, only thirteen charters were granted for manufacturing purposes and only nine to insurance companies.[12] Although the commonwealth quickly extended its mixed enterprise involvement to transportation by authorizing stock subscriptions in numerous turnpike, bridge and canal companies, it never played as active a role in these enterprises. This does not necessarily indicate any conscious hostility toward these groups, but only the limited demand for these types of charters. Prior to the 1830s, most manufacturing and mining concerns still were quite small and had little need of a more sophisticated form of corporate organization.[13]

The 1830s was a turning point in the development of corporate policy, a time of growing skepticism about direct state involvement in banking and transportation and of mounting hostility toward corporations in general. The number of bank and business charters increased markedly. (See Table 17.) The state was constantly in need of more and more money to finance the construction and administration of the Pennsylvania canal system, and the legislature continually succumbed to pressure to charter new banks to secure funds by way of bonuses, dividends and loans. The number of charters for manufacturing and mining companies grew due to the opening of the anthracite country and the development of new fuel markets.

While rumblings of discontent over the privileged and monopolistic character of banks had always surfaced during previous charter debates, the attack which took shape in the 1830s had a new twist. Those who had opposed banks earlier in the century had argued against the privileges of the existing banks and, as in 1814 and again in 1824, contended that more banks were needed to counteract their influence. Now those who took up the anti-bank crusade tended to attack not just specific banks, but <u>all</u> banks. This mounting hostility was fueled by President Jackson's veto of the Second Bank of the United States and by the Panic of 1837; when banks and businesses alike suspended their operations, ceased to deal in specie, and defaulted on payments to their creditors, this only confirmed their fears.

TABLE 17

NUMBER OF BANKS AND BUSINESS CORPORATIONS CHARTERED BY DECADE

Years	Number Banks Chartered	Number Businesses Chartered
1820-29	8	3
1830-39	34	40
1840-49	11	26
1850-59	70	100

Source: William Miller, "A Note on the History of Business Corporations in Pennsylvania, 1800-1860," *Quarterly Journal of Economics* 55(November 1940): 156-58.

Corporations in general became the objects of attack. Somewhere along the line, the opponents argued, corporations had lost their quasi-public character and were no longer acting as "agencies of government."[14] Rather than fulfilling a broad public mandate, they had come into direct conflict with individual rights. Powerful monopolies had acquired privileges and control that threatened the very sovereignty of the people. Granting corporate rights where unincorporated individuals had made investments was itself an infringement upon the rights of the individual, and the concept of limited liability absolved the corporation of responsiblities that should not be tolerated by a publicly-created institution in a democratic society.[15] "We [have] arrived at a crisis now," stated one anti-corporation legislator in 1839. "We must settle the question whether the Commonwealth of Pennsylania must be governed by corporate monopolies, or whether the honest yeomanry of the country [are] to remain free."[16]

The role of the corporation for both banking and business purposes was intensely debated over the next decade. The number of charters granted decreased significantly during the next ten years (see Table 17). The state slowly, but irrevocably, withdrew from its close relationship with incorporated banks, first by curtailing the bonus practice in 1842, and shortly thereafter by liquidating its stock in all banks.[17] Those in favor of the corporation continued to argue that an expanding economy needed the incentives provided by the corporate structure, while those opposed to the charter policy constantly threw up roadblocks by pushing for stricter individual liability, shorter time limits for charters, and other restrictions intended to strip the corporation of its most distinguishable yet controversial characteristics.

By the 1850s, the number of charters increased to unprecedented numbers as those opposed became less adamant and vocal. The memories of the debacles of the 1830s had faded in the face of improved economic conditions, and even those who continued to oppose certain corporate features had come to recognize that the corporation was an indispensable asset in a growing economy. Indeed, the terms of the debate now shifted away from the particulars of individual charters toward the advisability of enacting general incorporation laws which would make the acquisition of a charter more routine and easier.

These shifting sentiments toward banks and business corporations were reflected in the voting patterns of Pennsylvania's representatives. Legislators who demonstrated great interest in a more lenient and expansive banking policy during the 1820s came from those areas which became the centers of opposition toward all corporations in the late 1830s and 1840s. In contrast, those representatives who had displayed a more cautious approach toward expanded banking and corporate policies in the earlier decade were from districts which would send the most ardent corporate proponents to the legislature two decades later.

To some degree, regional self-interest served as a motivating factor when the legislators cast their roll-call votes. Representatives tended to favor chartering various banks and businesses when they directly benefited their region or district. Yet on the whole, the location of the various charters tended to reinforce already existing pro- and anti-corporation sentiments. During the 1830s and 1840s, petitions for charters came overwhelmingly from the areas of the state which demonstrated strong pro-corporation support. These districts were among the most commercial and economically-developed, and their representatives voted not only for charters in their own regions, but for the incorporation of most other banks and businesses and for broader powers for the corporation in general. By the late 1850s, those areas which had displayed such ardent opposition to charter enactments a decade earlier no longer demonstrated such overt hostility. Accepting the fact that the corporation had become a permanent fixture in American life, legislators from these counties voted increasingly in favor of charters, particularly for banks and enterprises that would enhance their region's economy, but also for the more lenient terms set forth in the general incorporation bills.

II

Pennsylvania state representatives debated and voted on acts of incorporation for numerous banks and business ventures as well as on extensions and alterations in existing charters. While specific sections of bills often came up for individual roll-calls, debated bills usually were subjected to a final vote after the third reading. Regardless of how individual legislators felt about specific sections and provisions, they were called upon to make a final judgment on whether or not the bill should pass.[18] Tables 18 and 19 give the percentage of pro-bank and pro-business votes on these final roll-calls.

Business incorporation bills were less controversial. With the exception of the 1838-39 session, the percent voting to charter business corporations averaged close to ten points higher than those in favor of bank charters for all regions and both sets of commercial-economic groups. The banks were perceived as more intimately involved with the health of the economy due to their close association with the commonwealth's financial affairs and through their role as suppliers of a circulating medium, as providers of much needed capital, and as repositories for individual deposits. They became much more susceptible to public criticism and much readier targets for legislators who chose to fulminate about the devastating affect corporations had on the public weal. Business corporations, while still arousing controversy, were viewed as much more limited and localized entities. They aroused less hostility on the part of those who questioned the legitimacy of the corporation.

Pro-corporation sentiment grew between the 1820s and the 1840s. Although no business charters were voted upon during the 1828-29 session, the pro-banking percentages point to clear patterns of support and opposition. Representatives from the interior regions and from the less-developed commercial-economic and commercial-economic aggregate groups were more in favor of extending banking facilities than were those from the more developed groups and areas like the Southeastern and Western regions which already had adequate banking facilities. By 1838-39, legislators from the Southeastern, Anthracite, and Western regions and from the most economically developed and commercial counties were moving toward a pro-bank and pro-corporation position.

This trend had become much more striking by 1849. In an almost complete reversal of the voting patterns of the 1828-29 session, representatives from the more economically-diverse regions and the most developed areas had become ardent supporters of banking and business incorporations. Hostility toward these institutions had become firmly lodged in the interior districts in the Northeastern, Allegheny Forest and Ridge and Valley regions and in the less-developed commercial-economic and commercial-economic aggregate groups. By 1859, however, opposition from these areas had clearly dissipated. While the most supportive representatives continued to come generally from the more commercial and economically advanced counties, those in the interior regions had become quite favorably disposed to granting additional banking and business charters.

TABLE 18
PERCENT PRO-BANK VOTES ON FINAL ROLL-CALLS
BY SESSION, REGIONS, AND GROUPS

Region	1829	1839	1849	1859	Region or Group Ave.
1. Southeastern	37.19	72.35	75.53	51.01	59.02
2. Anthracite	65.38	71.43	76.11	46.59	64.88
3. Pocono	---	100.00	100.00	0.00	66.67
4. Northeastern	100.00	100.00	9.30	60.52	67.46
5. Ridge/Vlly	33.33	67.57	48.09	95.65	61.16
6. Alghny.Frst.	50.00	75.00	26.15	64.71	53.97
7. Western	36.67	69.56	69.28	59.26	58.69
Session Ave.	53.76	79.42	57.78	53.96	
Commercial-Economic Group					
1	52.38	58.00	47.22	29.41	46.75
2	55.56	57.14	49.04	47.73	53.62
3	39.02	59.02	59.90	44.76	50.68
4	46.30	62.77	63.29	69.77	60.53
5	31.00	75.30	77.86	54.27	59.61
Session Ave.	44.85	62.45	59.46	51.19	
Commercial-Econ. Aggregate Group					
1	---	20.00	---	---	20.00
2	50.00	66.23	52.03	48.62	54.20
3	50.00	76.29	40.36	50.34	54.25
4	38.89	48.94	54.58	52.83	48.81
5	33.68	69.49	89.80	74.11	66.77
Session Ave.	43.14	56.17	59.19	56.48	

Source: Pennsylvania, House of Representatives. Legislative Journal. Vol. 1, 1828-29, 1838-39, 1849, 1859.

Map

TABLE 19

PERCENT PRO-BUSINESS VOTES ON FINAL ROLL-CALLS BY SESSION, REGIONS AND GROUPS

	1839	1849	1859	Region or Group Ave.
Region				
1. Southeastern	60.79	79.58	70.71	70.36
2. Anthracite	81.51	77.55	74.44	77.83
3. Pocono	89.47	100.00	18.18	69.22
4. Northeastern	98.18	33.33	82.61	71.37
5. Ridge/Vlly.	59.74	48.48	81.58	63.18
6. Alghny.Fst.	77.94	38.46	77.42	64.61
7. Western	62.74	79.33	74.43	72.17
Session Ave.	75.77	65.25	68.48	
Commercial-Economic Group				
1	55.49	64.71	100.00	73.40
2	50.40	59.09	30.77	46.75
3	55.25	69.31	58.33	60.96
4	70.72	54.08	46.67	57.16
5	73.34	83.06	86.11	80.84
Session Ave.	61.04	66.05	64.38	
Commercial-Econ. Aggregate Group				
1	0.00	---	---	0.00
2	66.80	65.55	50.00	60.78
3	79.89	53.64	57.89	63.81
4	39.03	56.25	60.00	51.76
5	70.98	91.34	82.76	81.69
Session Ave.	51.34	66.70	62.66	

Check which counties

Source: See Table 18.

To what extent are these patterns reflections of regional self-interest? To what degree did the location of the proposed bank or business influence legislative voting behavior? Regional location was a factor, although it was more in evidence in some regions and during some sessions. In the 1828-29 session, there were proposals to incorporate or extend the charter of three banks, one each in the Southeastern, Anthracite and Northeastern regions. (See Table 20.) While the Anthracite representatives voted unanimously to incorporate a bank in their region, those from the Southeastern counties could not even muster majority support to consider chartering the Manufacturer's Bank to be located in Northern Liberties, a suburb of Philadelphia. The reluctance of the single Northeastern representative to vote on the third bank is somewhat puzzling. Although he voted consistently in favor of incorporations in other districts, he chose not to vote on the revival of the charter of the Silver Lake Bank located in his own region which had been chartered under the 1814 act, but had subsequently lost its charter due to its failure to redeem in specie.[19]

Similar patterns emerged during the 1838-39 session. (See Table 21.) Although no banks applied for charters during this session, which is not surprising given the prevailing financial climate, the Miner's Bank in Schuylkill county (Anthracite Region) applied for a short extension of its charter, and the Philadelphia Savings Institution sought to alter its charter slightly. Both measures received strong support in the legislature as a whole and in their home region, although continued reticence on the part of some Southeastern legislators is detectable.

More interesting are the voting patterns surrounding the controversy over the Lumberman's Bank in Warren county in the Allegheny Forest Region. Pennsylvania banks had been forced to suspend their specie payments in the wake of the Panic of 1837. The banking acts of 1814 and 1824, however, had made charter revocation the automatic penalty for specie suspension. This penalty became difficult to enforce in the face of such widespread default. In July of 1838, Governor Ritner ordered the banks to resume their specie payments the following month, or run the risk of losing their charters. Most banks did resume payment, and most managed to continue until October of 1839 when they were forced to suspend payment once again.[20]

During the first period of specie resumption, the Lumberman's' Bank was unable to resume payment and appealed to the legislature to be allowed to continue business and to be given extra time to meet the governor's demands. The debate over the Lumberman's Bank resolution resulted in no less than eight roll-call votes and raised numerous constitutional questions concerning charter revocation. Although the resolution eventually passed, giving the bank until September of 1839 to resume its specie payments, the

Table 20

PERCENT PRO-BANK ON FINAL ROLL-CALLS BY REGION AND REGIONAL LOCATION OF BANKS, 1828-29

Regional Location	Regions 1	2	3	4	5	6	7
1. So.Estrn.	43.90	55.56	---	100.00	33.33	50.00	31.58
2. Antrcte.	50.00	100.00	---	100.00	55.56	50.00	54.55
4. No.Estrn.	15.79	50.00	---	---	10.00	50.00	21.05

Source: See Table 18.

Table 21

PERCENT PRO-BANK ON FINAL ROLL-CALLS BY REGION AND REGIONAL LOCATION OF BANKS, 1838-39

Regional Location	Region 1	2	3	4	5	6	7
1. So.Estrn.	77.14	100.00	100.00	100.00	100.00	100.00	90.48
2. Antrcte.	90.63	83.33	100.00	100.00	100.00	66.67	73.33
6. Algny.Frst.	65.05	59.09	100.00	100.00	53.85	71.43	63.29

Source: See Table 18.

Table 22

PERCENT PRO-BUSINESS ON FINAL ROLL-CALLS BY REGION AND REGIONAL LOCATION OF CORPORATIONS, 1838-39

Regional Location	Region 1	2	3	4	5	6	7
1. So.Estrn.	67.57	100.00	---	---	66.67	100.00	88.24
2. Antrcte.	58.94	83.91	100.00	100.00	53.09	76.32	51.77
4. No.Estrn.	64.63	70.00	100.00	100.00	75.00	83.33	70.73
5. Rdge/Vlly.	54.22	75.00	50.00	100.00	66.67	85.71	73.68
6. Algny.Frst.	66.43	76.92	100.00	100.00	65.63	69.23	69.14

Source: See Table 18.

bank was never able to meet this requirement and was eventually forced to close its doors.[21]

Support for the Lumberman's Bank was strong not only within the home region, but also in other interior, less-developed areas like the Pocono and Northeastern regions. Representatives from these areas tended to sympathize with the plight of country banks that faced a constant battle to prevent the draining of their specie reserves. Those legislators from areas where banks had been able to comply with the governor's demands like the Southeastern, Anthracite, and Western regions, however, gave much less supportive to waiving the specie suspension penalty.

The correlation between regional voting and the location of business corporations is equally uneven for the 1838-39 session. (See Table 22.) During this session, eighteen companies applied for charters of incorporation. Seventeen of these were coal or iron companies[22], or a combination thereof, and the remaining one was a Philadelphia mutual insurance company. Nine of the mining companies were located in the Anthracite Region, four in the Allegheny Forest Region, and two each in the Northeastern and Ridge and Valley regions. While each of these regions gave majority support to all of these proposed charters, clear regional motivation is evident only in the case of the Anthracite and Northeastern regions. Those in the Southeastern, Ridge and Valley, and Allegheny Forest regions, on the other hand, voted in favor of the corporations in their own areas, but were frequently more united in their support of charters located in other regions.

The voting patterns on both banking and business incorporations during the 1849 session are much more predictable and point to a growing regional identification on the part of Pennsylvania representatives. (See Tables 23 and 24.) The 1849 debates provide the most complete glimpse of legislative behavior on the banking issue. In that year, at least fifteen banks and one savings institution applied for re-charter, and one bank and one savings institution sought initial charters of incorporation.[23] With the exception of the Pocono Region representative who was an ardent bank proponent, legislators consistently cast the highest percentage of votes for banks located in their own region.

A similar pattern prevailed in the votes on business incorporations. During the 1849 session, charters for five coal companies, three manufacturing companies and one trans-state telegraph company came to some sort of final vote in the legislature. Six of these were located in the Anthracite Region, and one each in the Southeastern and Western regions. Leaving the telegraph company aside, the home region representatives once again demonstrated consistent and strong support for the enactment of charters for business ventures of direct benefit to their districts.

One must not read too much into these displays of regional self-interest. Legislators from areas seeking bank and business incorporations voted not only for charters for their home regions, but for <u>all</u> charters. Indeed, these representatives frequently supported corporations located in other parts of the commonwealth at levels as great or greater than that given to local enterprises. Regional self-interest votes, then, must be seen as part of a larger, general support for banks and businesses which was demonstrated across the board and not simply limited to charters which directly benefited the home district.

By 1859, the evidence for strong regional self-interest is less compelling. (See Table 25.) During that session, legislators voted on the incorporation of four banks and one savings institution. Two of these were in the Southeastern Region, two in the Ridge and Valley Region, and one in the Western Region. Ten years earlier, legislators from the Ridge and Valley Region had not been very enthusiastic about banks, yet now they unanimously supported the incorporation of two banks to be located in the region in 1859. While some regional self-interest is evident on the part of the Western representatives, Southeastern legislators showed lukewarm interest at best in establishing additional banks in their area.

Of the twenty-two manufacturing and insurance companies incorporated by special legislation during the 1859 session,[24] only seven required some type of roll-call vote.

Table 23

PERCENT PRO-BANK ON FINAL ROLL-CALLS BY REGION AND REGIONAL LOCATION OF BANKS, 1849

Regional Location	Region 1	2	3	4	5	6	7
1. So.Estrn.	78.24	77.46	100.00	18.18	47.19	30.23	70.68
2. Antrcte.	67.50	77.78	---	0.00	45.45	0.00	42.11
3. Pocono	85.71	71.43	100.00	50.00	57.14	0.00	65.00
7. Western	67.46	73.08	100.00	10.00	50.00	26.67	74.60

Source: See Table 18.

Table 24

PERCENT PRO-BUSINESS ON FINAL ROLL-CALLS BY REGION AND REGIONAL LOCATION OF CORPORATIONS, 1849

Regional Location	Region 1	2	3	4	5	6	7
1. So.Estrn.	88.00	80.00	100.00	0.00	33.33	25.00	92.86
2. Antrcte.	74.63	75.76	100.00	33.33	45.65	35.29	72.82
7. Western	96.43	83.33	100.00	100.00	62.50	0.00	88.89

Source: See Table 18.

Granting charters, then, had become a fairly routine and _pro forma_ legislative procedure. The fact that these bills came to a vote in a legislative climate that was predominantly pro-corporation sets them apart as controversial or objectionable in some way. In any case, neither Southeastern nor Anthracite representatives displayed regional self-interest in the voting. (See Table 26.) Legislators from other regions were frequently more supportive of these bills than were those who came from the area that would directly be affected by the charter enactments.

In legislative voting behavior, therefore, region _was_ a significant factor, but it was more important for some regions and during some sessions. Representatives rarely failed to cast majority support for corporations located in their home region and thus demonstrated some sense of regional identification. Yet voting patterns suggest a much broader perception of the corporation issue. If bargaining did occur, it was carried out within tightly circumscribed boundaries. Legislators had developed general ideas about the place of banking and business corporations in Pennsylvania society. They did not cast their votes willy-nilly simply to advance their own cause; if they supported banks and businesses in their own regions, they more than likely voted in favor of granting charters in other areas.

Table 25

PERCENT PRO-BANK ON FINAL ROLL-CALLS BY REGION AND REGIONAL LOCATION OF BANKS, 1859

Regional Location	Region 1	2	3	4	5	6	7
1. So.Estrn.	50.37	46.15	0.00	75.00	100.00	50.00	45.45
5. Rdg/Vlly.	55.04	51.28	0.00	52.38	100.00	76.92	69.70
7. Western	38.24	30.00	---	60.00	66.67	100.00	78.95

Source: See Table 18.

Table 26

PERCENT PRO-BUSINESS ON FINAL ROLL-CALLS BY REGION AND REGIONAL LOCATION OF CORPORATIONS, 1859

Regional Location	Region 1	2	3	4	5	6	7
1. So.Estrn.	74.30	80.00	20.00	85.00	94.74	84.62	83.13
2. Antrcte.	70.00	63.33	25.00	87.50	50.00	69.23	67.92

Source: See Table 18.

This fact is underscored by the voting patterns of both sets of commercial-economic groups. Rarely did legislators from a given region vote unanimously; a district's place on the commercial-economic continuum also strongly influenced voting behavior. Increasingly, representatives from the more commercially and economically advanced counties consistently voted for banking and business ventures. Although some representatives from the interior regions had overcome their hostility toward the corporation by the eve of the Civil War, the strongest proponents of charter enactments continued to come from those counties which were among the most economically developed in the commonwealth.[25]

III

The final votes on acts of incorporation, charter extensions and alterations, reveal only half of the controversy surrounding antebellum banking and business corporations. Many representatives who voted "yea" on the final vote did so only after attempting a variety of tactics that, in one way or another, restricted the powers of the corporations and made it, in their eyes, a more responsible, less dangerous institution. Conversely, those who were more favorably disposed to the idea of the corporation in general were frequently forced to accept restrictions simply to ensure passage of the bill.

Nothing nettled those suspicious of the corporation more than the question of the responsbility of the company to its creditors. The concept of limited liability of stockholders, the linchpin of corporate organization, was not always immediately accepted or automatically taken for granted. Indeed, the idea that the investor could be freed from corporate obligations beyond the amount of his original commitment was anathema to many.[26] Individuals and partnerships, after all, were held responsible for all of their debts and contracts. What could be better proof of the monopolistic, undemocratic character of the corporation than a principle which absolved its members from the most basic of responsibilities?

To proponents, on the other hand, limited liability was crucial in enabling the corporation to foster the state's economic development. "There was a great distinction to be made between corporations that interfered with the enterprise of private citizens and which only obtained charters with a view of benefiting the corporators, and corporations which were instituted solely with a view of fostering the resources of the Commonwealth, and of benefiting the community at large." Unlimited liability of individual stockholders would

> have the effect of stopping all corporations now and for time to come. It would stop all future applications for corporations, because . . . there was not a company of men in the Commonwealth who would apply for an act of incorporation when their private fortunes would be made liable for the debts of the company. In truth, the great object in obtaining an act of incorporation

> was, that the company should only be liable to the amount of their capital stock, and that the corporators might be exempted individually from suits brought for payment of debts of the company.[27]

Stockholders themselves were little more than innocent investors. "It was impossible that a large number of the stockholders in any company could have the slightest voice in the management of their affairs, except so far as the election of directors went," the proponents claimed. "The majority of the stockholders know nothing of the operations of the company. . . . Make the stockholders responsible for the debts of the company, and the consequence of it will be that the innocent and the ignorant will be entrapped, while those who are most conversant with the affairs of the company will escape entirely."[28]

The question of stockholder liability occasioned repeated attempts by opponents to include some provision for individual liability, leading inevitably to innumerable roll-calls. Limited liabilty became a central issue during the 1839 session, for example, with respect to coal companies. How much individual liability could be imposed? Those suspicious of corporations favored a strict clause stating that, "The stockholders of said company, shall be individually liable for all the debts and contracts entered into, and contracted for by the same."[29] Pro-corporation members were ultimately forced to compromise on a provision included in the majority of charters eventually granted in 1839: "Each stockholder shall be liable in his individual capacity for the debts and performance of all contracts entered into by said company, to the amount of the balance unpaid on the stock held by him, so that the whole capital stock of said company, whether paid in or not, shall be liable for the said debts and contracts."[30]

The debate over liability for coal and manufacturing companies was still raging a decade later. Tables 27 and 28 compare the percentage of pro-business votes on the liability issue with the final votes on incorporation for the 1839 and 1849 sessions. The broader trends outlined earlier are evident on the limited liablity roll-calls for the regions and both types of commercial-economic groups, yet the percent voting pro-business on these roll-calls in almost all cases is less than that for the final votes. This pattern could indicate one of two things, both of which probably occurred simultaneously: many from across the state and at all levels of commercial-economic development had serious reservations about the extent of stockholder liability or those seeking charters occasionally voted to include some sort of liability clause in the belief that compromise with the opposition was the only way to secure the charter.

Limited liability became an intensely controversial issue during debates over banking charters. Banks not only conducted business transactions, but they also received the savings of countless individuals in the form of deposits. While the question of individual liability was raised briefly during the 1829 session in conjuction with the incorporation of the Wyoming Bank,[31], it wasn't until 1834 that individual liability clauses became more common in banking charters. Total liability was rarely imposed: individual stockholder responsibility for the unpaid balance on stock subscriptions became the rule.[32] The financial crisis of the late 1830s led to demands for more stringent liability clauses. One 1839 proposal required that stockholders "be liable in their individual capacity, for all debts in proportion to the amount of stock by them severally held." This measure was ultimately defeated, but the law as eventually passed contained a rather unique liability clause which implicitly acknowledged the stockholder's restricted role in the actual direction of the bank. Stockholders were only liable for debts if they personally had advised or consented to the policies which contributed to the inability of the institution to pay.[33]

By the mid-1840s, clauses such as the type defeated in 1839 became commonplace and were included in most charters. Opponents, however, continually pushed for tougher liability provisions. In 1849, for example, there were numerous attempts to make stockholders individually liable to an unlimited extent for the debts of the bank. This provision was, in fact, eventually included in the Banking Act of 1850 which set forth a model charter to be followed in future bank incorporations, and was ultimately one of the causes of the act's failure.[34]

TABLE 27

PERCENT PRO-BUSINESS BY ISSUE, REGIONS AND GROUPS, 1838-39

Issue	Regions 1	2	3	4	5	6	7
1. Final Votes	60.79	81.51	89.47	98.18	59.74	77.94	62.74
2. Limited Liability	57.67	82.10	44.44	100.00	57.14	75.00	52.25

	Commercial-Economic Groups 1	2	3	4	5
1. Final Votes	55.49	50.40	55.25	70.72	73.34
2. Limited Liability	47.83	38.51	43.56	55.79	71.73

	Commercial-Economic Aggregate Groups 1	2	3	4	5
1. Final Votes	0.00	66.80	79.89	39.03	70.98
2. Limited Liability	0.00	53.80	67.08	31.67	66.93

Source: See Table 18.

TABLE 28

PERCENT PRO-BUSINESS BY ISSUE, REGIONS AND GROUPS, 1849

Issue	Regions 1	2	3	4	5	6	7
1. Final Votes	79.58	77.55	100.00	33.33	48.48	38.46	79.33
2. Limited Liability	54.10	70.00	50.00	0.00	24.14	4.35	44.09

	Commercial-Economic Groups 1	2	3	4	5
1. Final Votes	64.71	59.09	69.31	54.08	83.06
2. Limited Liability	41.67	21.35	40.23	25.51	63.41

	Commercial-Economic Aggregate Groups 2	3	4	5
1. Final Votes	65.55	53.64	56.25	91.34
2. Limited Liability	29.57	20.00	31.25	75.77

Source: See Table 18.

Support for limited liability was, in most cases, lower than those voting pro-bank on the final votes for the 1849 session. (See Tables 29 and 30.) In 1839, however, the pro-bank voting percentages on liability roll-calls were frequently higher than those on the final votes and were, in general, greater than the 1849 percentages. Many representatives were unwilling to push the individual liability issue and saw no reason to demand stricter provisions. In the face of repeated bank suspensions which continued into the early 1840s, however, more and more legislators sought to protect themselves and their constituents from irresponsible banking practices.

In a few instances, a section was included in 1849 charters which provided for the collection of debts in the case of the insolvency of the current stockholder and extended liability back to previous stockholders for a period of up to one year. This highly restrictive measure which implicitly placed direct responsibility for banking policy on all stockholders read as follows:

> If the amount assessed . . . shall not be collected from such stockholder by reason of his insolvency or his absence from this State, the sum remaining due on such assessment shall be recoverable against the person from whom the delinquent stockholder, at any time within one year previous to the assignment of the said bank, shall have received a transfer of the shares, or any portion of the shares then held by him.[35]

As the vote on "Collection from Stockholders" in Table 30 demonstrates, this was not a particularly popular measure except in the most anti-bank regions. The measure came up for a roll-call vote only once and was defeated. When it was included in a charter, it was probably accepted reluctantly as a compromise measure deemed necessary to ensure passage of the act.

On both business and banking roll-calls, the gap between those voting pro-corporation on final votes and on individual liability tended to narrow the higher the group on the commercial-economic continuum. Representatives from less commercial, less economically-developed districts were more concerned about protection from banking and business ventures than those from areas where capital was more plentiful and more fluid. The more developed commercial-economic areas, on the other hand, voted not only for corporations, but for corporations with fewer restrictions for stockholders and, hence, greater incentive for investment.

Length of the terms of charters was also a hotly contested issue during the 1849 session.[36] Limiting the length of the charter, bank reformers believed, was yet one further way of making banks more reliable and responsible. Bank proponents, and particularly bank directors, on the other hand, sought longer charters to give them the freedom to develop long-range financial policies and to avoid the arduous process of continually appealing to the legislature for charter renewals. Most charter extensions granted in 1849 were fifteen years, although longer charters of twenty years and shorter ones of ten years were both proposed and

TABLE 29

PERCENT PRO-BANK BY ISSUE, REGIONS AND GROUPS, 1838-39

	Regions						
Issue	1	2	3	4	5	6	7
1. Final Votes	72.35	71.43	100.00	100.00	67.57	75.00	69.56
2. Limited Liability	61.54	100.00	0.00	50.00	66.67	66.67	85.71

	Commercial-Economic Groups				
	1	2	3	4	5
1. Final Votes	58.00	57.14	59.02	62.77	75.30
2. Limited Liability	75.00	58.33	66.67	85.71	69.70

	Commercial-Economic Aggregate Groups				
	1	2	3	4	5
1. Final Votes	20.00	66.13	76.29	48.94	69.49
2. Limited Liability	---	91.67	73.33	52.94	73.53

Source: See Table 18.

TABLE 30

PERCENT PRO-BANK BY ISSUE, REGIONS AND GROUPS, 1849

	Regions						
Issues	1	2	3	4	5	6	7
1. Final Votes	75.53	76.11	100.00	9.30	48.09	26.15	69.28
2. Limited Liability	68.17	74.55	33.33	23.08	31.25	6.45	51.63
3. Clltn.frm.Stkhldrs.	75.69	71.43	0.00	0.00	50.00	0.00	47.37
4. Charter Length	64.89	73.91	28.57	4.76	43.68	2.38	55.26
5. Par Value	63.14	57.58	100.00	4.55	55.26	42.86	65.93
6. Director's Borrowing	53.77	55.56	100.00	0.00	23.81	0.00	37.04
7. Specie Redemption	61.19	72.73	---	0.00	23.08	0.00	47.06

	Commercial-Economic Groups				
	1	2	3	4	5
1. Final Votes	47.22	49.04	59.90	63.29	77.86
2. Limited Liability	31.58	28.00	53.61	40.68	73.87
3. Clltn.Frm.Stkhldrs.	50.00	28.57	46.67	53.33	78.79
4. Charter Length	42.31	32.35	45.52	44.52	71.50
5. Par Value	18.18	51.56	50.00	59.72	67.92
6. Director's Borrowing	20.00	18.92	29.41	41.30	42.31
7. Specie Redemption	20.00	26.92	27.78	53.33	62.90

	Commercial-Economic Aggregate Groups			
	2	3	4	5
1. Final Votes	52.03	40.36	54.58	89.80
2. Limited Liability	26.52	34.26	36.11	88.56
3. Clltn.frm.Stkhldrs.	33.33	43.75	41.18	92.86
4. Charter Length	35.05	31.33	42.63	83.28
5. Par Value	49.41	36.84	58.33	78.13
6. Director's Borrowing	20.00	25.00	32.14	69.51
7. Specie Redemption	29.41	22.73	36.11	81.63

Source: See Table 18.

voted upon. Votes on charter length paralleled the final votes, but were generally not as strongly pro-bank, particularly among the lower commercial-economic and commercial-economic aggregate groups. This too, then, was an area where some compromise was possible.

During the debate on four of the bills before the legislature in 1849, attempts were made to compel the banks to keep their notes at par for a period of 15-20 days in Philadelphia or Pittsburgh, depending upon the proximity of the bank in question. Failure to do so, the provision mandated, would result in the automatic revocation of the bank's charter. This was an effort to institute something like the Suffolk Bank system which had worked so successfully in New England and which helped to keep the more volatile country banks solvent. Although a measure of this sort was eventually included in the "Act Regulating Banks" passed in 1850, none of the individual proposals passed in 1849.[37]

For the purposes of comparing these votes with the other banking issues listed in Table 30, a vote in favor of the requirement was perceived as an anti-bank or reform bank position. The interior and western regions, with the notable exception of the Northeastern Region, as well as most of the lower level commercial-economic and commercial-economic aggregate groups showed a stronger pro-bank position on this issue than on many others. These were the regions and groups that would be most seriously affected by the passage of the par value requirement and they recognized it for what it was--a restriction that would be difficult to meet. Conversely, the Southeastern and Western Regions and the upper level groups, while not overwhelmingly in favor of the measure, were not as opposed to this requirement as they were to others. Demanding that banks keep their notes at par in the two major commercial centers of the commonwealth would not only further enhance the position of these regions, but would also bring some much-needed stability and uniformity to the state's banking system.

Two other reform provisions were occasionally introduced and were, in general, less controversial than the more important issues of individual liability or length of charter. Most charters, for example, contained clauses limiting the amount the directors individually and collectively could borrow. As Table 30 indicates, this issue was not nearly as important to those regions and groups who were generally pro-bank.[38] While the pro-bank counties still voted in favor of more lenient borrowing privileges for directors than did those who usually voted anti-bank, the comparatively low pro-bank percentages indicates that the legislators haggled more over the amount directors should be allowed to borrow or over the provisions required to alter the measure, rather than over the principle of the restriction itself.

Some of the charter extensions enacted in 1849 contained a section stating that, "if the said bank shall at any time fail or refuse to redeem its notes and pay its liabilities in gold and silver coin, upon the demand being made at the banking house of said bank during banking hours, such failure or refusal shall be deemed and held to be an absolute forfeiture of the charter of said bank."[39] For the most part, this was an overly precautionary and redundant measure since the act of March 12, 1842, "To provide for the Resumption of Specie Payments by the Banks of the Commonwealth, and for other purposes," made this point abundantly clear.[40] Opposition to these proposed clauses, which is reflected in the pro-bank votes in Table 30, therefore, was in large part a visceral reaction against including unnecessary and redundant measures that merely cluttered an already complicated legislative process.[41]

No issue more clearly demonstrates the shifting regional and commercial-economic group sentiment toward banks than the roll-calls taken on the circulation of small notes during the 1829 and 1849 sessions. (See Table 31.) The clamor to establish banks in the interior regions which occurred both before and after the Panic of 1819 was due, in large part, to a desperate need for some type of circulating medium in these areas, and particularly for notes of low denominations which could be used in day-to-day transactions. Others, however, were more concerned with promoting bank stability and with developing policies which would prevent another debacle like that of 1819. Restricting the issue of small notes and requiring the use of specie would provide better security for the monetary foundation of the entire banking system. Although the act of 1824 allowed for the circulation of small notes, opponents succeeded in enacting a law prohibiting banks from issuing these notes in 1828.[42]

Early in the 1829 session, a motion was made to repeal this restriction. "Whereas, it is the duty of this house to interpose its legislative powers, so that one part of the community may not be sacrificed to the interest or caprice by another," the resolution began,

> And whereas many of the counties have no other currency below five dollars, and if you take this from them they have none . . . . And whereas, in conclusion it may be remarked, that the demand for a currency of this kind, in particular districts, for the purpose of change and transmission in small sums, is too important to be neglected
>
> Resolved, That in consequence of the unequal operations of the act, to restraining the circulation of small notes, as well as from doubts entertained of its constitutionality, it is considered most conducive to the public peace and general welfare, that the law be repealed.[43]

The voting patterns on this measure, which ultimately failed to be sent to a select committee for consideration, are starkly clear. Interior regions and the lower level commercial-economic and commercial-economic aggregate groups favored the circulation of small notes. The Southeastern Region and the most commercial and economically developed counties were firmly opposed to even considering the resolution.

TABLE 31

PERCENT IN FAVOR OF SMALL NOTE CIRCULATION BY REGIONS AND GROUPS IN THE 1828-29 AND 1849 SESSIONS

Region	1829	1849
1. Southeastern	27.08	43.75
2. Anthracite	50.00	70.59
3. Pocono	---	0.00
4. Northeastern	100.00	30.00
5. Ridge and Valley	66.67	40.00
6. Allegheny Forest	50.19	0.00
7. Western	76.19	47.92
Commercial-Economic Group		
1	57.14	33.33
2	66.67	17.24
3	64.29	52.94
4	55.00	20.59
5	29.27	59.04
Commercial-Economic Aggregate Group		
2	63.64	34.89
3	78.57	32.59
4	48.15	41.33
5	28.21	81.49

Source: See Table 18.

Twenty years later, this pattern had almost directly reversed itself. During the boom years of the 1830s, the restrictions against circulating small notes had been relaxed and the banks themselves had come to see the advantage of issuing notes in small denominations. The Panic of 1837 coupled with the recurrent bank suspensions of the early 1840s, however, pumped new blood into the small note debate and restricting their circulation became one of the major crusades of the anti-bankers. Hard money, according to bank reformers, was the only true circulating medium. Specie would act, as James Sharp explained it, "as a kind of perpetual and infallible balance wheel, regulating the workings of the banking system." The circulation of small notes was a constant impediment to the reformers' goal and should be prohibited in order to force the use of specie for daily monetary exchange.[44] The hard-money advocates were quite successful for a time. Indeed, most of the banking incorporations and charter extensions enacted in the 1840s contained a section which read as follows: "Neither the said bank, nor any other bank hereafter chartered, shall issue and put in circulation any bill or note of said bank, payable at any other place than at said bank, nor otherwise than payable on demand, nor of a denomination of less than five dollars; . . ."[45]

The inclusion of such measures, however, did not deter pro-bank advocates from attempting to repeal these restrictions. Banks, for example, frequently tried to exact this privilege from the legislature in return for loaning funds to the state for the completion of various portions of the public works.[46] In 1849, a rider allowing banks to issue small notes was attached to a bill providing for the completion of the North Branch Canal. Work on the canal had been suspended in 1841 and the residents of the regions which would be the primary beneficiaries of the canal--the Anthracite and Northeastern Regions--were constantly agitating for its completion. The proposed rider stated that the banks would loan the state the $1.2 million necessary for the completion of the canal, _if_, in return for the loan, the banks were given the privilege of issuing small notes.

The small note provision passed the House of Representatives on one of the two occasions it came up for a vote, although the canal bill itself never did. As Table 31 so clearly demonstrates, the sources of support for the circulation of small notes had shifted dramatically from those of 1829. In 1849, the eastern and western regions gave most support to the measure, while the interior regions had become decidedly opposed. Even the representatives from the Northeastern Region, a region that stood to gain the most from the completion of the canal, stood steadfast. While the percent of Northeastern legislators voting for the circulation of small notes is somewhat higher than the vote on other banking measures, these representatives, for the most part, remained intransigent in their opposition to banks.

The voting patterns among the commercial-economic and commercial-economic aggregate groups is even more striking. Support for a less-restricted circulating medium had shifted to the more developed, more commercial counties by 1849. While the votes cast by commercial-economic group 4 legislators reflect a break in the pattern,[47] the strongest support came from the counties that ranked highest on the continuum in 1849. Representatives who came from counties that continually ranked among the most economically-developed (commercial-aggregate group 5) were overwhelmingly in favor of allowing banks to circulate notes in small denominations. As with other banking and business issues, these groups were willing by 1849 to pursue policies which were less restrictive and gave more power and, ultmately, independence to the corporation.

IV

By the fifth decade of the nineteenth century, it had become abundantly apparent to all concerned that the corporation had evolved into a permanent form of business organization. As the average number of individual acts of incorporation passed during each session mounted from 14.5 in the 1820s, to 40 in the 1840s, to 116 by the 1850s, [48] the idea of enacting general incorporation laws, which would require charter-seekers to go through the courts rather than the legislature, became more and more appealing. The concept of the general incorporation law was not a new one. As early as 1791, the legislature had passed a general law for literary, charitable, and religious corporations and the provisions of this act were later extended to include beneficial associations and fire-engine companies. The legislature, however, remained reluctant to enact such laws for banking and business. A general measure covering virtually all types of business corporations was not passed until 1874, but general laws for banking and other specific categories of enterprise surfaced much earlier.[49]

During the sessions under examination, three types of general incorporation laws were debated. In 1849, a general manufacturing law covering textiles, iron, paper, lumber, and salt companies was passed. Surprisingly, this bill gave rise to very little discussion on the floor, and relatively few roll-calls. The initial attempt to pass the bill was unsuccessful. But when a bill for the incorporation of the Reading Manufacturing Company was taken up before the Committee of the Whole, it was replaced with a more general bill to encourage the manufacturing, mining, mechancial, and chemical purposes. Mining companies were subsequently omitted without a vote, and the bill passed by a margin of 52 to 37.[50] In 1859, a general act covering mutual savings fund, land and building associations which had been enacted for the county of Philadelphia in 1850 was extended to the whole commonwealth. Again, this act passed with relative ease by a vote of 53-27.

The third general incorporation act, the free banking law, however, met more resistance. The 1850 act establishing a model bank charter still required prospective incorporators to petition the legislature to obtain their charter.[51] The strict provisions of the act, moreover, had not been very popular among bankers. Toward the end of the 1850s, interest came increasingly to center on a free banking law which would allow petitioners to by-pass the legislature and apply directly to the attorney general. The law was much less restrictive than that of 1850 allowing for longer charters and significantly, limited liability. The most objectionable provision of the bill was the requirement that notes be uniform and backed by specie equal to eight percent of all circulating notes.[52]

When the bill was introduced early on in the 1859 session, legislators became hung up on the method of appointing or electing the Superintendent of the Banking Department and on the amount of initial capital required of the banks. The proponents of the bill had not yet worked out the details carefully enough to ensure its passage. As one sympathetic editor put it, "A strong impression that something must be done is the origin of many bad measures. It is easy to do something, but the object is to do something useful. It is better to do nothing than to do mischief. It is better to make no bank than to pass the bill as it now is."[33] Stalled in 1859, the bill was finally passed the following year.

The voting patterns on general incorporation bills reflected in Table 32 are familiar. Opposition of the interior regions to corporations in 1849 had dissipated by 1859. The upper level commercial-economic groups, and commercial-economic aggregate group 5 voted consistently and overwhelmingly for general incorporation laws. The 1859 banking law votes reflected the strong pro-bank position which had emerged in some of the interior regions and the lower level commercial-economic and commercial-economic aggregate groups; it also indicated a slightly more hesitant policy among those upper level groups and regions that had previously been banking's most ardent supporters.

These voting patterns run counter to the belief that those who sought incorporation preferred special enactment and found the general laws too restrictive.[34] If this were the case, these voting trends should deviate significantly from those on the special incorporation roll-calls. Such reticence is simply not apparent from these roll-call votes. It may be, as L. Ray Gunn has suggested, that historians have tended to over-emphasize the regulatory aspects of general incorporation laws at the expense of other themes. In New York, he argues, "demands for the expansion of the corporation to stimulate growth and development were as important . . . as demands for regulation" among advocates of general incorporation laws.[35]

The special charters granted to corporations were, in reality, not very "special." Time and time again, already enacted charters were expressly duplicated verbatim, with only the name of the new company inserted in place of the old. In 1849, over one-half of the bank charter extensions granted openly used the Bank of Montgomery County bill as a model, merely substituting the name of the bank in question. While individual incorporators might occasionally find it desirable to appeal to the legislature in unusual instances, the majority of those from the regions and groups who most frequently sought incorporation favored and welcomed the general laws. The advantages of by-passing the legislature outweighed any minor special benefits achieved through special enactment. The charter was the ultimate goal, and by the late 1840s, general incorporation was the easiest way to obtain the desired end.[56]

V

Attitudes toward the corporation shifted dramatically during the antebellum years as state representatives struggled to promote economic development in a way that was equitable, responsible, and hopefully designed to prevent wild fluctuations in the financial well-being of both commonwealth and constituents. In the early decades of the nineteenth century, the relationship between the state and the corporate bodies it created was tightly interwoven and much more specific than it had become by the eve of the

TABLE 32

PERCENT IN FAVOR OF GENERAL INCORPORATION LAWS BY REGIONS, GROUPS AND SESSIONS

Region	1849 (General Manufacturing)	1859 (Mutual Savings)	1859 (Free Banking)
1. Southeastern	63.31	76.47	49.79
2. Anthracite	80.77	70.00	63.01
3. Pocono	---	100.00	46.15
4. Northeastern	13.33	80.00	88.10
5. Ridge/Valley	38.89	25.00	75.68
6. Allegheny Frst.	0.00	100.00	39.40
7. Western	50.00	40.00	63.06
Commercial-Economic Group			
1	42.86	100.00	60.00
2	23.53	30.77	80.95
3	54.55	58.33	46.39
4	32.79	46.67	53.45
5	74.24	86.11	56.30
Commercial-Economic Aggregate Group			
2	37.50	50.00	66.10
3	27.78	57.89	58.11
4	39.19	60.00	49.59
5	86.79	82.76	60.00

Source: See Table 18.

Civil War. Corporations, and banks in particular, were perceived as public agencies. Private capital and private initiative may have been necessary to organize these endeavors, but the functions they performed were expressly public. Those areas of the state that had not yet benefited from the establishment of local institutions actively petitioned for their own charters and for more lenient privileges they believed would serve the public need.

The events of the 1830s, and particularly the devastating effects of the Panic of 1837, called into question the very essence of the corporation. Somehow, these organizations had lost their public quality. Rather than serving the needs of the commonwealth, they sought to promote their own private interests at the expense of innocent creditors and the financial security of the state itself. Slowly over the next two decades, the corporation became a much more strictly private institution which still owed its existence to the state, but operated much more independently. There were those who readily embraced and promoted this change, just as there were those who found it more difficult to shed the inimical perception of the corporation that had emerged during the 1830s. By the late 1850s, the state had divorced itself from its intimate association with both banks and corporations, and the growing interest in general incorporation laws reflects the increasing acceptance of the corporation as an indispensable way for private citizens to organize to promote economic development.

These shifting perceptions of the corporation are clearly reflected in the regional, commercial-economic and commercial-economic aggregate group voting patterns of Pennsylvania's legislators. Both the regional location of the corporation and the level of commercial-economic development of the districts influenced the representives' legislative decisions. Legislators from the less-developed counties and the interior regions actively petitioned for local banks and lenient banking policies during the 1820s. Yet it was precisely these areas that were hardest hit during the depression of the late 1830s. The hardships endured by these counties at the hands of what they saw as irresponsible, greedy entrepreneurs bred a suspicion of both banks and corporations that would take close to two decades to erase.

Those from the more economically developed regions and commercial-economic groups, on the other hand, became ardently pro-corporation. Although representatives from these areas voted for a more cautious and restrained charter policy in the 1820s, the prosperity of the early 1830s had convinced them of the potential of the corporation. By 1849, those from the most economically-advanced counties in the commonwealth had become the leading proponents of granting charters with provisions that increasingly benefited the individual investor.

Some exchange of votes between representatives took place to gain the passage of specific charters. But the consistency of legislative behavior within each session suggests deeper influences. A legislator's position was profoundly shaped by the level of commercial-economic development of his district as well as his perceptions of the needs of the commonwealth as a whole. Representatives cast their votes across a wide array of banking and business issues and they debated and voted upon the same questions time and time again. In the end persistent support on the part of legislators from the more populous and economically-advanced areas led to the development of a policy that made it easier to obtain charters and granted a degree of independence to the corporation that would have been unthinkable some thirty years before.

FOOTNOTES

[1]William Miller, "A Note on the History of Business Corporations in Pennsylvania, 1800-1860," Quarterly Journal of Economics 55(November 1940): 154. See also Louis Hartz, Economic Policy and Democratic Thought: Pennsylvania, 1776-1860 (Cambridge: Harvard University Press, 1948; reprint ed. Chicago: Quadrangle Paper Books, Inc., 1968), pp. 37-128 for a discussion of the development of the corporation in Pennsylvania.

[2]The role of the state in creating a transportation network for antebellum Pennsylvania will be examined in depth in the following chapter.

[3]Hartz, Economic Policy and Democratic Thought, p. 37.

[4]John Thomas Holdsworth, Financing an Empire: History of Banking in Pennslvania, 4 vols. (Chicago and Philadelphia: S. J. Clarke Publishing Co., 1928), 1:52-55.

[5]Ibid., p. 56.

[6]Ibid., p. 59.

[7]Hartz, Economic Policy and Democratic Thought, pp. 54-56, 97-98; Holdsworth, Financing an Empire, 1:61, 133-36.

[8]Holdsworth, Financing an Empire, 1:136-37, 161-65.

[9]Ibid., pp. 313-15.

[10]Ibid., pp. 313-23.

[11]Ibid., pp. 323-26; Joseph Van Fenstermaker, The Development of American Commercial Banking, 1782-1837 (Kent, Ohio: Kent State University Press, 1965), pp. 18-19.

[12]Miller, "Business Corporations in Pennsylvania," pp. 156-57.

[13]Hartz, Economic Policy and Democratic Thought, pp. 37-38. See also John W. Cadman, Jr., The Corporation in New Jersey: Business and Politics, 1791-1875 (Cambridge, Mass.: Harvard University Press, 1949), pp. 34-38.

[14]Oscar Handlin and Mary Flug Handlin, "Origins of the American Business Corporation," Journal of Economic History 5(May 1945): 22.

[15]See Hartz, Economic Policy and Democratic Thought, pp. 69-79, for a full discussion of the anti-charter doctrine.

[16]Pennsylvania Telegraph, 13 February 1839.

[17]Hartz, Economic Policy and Democratic Thought, pp. 56, 89-90.

[18]On occasion, other types of roll-calls which reflected clear-cut sentiment on the bill as a whole were used. For example, if a vote was taken after the second reading, but not after the third, the second reading roll-call was used. Motions to postpone indefinitely were also included if it was clear from the terms of the debate that this reflected general positions on the bill.

[19]Holdsworth, Financing an Empire, 1: 321.

[20]Hartz, Economic Policy and Democratic Thought, pp. 257-58; Holdsworth, Financing an Empire, 2:509-10, 553.

[21]Holdsworth, Financing an Empire, 2:531; Pennsylvania, Laws of the Commonwealth of Pennsylvania, 1838-39, p. 686.

[22]A good number of combination railroad-coal companies were chartered during these years. These corporations were given the right to own land, to mine the coal, and to construct a short railroad to connect with a major transportation artery. Given the fact that the main purpose of these companies was to obtain the coal rather than to transport the product over long distances, they have been included in this discussion rather than in the treatment of transportation policy in the following chapter.

[23]Other banks and savings institutions may have applied and received recharter and incorporation. This chapter, however, deals only with those instances which resulted in debate and in at least one roll-call vote.

[24]Miller, "Business Corporations in Pennsylvania," p. 158. Four of these corporations were located in the Southeastern region and three in the Anthracite region. A general incorporation act for manufacturing companies passed in 1849 had shifted some of the burden of reviewing and granting charters to the courts. This general incorporation act will be discussed below.

[25]See Tables 18 and 19. Although support for bank charters had slipped somewhat for commercial-economic group 5 representatives by 1859, commercial-economic aggregate group 5 legislators remained overwhelmingly the most pro-charter group for both banking and business incorporations during this session.

[26]Handlin, "Origins of the American Business Corporation," pp. 8-17.

[27]Pennsylvania Telegraph, 13 February 1839.

[28]Ibid.

[29]See, for example, Pennsylvania, House of Representatives, Legislative Journal, vol. 1, 1838-39, pp. 303-4.

[30]Emphasis mine. See, for example, Laws of the Commonwealth of Pennsylvania, 1838-39, p. 278.

Stockholders frequently subscribed to a certain amount of shares without actually paying in full. Arrangements were made to pay the remaining balance in installments. This provision assured opponents that stockholders were resonsible for the par value of their stock if the corporation should fail, and not simply the amount they had paid to date.

[31]Harrisburg Chronicle, 19 March 1829.

[32]Douglas E. Bowers, "The Pennsylvania Legislature, 1815-1860: A Study of Democracy at Work" (Ph.D. dissertation, University of Chicago, 1974), p. 143.

[33]Legislative Journal, vol. 1, 1838-39, pp. 422-23; Laws of the Commonwealth of Pennsylvania, 1838-39, pp. 515-6.

[34]Bowers, "The Pennsylvania Legislature," pp. 143-6; Holdsworth, Financing an Empire, 2: 577-59, 583-5.

[35]Legislative Journal, vol. 1, 1849, p. 551; Laws of the Commonwealth of Pennsylvania, 1849, pp. 433-40.

[36]Limiting the length of the charter had initially served as yet another way to bring additional money into the state coffers. Each time a bank applied for recharter, it very likely had to pay, once again, a sizeable premium for the privilege. Although the bonus system was curtailed in 1842, banks were still required to disburse a small percentage of their capital stock paid in to the state treasury. This provision coupled with the belief that shorter charter terms exacted greater responsibility from corporate directors led bank reformers to push for shorter time limits than many proponents desired.

See, for example, the law extending the charter of the Bank of Montgomery County which served as a model for numerous other bank recharter bills during the 1849 session. Laws of the Commonwealth of Pennsylvania, 1849, p. 436.

[37]Holdsworth, Financing an Empire, 2: 577-79.

[38]Votes for limiting the directors' borrowing privileges were perceived as anti-bank. The percentages

listed on the table, therefore, reflect those who voted in favor of more liberal borrowing privileges.

[39]See, for example, Laws of the Commonwealth of Pennsylvania, 1849, p. 423.

[40]Laws of the Commonwealth of Pennsylvania, 1842, pp. 68-72.

[41]The "Specie Redemption" votes on Table 30 reflect the votes of those opposed to including specific specie redemption clauses.

[42]Holdsworth, Financing an Empire, 1:325.

[43]Harrisburg Chronicle, 5 Feburary 1829.

[44]James Roger Sharp, The Jacksonians Versus the Banks: Politics in the States after the Panic of 1837 (New York: Columbia University Press, 1970), pp. 17-18.

[45]See, for example, Laws of the Commonwealth of Pennsylvania, 1849, pp. 433-40.

[46]Peter Andrew Wallner, "Politics and Public Works: A Study of the Pennsylvania Canal System, 1825-1857," (Ph.D. dissertation, Pennsylvania State University, 1973), pp. 198-99, demonstrates that this had become a favorite bank tactic as early as 1839. See also, Laws of the Commonwealth of Pennsylvania, 1838-39, p. 634.

[47]This deviation in the pattern on the part of the commercial-economic group 4 legislators is largely explained by this group's party affiliation. See Chapter 7 for a full discussion of parties and banking issues.

[48]Miller, "Business Incorporations in Pennsylvania," p. 155.

[49]Hartz, Economic Policy and Democratic Thought, pp. 38-42.

[50]Pennsylvania Telegraph, 31 March 1849.

[51]Cadman refers to these laws which established model charters as "general regulating statutes." Although petitioners were still required to appeal to the legislature for incorporation, these laws set up a standard charter to be used in all appropriate circumstances. As such, they represented an intermediate step between special enactments and general incorporation laws. See Cadman, The Corporation in New Jersey, pp. 15-17.

[52]Bowers, "The Pennsylvania Legislature," pp. 145-46; Holdsworth, Financing an Empire, 2: 583-5.

[53]Pennsylvania Daily Telegraph, 30 March 1859.

[54]Douglas E. Bowers, "From Logrolling to Corruption: The Development of Lobbying in Pennsylvania, 1815-1861," Journal of the Early Republic 3(Winter 1983): 439-74; Hartz, Economic Policy and Democratic Thought, p. 40.

[55]Gunn, "Political Implications of General Incorporation Laws," p. 188.

[56]Daniel J. Dykstra has pointed this trend out in his discussion of the Wisconsin lumber industry between 1861 and 1871. Most special charters were alike in all materal respects, he argues. "While the charters were less restrictive than were the general acts of incorporation, the obtaining of such legislative authorization was considered a means to an end, and not as a vehicle by which countless individual special favors could be secured." See Daniel J. Dykstra, "Corporations in the Day of the Special Charter," Wisconsin Law Review (March 1949): 312.

CHAPTER SIX

PUBLIC WORKS, MIXED ENTERPRISES AND PRIVATE CORPORATIONS: BUILDING A TRANSPORTATION SYSTEM FOR ANTEBELLUM PENNSYLVANIA

No single topic dominated the legislative agenda of the Pennsylvania General Assembly between 1820 and 1860 as did the issue of transportation. As the commonwealth became more involved in directing and constructing the state's transportation network, the time the legislature spent debating the merits of proposed methods and routes mushroomed proportionately. Almost thirty percent of all laws passed in each of the four sessions had to do with some type of transportation. Already by the 1828-29 session, roughly forty percent of all roll-call votes were taken on the issue. This preoccupation continued during the 1838-39 session, but diminished by 1849 to eighteen percent, and then by 1859, rose to over twenty-five percent.[1]

In the 1790's the legislature granted its first turnpike charters. Chartering private companies for transportation purposes continued to be a major undertaking of the General Assembly throughout the antebellum period. Over 64% of all acts of incorporation passed between 1790 and 1860 were for turnpike, bridge, canal, steamboat, or railroad companies.[2] The state expanded even further its role and control over transportation by extending its mixed enterprise policy, already used for banking, to transportation. In 1806, the legislature authorized the governor to subscribe one-fifth of the shares of all turnpike companies chartered during that session. By 1810, the total state investment in turnpike corporations reached $61,937, a figure which climbed to $2.3 million in 1843. By the early 1840's, state stock subscriptions amounted to roughly $500,000 in bridge corporations, $600,000 in canal companies, and $300,000 in railroads.[3]

As neighboring New York state pushed the Erie Canal westward toward completion in 1825, and as Baltimore stretched her commercial tentacles further northward, Philadelphia became fearful of losing its competitive place on the eastern seaboard and sought some means of retaining the city's commercial advantage. The decision to build the state-owned and operated Pennsylvania Canal system was the result.[4] Because of the state's geographical barriers, the construction of the Main Line of the canal and many of its branches proved to be an engineering nightmare and a source of acute financial embarassment to the commonwealth.

Although the state was in excellent financial shape when the public works were commenced in 1826, the commonwealth failed to develop a safe fiscal policy backed by a sinking fund as was done in New York state. The interest fund was soon exhausted and the tolls themselves did not begin to cover the interest payments. In 1835, the year the canal opened, the tolls amounted to $684,357. Interest payments alone, however, were close to $1.2

million. Beginning in the early 1830's, the legislature resorted to a tax on personal and real property in an attempt to keep the state solvent, a measure that caused Pennsylvanians to cast a skeptical eye on the administration of the public works.[5] By 1842, the state had spent well over $53 million on internal improvements and the legislature decided that its involvement should be curtailed. One year later, the massive sale of over $2 million worth of public stocks in transportation companies marked the beginning of the withdrawal of the state from the internal improvments arena; this culminated in 1857 with the sale of the Main Line and the passage of an anti-investment amendment which prohibited the commonwealth, counties, cities, boroughs, and townships from becoming joint owner or stockholder of any corporation or partnership.[6]

Historians have long argued that clashing sectional and local interests prevented the legislature from concentrating on strategically crucial lines. The General Assembly was deluged by hundreds of petitions for local routes; many petitioners and legislators were simply unwilling to support transportation improvements elsewhere unless their locale, too, grabbed a portion of the public pie.[7]

The effect of these conflicting demands was most evident in the escalating battles over the extension of the public works. Initial intentions to concentrate on completing the Main Line were immediately undercut. With only two short sections of the east-west route under construction, the second major public works act of April 9, 1827 provided that work begin on six different parts of the state system. Of these, only two were on the Main Line. Scarcely one year after the public works project had been launched, demands for regional aggrandizement were already putting pressure on the legislature.[8]

This dominant sectional theme suggests that some sort of regional or sectional consciousness existed in antebellum Pennsylvania and that it became a prominent force in shaping transportation battles. Regional self-interest exercised occasional influence over voting behavior on banking and business issues. It is logical to expect regional motivation to be more in evidence on transportation roll-calls given the highly competitive nature of the debate and the sheer number of routes proposed. Regional self-interest, however, was <u>not</u> always a clear motivating factor when representatives cast their votes on transportation issues.

Unlike the banking and business corporations, a transportation system which relied heavily on state investment in mixed enterprises and on publicly-owned routes, involved dividing up finite public funds. While an untold number of charters could theoretically be granted by the legislature, there were only limited funds available for transportation. This led representatives to make difficult choices. While some regions managed to develop a fairly consistent policy toward all internal improvements, members from other regions could not even present a united front when voting on routes which directly traversed their backyards.

These patterns were influenced by both the pull of conflicting markets, and the level of commercial-economic development. Less-developed counties supported transportation improvements as did the economically advanced areas. Counties which fell roughly mid-way on the commercial-economic continua, however, were less enthusiastic. While generalizing about transportation voting trends _is_ possible, legislative behavior fluctuated significantly between regions, commercial-economic groups, issues, and sessions.

II

Transportation issues of the 1828-29 session presaged those that continued to plague and frustrate future legislatures. The most pressing topic on the 1828-29 agenda was the authorization of the first sizeable loan to continue the public works. Although construction on the state system had just barely begun, already ominous signs loomed over the attempts to fund it.

The tone of the entire fiscal debate was set within the first few days of the session. The second law passed by the legislature was "An act authorising a loan for the continuance of the Pennsylvania canal and railroad and for other purposes."[9] The intent of this act was to authorize an emergency loan of $800,000 to allow the canal commissioners to continue work on the state system. The $2 million appropriated by the 1827 act had simply not stretched as far as had been hoped. As one representative put it, "new routes had been explored and located, and new contracts entered into, all which required the expenditures of large sums . . . These contracts had been made on the faith of the state and it was the duty of the state to be prepared to comply with them."[10] While this bill passed with relative ease and was seen as an emergency expedient, it also was one of the first indications that state expenditures needed to be monitored more closely.

In February of 1829, the committee on internal improvements submitted a report asking for a loan of $3.2 million to allow public works construction to continue. Already leery about the need for the additional $800,000, some members attempted to limit the amount of the loan and the authorization of further surveys that would commit the state to future contracts. Certain lines such as the Delaware Canal between Bristol and Easton, and the section on the North Branch division between Northumberland and Nanticoke Falls, had received a previous commitment from the legislature. There was little opposition to completing these sections, but there was amendment after amendment to restrict further commitments. Attempts were made to limit the amount expended on new contracts, to confine the length of newly-contracted routes to less than twenty miles, and to make certain that no new contracts were entered into before October 1, 1829, or in more extreme proposals, until 1830.

Although several improvements were put to a roll-call vote, in the end, only two routes were specifically mentioned in the act, and these received only vague commitments for future action. The canal commissioners were authorized to locate a route either by canal or by canal and slackwater between Pittsburgh and Erie, and in an even more obscure promise, were given permission "to improve the navigation of the Monongahela river, from the city of Pittsburg to the Virginia state line, at such time and in such manner as the legislature may hereafter direct."[11]

Just as attempts were made to limit the number of contractual commitments the legislature, efforts were also made to decrease the amount of the proposed loan. There were those, among them the majority of the committee on ways and means, who assured the legislature that "the resources of the commonwealth . . . are in a flourishing condition. . . The extensive system of internal improvement in which the commonwealth has embarked, has created new wants, and given to a portion of the revenue a new direction."[12] While the committee recommended that the whole $3.2 million be granted, there were a vocal few who felt otherwise. Amendments were proposed which reduced the amount of the loan by as much as one million dollars. These failed to be adopted, however, and the bill appropriating the larger amount passed the House of Representatives. In the end,

Governor Shultze vetoed the act. The governor's objections to the bill were confined exclusively to the amount of the loan. "Should we not in authorising loans upon [the commonwealth's] credit and for her use, have a watchful care that we do not exceed the amount, which, calculating from the largest expenditure of former years, will be amply sufficient to meet the demand of the present, and by that means avoid the payment of unnecessary interest upon an unnessarily large principal, " he asked. "The last season was particularly favourable for constructing public works," Shultze optimistically continued, "and the sum required did not far exceed two millions; it is therefore not probable that a sum much exceeding the loan of last year will be necessary the present season."[13]

Eventually, the governor's recommendations were accepted and the legislature passed a new bill authorizing a $2.2 million loan to continue the public works. Even with the considerable reduction in the amount of the loan, however, not a single bid was immediately forthcoming. Alarmed by the lack of an adequate interest fund and at the constant demand for additional appropriations, Pennsylvania banks had to be cajoled into loaning the state more money to complete the transportation system. By the end of the session, "Pennsylvania groans under the millions of her loans" had become a familiar refrain among bankers and skeptics alike.[14]

Which regions and which types of commercial-economic districts tended to support and push for extension of the public works and which advocated a more cautious policy? Table 33 lists the percent voting in favor of a more expansive policy by region and issue or route. The "general extension" category includes all roll-calls which dealt broadly with issues such as the authorization of new contracts and time limits for completion. The "general appropriations" classification refers to all votes taken on the authorization and amount of the loan, including the $800,000 emergency loan passed at the beginning of the session.

All regions, with the exception of the Allegheny Forest Region, were more in favor of extending public works than they were in appropriating money for them. Strongest support for both general categories came from the interior regions--the Northeastern, the Ridge and Valley, and the Allegheny Forest regions. These voting patterns underscore the difference between the "Main Liners" and the "Branch Men," between those who wanted to focus solely on completing the major east-west route and those who pushed for the simultaneous construction of branch lines. The Southeastern and Western regions were the primary beneficiaries of the Main Line route and their representatives were least willing to authorize expenditures or extensions that might jeopardize their region's future by delaying the completion of the line. The interior regions stood to gain the most from a more expansive financial and branch policy, and their legislators voted accordingly.

Interior region representatives continued to demonstrate their support by their votes on the specific routes. While Southeastern legislators had become less enthusiastic about the construction of additional lines, Western members were acting out of a well-developed regional self-interest. Even though the region was tied directly to the fate of the Main Line, its representatives were not adverse to making a pitch, and a marginally successful one, for state-funded improvements that would open up valuable north-south routes within the region. The improvement of the Monongahela River, in particular, would tap the valuable east-west traffic on the National Road and divert some of the traffic upstream toward Pittsburgh.

Regional self-interest, however, was not always an overriding factor for representatives from other regions. While regional promotion is somewhat in evidence on the West Branch roll-calls which would benefit the Ridge and Valley Region, the voting patterns on the Delaware and North Branch divisions are not as revealing. These two routes received legislative approbation with relative ease. Yet the regions which they directly benefited--the Southeastern and Anthracite regions, respectively--were not always the regions which gave them the greatest support.

The Northeastern and Allegheny Forest regions, on the other hand, and to a slightly lesser extent, the Ridge and

TABLE 33

PERCENT IN FAVOR OF THE PUBLIC WORKS BY REGION, ISSUE AND ROUTE, 1828-29

Issue/Route	Reg. Lctn.	Region 1	2	3	4	5	6	7	Ave.
General Extension		65.88	65.15	---	100.00	73.61	85.71	66.67	76.17
General Approprtns.		54.17	57.98	---	83.33	71.31	95.83	51.03	68.94
Delaware Division	1	66.67	57.14	---	83.33	70.77	63.64	71.09	68.77
North Branch	4,2	68.79	62.16	---	100.00	69.77	71.42	74.12	74.38
Susquehanna River	1,5,2	17.02	50.00	---	0.00	40.00	50.00	14.29	28.55
West Branch	5	39.29	57.89	---	100.00	68.18	100.00	58.14	70.58
Monongahela River	7	29.26	43.86	---	33.33	57.38	60.00	92.98	52.80
French Creek Ext.	7	25.44	41.67	---	75.00	45.23	62.50	60.76	51.77
Pittsburgh-Erie	7	41.52	55.00	---	75.00	69.77	83.33	71.43	66.05
Route Average		41.14	52.53	---	66.67	64.44	70.13	63.26	

Source: Pennsylvania, House of Representatives, Legislative Journal, Vol.1, 1828-29 .

Valley Region, consistently supported policies and routes that did not even directly affect their area. These three regions (along with the Pocono Region which did not even send a representative of its own to the General Assembly in 1828) were desperate for any kind of transportation improvement. Only one of the proposed routes, the West Branch, directly traversed any of these regions. Representatives from these areas supported almost all transportation improvements in the hopes of attaining something for their region.

Voting patterns for the commercial-economic and commercial-economic aggregate groups reinforce these findings. (See Table 34.) The greatest support on both the "general extension" and "general appropriations" issues came from those areas that were least developed as well as those that were more commercially oriented. The patterns are somewhat different on roll-calls for specific routes. The strongest support was concentrated in the lower two commercial-economic and commercial-economic aggregate groups. None of the routes voted upon during the 1828-29 session was part of the Main Line and it is not surprising that these counties, which tended to be in more isolated areas, favored the extension of branch lines. Conversely, the groups at the upper end of the both spectrums had been willing to vote for general extension and appropriation measures, but were less anxious to support branch routes, with the exception of the Delaware and North Branch divisions.

With only a few exceptions, representatives from commercial-economic group 3 and from commercial-economic aggregate group 4 gave the least support to internal improvement proposals. The reason for this is not altogether clear. It is possible that those residing in these counties felt they had acceptable access to necessary markets, did not feel the desperate need for improvements felt by less-developed counties, and may even have feared that long-range routes would flood the market with competing products from the west and threaten their own financial security.[15]

If questions about the methods used in financing the state works and about the order of the construction priority were already being raised in the 1828-29 session, there was also evidence of dissatisfaction with the administration of the state works. The construction of the works had been under the direction of a governor-appointed Board of Canal Commissioners. Disappointment with the financial situation and the slow pace of construction coupled with a desire to wrest control of the Board from the executive office led legislators to attempt to change the method of selecting the Canal Commissioners. Some wanted to shift the appointive power from the governor and to the legislature. A more radical proposal was for the popular election of commissioners. Table 35 indicates that the legislature was

TABLE 34

PERCENT IN FAVOR OF THE PUBLIC WORKS BY COMMERCIAL-ECONOMIC GROUP, COMMERCIAL-ECONOMIC AGGREGATE GROUP, ISSUE AND ROUTE, 1828-29

	Commercial-Economic Group					
Issue/Route	1	2	3	4	5	Ave.
General Extension	85.45	69.57	64.89	56.49	70.40	69.36
General Appropriations	78.49	65.22	46.06	48.09	59.65	59.50
Delaware Division	72.34	63.16	65.96	67.54	67.92	67.38
North Branch	77.42	70.27	70.97	65.38	70.21	70.85
Susquehanna River	42.86	30.00	0.00	26.32	25.65	24.96
West Branch	81.25	50.00	38.71	43.59	52.94	55.30
Monongahela River	60.00	67.31	39.29	59.32	40.18	53.22
French Creek Ext.	48.28	55.26	31.03	44.16	33.82	42.51
Pittsburgh-Erie	81.25	70.27	42.11	44.30	55.94	75.02
Route Average	66.20	59.47	41.15	50.09	49.52	

	Commercial-Economic Aggregate Group				
	2	3	4	5	Ave.
General Extension	67.82	78.50	50.89	75.00	68.05
General Appropriations	55.94	73.08	39.93	63.11	58.02
Delaware Division	69.74	67.35	59.06	72.64	67.20
North Branch	72.00	75.00	56.44	76.87	70.10
Susquehanna River	41.67	11.76	20.00	24.32	24.44
West Branch	65.38	64.71	30.61	55.38	54.02
Monongahela River	77.27	54.84	42.95	41.43	54.12
French Creek Ext.	54.35	46.77	33.67	34.85	42.41
Pittsburgh-Erie	72.00	65.63	37.37	56.30	57.83
Route Average	64.63	55.15	40.01	52.68	

Source: See Table 33

very interested in gaining control over the Board. The voting patterns on the issue of legislative appointment parallel those found on the votes for the general appropriations and extension of the public works. The interior and western regions, which sought a greater piece of the action, were very interested in the idea of legislative appointment. The eastern regions, on the other hand, had received quite favorable treatment under the old system and were less anxious to alter the method of selecting the Board. The commercial-economic and commercial-economic aggregate group patterns are more muddled. Very generally speaking, groups at either end of the continua were more interested in gaining control over the appointment process than were those in the middle.

These patterns almost reversed themselves on roll-calls dealing with the popular election of the commissioners. While the idea of allowing the people to elect the Canal Commissioners was generally not a very popular one, representatives from the most populous region, the Southeastern Region, were those least opposed to electing the Board by a popular vote. Members from other areas of the state, however, realized that they would have much more leverage under the legislative appointment method and gave less support to popular election.

The commercial-economic and commercial-economic aggregate group trends on these issues are much less clear, indicating the overriding importance of region on this

TABLE 35

PERCENT IN FAVOR OF THE APPOINTMENT OR POPULAR ELECTION OF CANAL COMMISSIONERS, 1828-29

Region	Legislative Appointment	Popular Election
1. Southeastern	72.09	44.07
2. Anthracite	70.00	41.37
4. Northeastern	100.00	33.33
5. Ridge and Valley	80.00	37.50
6. Allegheny Forest	100.00	40.00
7. Western	80.00	38.09
Average	83.68	39.06
Commercial-Economic Group		
1	50.00	40.91
2	100.00	46.43
3	73.33	42.22
4	64.71	39.29
5	80.56	40.40
Average	73.72	41.85
Commercial-Economic Aggregate Group		
2	92.31	37.84
3	58.82	37.21
4	68.18	52.50
5	82.36	34.44
Average	75.42	40.50

Source: See Table 34.

topic. The most striking result revealed by these roll-calls is the majority support for popular election cast by commercial-economic aggregate group 4. This group was consistently opposed to the extension of public works and to appropriating money for them. Perhaps they believed that the populace would select commissioners who would be more parsimonious in their handling of the public purse and who would create a transportation system more to their liking.

In the end, the legislature succeeded in gaining control over the appointment of the Board of Canal Commissioners.[16] Commissioners appointed by the legislature, however, were to fare little better than those selected by the governor. As we shall see, the conduct and method of selecting the Board became a chronic theme in the history of the public works.

The cautious attitude toward government spending was even more evident in the legislature's treatment of mixed enterprises, or subsidized routes. Appropriations for a total of nine turnpike companies, bridge corporations, or state roads were voted upon during the course of the session.[17] Only one-third of these received any money at all. Although petitioners had asked for sums as high as $5000, in the end, the more niggardly amounts of $2000 and $500 were granted to help in the construction of two state roads in the Anthracite Region, and $200 for improvement of Penn's Creek, Centre County in the Ridge and Valley Region.

While two of the proposed routes traversed the Anthracite Region and one ran between the Anthracite and Southeastern regions, the majority of the appropriations voted upon were for routes in interior and western regions. Petitioners appealed for financial aid for one route in the Allegheny Forest Region, two in the Ridge and Valley Region, and three in the Western Region. The majority of the proposed routes were located in sparsely inhabited areas of the commonwealth. If attainment of a major public works project was beyond the immediate grasp of these areas, they nevertheless felt that they deserved a small portion of the public largesse.

Those from the northwest corner of the state were particularly active in their efforts to secure appropriations for local routes. George Moore, representing both Erie and Warren counties, placed the blame for his district's lack of development squarely upon the legislature. According to Moore, "the commonwealth of Pennsylvania has deprived the people of that section of the state of being comfortable, and the means of making their roads. Had it not been, sir, for the frauds and delusions practised upon the people by the commonwealth, it would not now be necessary for them to ask aid for this or any other purpose. . . . But sir, those people are poor."[18] An attempt was made to include an amendment in the canal bill to authorize state subscriptions to the stock of certain western turnpike companies. With passage of the canal bill, the members from the Northwest corner argued, this section of the state would not receive one dollar directly or indirectly of the entire $8.5 million that had been appropriated for the public works. Such neglect, they threatened, would force the trade of these western territories toward neighboring states.[19] All of these efforts were unsuccessful. Although the canal bill made vague and grandiose promises of surveying water routes between Pittsburgh and Erie and along the Monongahela River, aid for turnpike roads was not forthcoming.

The voting patterns on the local mixed appropriations roll-calls reflect the divisions and needs of the various regions and economic groups. As Table 36 demonstrates, Southeastern Region representatives were simply not interested in providing funds for turnpikes and local roads that had little tangible benefit to them. The remaining regions, on the other hand, generally supported aid to turnpikes and state roads. These patterns emphasize the enormous legislative clout of the Southeastern Region. Even though all other regions were strongly in favor of the proposed appropriations, the Southeastern Region sent the most representatives to the lower house. Their general opposition was sufficient to block the passage of aid to local routes.

Commercial-economic and commercial-economic aggregate group voting trends reinforce these findings. Along the commercial-economic continuum, the least supportive groups were the most-developed group 5 and again, the persistently opposed middle group 3. Commercial-economic aggregate group support is even more precise. Those groups which remained among the least developed throughout the antebellum period, and hence those which were most desperately in need of additional roads, supported state aid most strongly. As with the commercial-economic groups, those at the upper end of the spectrum did not cast the majority of their votes in favor of the proposed appropriations. These more advanced districts already had adequate overland transportation. Their sights were set on long-range routes like those allegedly being constructed as part of the public works and reduced transportation costs that the completion of these lines would bring.

As the policy toward transporation improvements unfolded, the enhancement of Pennsylvania's, and more particularly, Philadelphia's position in the interstate competition for markets continuted to be a dominant theme. Most of the improvements that received financial aid could at least loosely be justified in this way. Those that were perceived as more purely local, like the western turnpikes, failed to receive the necessary support. Since one of Philadelphia's prime competitors was Baltimore, appeals from Baltimore railroad companies to penetrate the Susquehanna Valley were denied. Table 37 gives the percent voting in favor of referring a petition for the incorporation of a railroad from York Haven to the Maryland line to the

TABLE 36

PERCENT IN FAVOR OF APPROPRIATIONS FOR LOCAL ROUTES, 1828-29

Region	Percent in Favor
1. Southeastern	37.44
2. Anthracite	62.92
4. Northeastern	87.50
5. Ridge and Valley	63.54
6. Allegheny Forest	88.89
7. Western	60.64
Average	66.82

Commercial-Economic Group	
1	51.43
2	76.54
3	34.48
4	53.04
5	48.58
Average	52.81

Commercial-Economic Aggregate Group	
2	65.38
3	64.86
4	37.10
5	48.33
Average	53.92

Source: See Table 34.

committee on corporations by region, commercial-economic and commercial-economic aggregate group.

Those regions that were traditionally torn in their allegiance to Philadelphia and Baltimore, the Southeastern and Ridge and Valley regions, appropriately split their vote on this roll-call. The Western Region was decidedly opposed. While this region had some Baltimore connections via the National Road, its future, at least for the present, was wrapped up in the Main Line and in its north-south intra-regional routes. Among both sets of commercial-economic groups, greatest support clustered toward the bottom of each scale while upper level group representatives who were probably tied more closely to commercial interests in Philadelphia tended to oppose considering the petition. The Anthracite, Northeastern, and Allegheny Forest regions, on the other hand, overwhelmingly supported the measure even though these areas would not directly benefit from the construction of the proposed railroad. Although this roll-call only reflects sentiment on whether or not to refer the petition to committee, the pattern of support on the part of these three regions is one that was repeated time and again in the sessions to come.

III

The problems and issues the 1828-29 legislators confronted continued to surface during each legislative session throughout the 1830's. By 1839, the state was in

TABLE 37

PERCENT IN FAVOR OF EXTENDING THE YORK HAVEN-BALTIMORE RAILROAD, 1828-29

Region	Percent in Favor
1. Southeastern	42.55
2. Anthracite	70.00
4. Northeastern	100.00
5. Ridge and Valley	50.00
6. Allegheny Forest	100.00
7. Western	20.00
Average	63.76
Commercial-Economic Group	
1	87.50
2	55.56
3	42.86
4	19.05
5	44.74
Average	49.95
Commercial-Economic Aggregate Group	
2	45.45
3	68.75
4	22.22
5	47.22
Average	45.91

Source: See Table 34.

deep financial trouble, yet the public works system and the policy of subsidizing private companies seem to have taken on lives of their own. Attempts to limit appropriations to primary routes met little success as members and non-members from across the state continued to push for subsidisies for their own favorite lines. During the 1838-39 session, proposals to appropriate funds for thirty-four separate routes came to a vote. Fourteen of these fell under the umbrella of the public works administration, sixteen were mixed corporations, and only four were privately-owned companies seeking incorporation or charter extensions.[20] While the legislature seemed unable or unwilling to shed the major responsibility for constructing the transportation network, the representatives had become demonstrably more parsimonious and were more concerned with keeping a strict accounting of transportation expenditures. During the 1829 session, the public works bill authorized a lump sum for the annual loan and vaguely indicated upon which lines that amount was to be spent. The 1839 law, in contrast, specifically designated how much was to be allocated to each, individual route.[21]

By the 1838-39 session, members of the House of Representatives had become accustomed to, if not altogether happy about, the constant demands for more money from the Board of Canal Commissioners. At the beginning of the session, as in 1828, the legislature was asked to make an emergency loan, this time to the tune of $1.2 million. The

House authorized this amount without even taking a roll-call vote.[22] Passing the annual public works bill, however, proved to be a more difficult task. One of the thorniest issues involved how much to appropriate for construction and for repairs on already existing lines. At the outset of the session, the President of the Canal Board, James Clarke, recommended that $1,676,992 was needed to return the canals to full working order.[23] Many representatives found it inconceivable that repairs for a canal system that had been in total operation for less than five years could approach two million dollars. Many of the lines, most notably the North Branch and Erie Extensions, had not yet been completed.

To come to terms with these issues, both houses remained in Harrisburg until mid-July rather than adjourning at the conventional time in late April. The House version of the first "Act to provide for the repairs of the canals and railroads and to continue the improvement of the state," reduced appropriations for repairs from a little over $1 million to $.5 million. Even with this reduction, the bill failed to pass through the lower house. Debate over the second bill, which was introduced in a somewhat unorthodox fashion as a joint resolution, continued until the final days of the <u>extra</u> session. The public works law, as eventually passed, appropriated $700,000 for repairs and authorized the governor to borrow $2,054,000 to continue the state system.[24]

Table 38 compares the voting patterns on general appropriation roll-calls for the 1828-29 and 1838-39 sessions. Overall support for the public works system declined dramatically during the decade. The average support for all regions was close to 70% in the late 1820's, but dropped to just 51% by the 1838-39 session. While the percent voting in favor of appropriations to continue the public works remained roughly the same for the Southeastern and Western regions, support declined in all of the other regions. In all regions, representativies split their votes almost equally which explains, in part, why it required an extra session to adopt a public works bill.

Although the commercial-economic and commercial-economic aggregate group averages did not decline as markedly as the regional average did, the range in percentage points between those groups supporting and those opposing appropriations had narrowed significantly. Both commercial-economic group 5 and aggregate group 5 representatives demonstrated a decided shift away from support of the state system. While the upper groups had been in favor of granting financial aid for the construction of public routes in 1829, these representatives voted against increased appropriations more frequently than those from any other group. By 1839, the Main Line had been completed. This was the route that had most interested the more developed commercial-economic districts in 1829. Representatives from less-developed districts continued to vote in favor of aid for a public

TABLE 38

PERCENT IN FAVOR OF PUBLIC WORKS APPROPRIATIONS, 1828-29, 1838-39

Region	1828-29	1838-39
1. Southeastern	54.17	50.38
2. Anthracite	57.98	45.95
3. Pocono	---	55.56
4. Northeastern	83.33	52.63
5. Ridge and Valley	71.31	49.35
6. Allegheny Forest	95.83	53.33
7. Western	51.03	50.00
Average	68.94	51.03
Commercial-Economic Group		
1	78.49	56.58
2	65.22	51.28
3	46.06	59.06
4	48.09	50.00
5	59.65	44.41
Average	59.50	52.27
Commercial-Economic Aggregate Group		
1	---	62.50
2	55.94	48.62
3	73.08	53.45
4	39.93	54.80
5	63.11	45.61
Average	58.02	53.00

Source: Pennsylvania, House of Representatives, Legislative Journal, Vol. 1, 1828-29, 1838-39.

works system that would now concentrate on constructing branch lines. In contrast, members from the more commercial districts were increasingly concerned with keeping the financial commitment of the commonwealth to a minimum.

Continuing apprehension over the state debt coupled with concern over the cost for repairs came to focus on the conduct and method of selecting the Canal Commissioners. The power of appointing the commissioners had been returned to the governor in the early 1830's, and the close ties between the executive and the Board became an easy target for opponents. So grave were the accusations of corruption and mismanagement that the Senate carried out a full-scale investigation of the activities of the Canal Board throughout the 1838-39 session, an investigation which failed to substantiate any charges against the commissioners.[23]

At the same time, there were those who maintained, as in 1829, that the commissioners should not be appointed by the governor or the legislature, but should be elected by the people themselves. As Table 39 demonstrates, support for the popular election of the Canal Commissioners had not increased much between 1829 and 1839. The greatest support for the idea continued to be located in the most populated regions and districts--the Southeastern, Anthracite, Western, and Ridge and Valley regions. Whereas representatives in the interior areas had been marginally opposed to the idea in 1829, they came out firmly against

TABLE 39

PERCENT IN FAVOR OF THE POPULAR ELECTION OF CANAL COMMISSIONERS, 1828-29, 1838-39

Region	1828-29	1838-39
1. Southeastern	44.07	44.44
2. Anthracite	41.37	40.91
3. Pocono	---	0.00
4. Northeastern	33.33	12.50
5. Ridge and Valley	37.50	47.83
6. Allegheny Forest	40.00	11.11
7. Western	38.09	52.54
Average	39.06	29.90
Commercial-Economic Group		
1	40.91	47.83
2	46.43	46.15
3	42.22	28.95
4	39.20	30.19
5	40.40	50.52
Average	41.85	40.73
Commercial-Economic Aggregate Group		
1	---	33.33
2	37.84	47.22
3	37.21	27.45
4	52.50	48.84
5	34.44	50.49
Average	40.50	41.47

Source: See Table 38.

it by 1839. This shift was undoubtedly a recognition of political and demographic reality rather than a tacit vote of confidence in the present Board.

A similar shift in support took place in the commercial-economic and commercial-economic aggregate group patterns. Although there was a slight increase in support of popular election in both of the least-developed groups, the middle groups were less in favor of the idea than they had been in 1829. It was the upper groups--again, the most populous districts--that had significantly shifted their support toward the popular election of the Canal Commissioners. The idea of allowing the people to elect the members of the Canal Board, then, was gaining greater acceptance within the areas that counted. The popular election of the Board did not become a reality until 1844 after yet another attempt at appointment by the General Assembly. As time would tell, Pennsylvanians were no more satisfied with commissioners who were popularly elected than they were with those selected by the legislature or the chief executive.[26]

Despite all this, numerous attempts to obtain funds to construct specific transportation lines continued. While appropriations for fourteen public works routes were voted upon during the 1838-39 session, in the end only six received financial aid.[27] Table 40 lists the percent voting in favor of appropriations by region and location of route. The regional averages indicate a significant decline in the

TABLE 40

PERCENT IN FAVOR OF THE PUBLIC WORKS ROUTES BY REGION AND REGIONAL LOCATION OF ROUTE, 1838-39

Regional Location of Routes*	Region 1	2	3	4	5	6	7	Ave.
1. Southeastern	41.91	55.23	14.67	39.73	46.19	35.28	51.91	40.70
2. Anthracite	47.73	84.08	33.33	66.67	54.76	54.56	63.98	57.87
3. Pocono	---	---	---	---	---	---	---	---
4. Northeastern	53.52	73.68	100.00	100.00	42.86	87.50	57.41	73.57
5. Ridge/Valley	38.34	50.01	10.00	42.86	58.69	57.78	59.05	45.25
6. Allegheny Frst.	28.15	39.58	16.67	33.33	45.74	100.00	45.18	44.09
7. Western	33.49	49.96	20.00	40.20	50.31	67.15	46.41	43.93
Average All Routes	37.23	49.89	23.10	43.76	49.06	57.35	47.84	

*If a route traversed any part of a region, it was counted as being located within that region.

Source: Pennsylvania, House of Representatives, Legislative Journal, Vol. 1, 1838-39.

support for public works construction since the 1828-29 session. (See Table 33.) As in the earlier session, however, greatest support came from the interior regions and, to a greater extent than in 1829, from the Anthracite Region. Opposition to the extension of the state system was most prevalent in the Southeastern and Pocono regions.

Did the regions' representatives, however, vote in favor of appropriations for routes that directly traversed their home turf? Regional self-interest was a motivating factor for legislators from the Anthracite, Northeastern and Allegheny Forest regions. Members from the latter two areas voted unanimously for routes which crossed their region while the Anthracite representatives voted in favor of their region's routes close to 85% of the time. While Ridge and Valley legislators cast the majority of their votes for their region's proposed routes, the same cannot be said of representatives from the Southeastern and Western regions. Indeed, there is little evidence of any cohesive regional self-interest on the part of these two regions for these roll-calls.

Patterns of legislative behavior on appropriations for mixed enterprises parallel these findings. Although a bill for appropriations to 127 local routes in amounts ranging from $200 to $10,000 was vetoed by the governor, the House did vote on aid or stock subscriptions for sixteen transportation companies.[28] As Table 41 indicates, the average percent voting in favor for subsidies on all routes

TABLE 41

PERCENT IN FAVOR OF MIXED ENTERPRISE ROUTES BY REGION AND REGIONAL LOCATION OF ROUTE, 1838-39

Regional Location of Routes*	1	2	3	4	5	6	7	Ave.
1. Southeastern	61.51	79.17	37.50	60.42	61.19	77.08	57.57	62.06
2. Anthracite	68.68	92.05	27.78	87.50	81.06	96.67	69.80	74.79
3. Pocono	15.38	0.00	100.00	---	33.33	33.33	17.65	33.28
4. Northeastern	38.09	73.08	0.00	100.00	38.71	80.00	57.14	55.29
5. Ridge and Valley	45.81	96.88	0.00	90.00	65.24	100.00	72.56	67.21
6. Allegheny Forest	36.08	79.21	0.00	95.00	24.80	95.00	45.00	53.58
7. Western	51.32	47.72	62.50	66.07	60.70	66.03	58.17	58.93
Average All Routes	51.81	65.72	43.89	72.72	55.29	75.52	58.24	

*If a route traversed any part of a region, it was counted as being located within that region.

Source: See Table 40.

was particuarly strong in the Anthracite, Northeastern and Allegheny Forest regions. Representatives from these areas gave almost unanimous support to the lines which criss-crossed their own regions. While these representatives were somewhat reticent to vote for public works appropriations outside of their area, they favored stock subscriptions or out-right grants for mixed transportation enterprises to be built both within or outside of their own region. The Pocono Region legislator was not enthusiastic about any other region's routes, but clearly had no misgivings about demanding state aid to construct lines within his own backyard.

The average percent voting in favor of subsidies for all routes was significantly lower for the Southeastern, Ridge and Valley and Western regions. As on the public works roll-calls, representatives from these regions did not vote cohesively even on routes directly affecting their area. While these legislators were more favorable to subsidized routes than they were to public works projects, they still seemed unable to come to any agreement amongst themselves and frequently cast more unanimous support for lines in other parts of the state than for routes in their own region.

Several explanations can be offered to explain these persistent voting patterns. To begin with, the Southeastern and Western regions were by far the most populous areas which meant that there were simply more people, with more demands, and more conflicting interests to satisfy, not to mention more representatives to coordinate. More important, the Anthracite, Northeastern, and Allegheny Forest regions were more economically and geographically homogeneous than the Southeastern, Ridge and Valley, and Western regions. In addition, the Anthracite and Northeastern regions had only one major market orientation making the decision of which routes to support less complicated. Although products from the Allegheny Forest Region travelled down both the Susquehanna River in the east and the Allegheny River in the west, the region was so utterly devoid of any kind of transportation improvements that representatives from the area believed that any improvement was better than none at all. Just as they were able to agree on transportation issues which directly affected the home region, representatives from these three regions supported mixed enterprise proposals to improve the transportation system in other parts of the state. The Southeastern, Western, and Ridge and Valley regions, on the other hand, felt the pull from various competing markets, most notably Baltimore and Philadelphia, more acutely. Attempts by interests within each region to improve access to competing markets increasingly made compromise on any transportation issue, even those which did not directly affect the home region, next to impossible.

A third type of transportation organization was making its presence increasingly felt--the privately-owned railroad. Pennsylvania, unlike Maryland, chose to build a canal rather than a railroad in an effort to open up the east-west avenues of trade. While the canal alternative worked well in neighboring New York because of the state's even topography, it did not in mountainous Pennsylvania. By the late 1830's, this fact was becoming painfully apparent.[29] Although the legislators tried to keep the issue of competing railroads from surfacing, proposals for long-distance rail lines which would seriously undercut the marginal effectiveness of the public works crept into the debate time and again.

The 1838-39 legislature was not indiscriminately hostile towards all railroads, merely those which would compete directly with the public works. Rail lines which would open up new areas, in fact, received quite favorable treatment. Provisions were made for the Williamsport and Elmira Railroad to extend its line and the time required for completion of construction. This railway, it was argued, would tap the valuable trade of southern New York state.[30] A similar extension was granted to the Baltimore and Ohio Railroad which still hoped to establish connections with Pittsburgh, a connection that southwestern Pennsylvanians ardently desired.[31] Likewise, a petition requesting the governor to open negotiations with other states to promote a railroad to St. Louis was debated until the discussion became bogged down over the location of the eastern terminus of the route, causing the resolution to be postponed indefinitely.[32]

Proposals for authorizing a survey of a railroad between Philadelphia and Pittsburgh and for providing appropriations for the Hollidaysburg and Huntingdon Railroad aroused much more opposition. The debate surrounding the Hollidaysburg and Huntingdon was put before the legislature under two separate guises during the 1838-39 session. Initially, an attempt was made to secure $300,000 for the construction of the line as part of the public works bill. The proposed route paralleled the Main Line for over forty miles, however, and was strongly opposed on these grounds. When the appropriation was denied, the railroad's proponents regrouped their forces and applied to the legislature for an act of incorporation. The original petition requested a stock subscription of $150,000 which was denied, and in the end, the petitioners had to settle for a charter for a privately-owned corporation.

Table 42 compares the percent voting in favor of the public works appropriation with the percent supporting the act of incorporation for the Hollidaysburg and Huntingdon for the seven regions. The difference in the two sets of votes could hardly be more striking. The only area to cast majority support for the public works proposal came from within the Ridge and Valley Region itself. The remaining six regions were all opposed to the appropriation. As a private corporation, however, the Hollidaysburg and

TABLE 42
PERCENT IN FAVOR OF THE HOLLIDAYSBURG AND HUNTINGDON RAILROAD, 1838-39

Region	Public Works Bill	Private Incorporation
Southeastern	23.46	47.22
Anthracite	0.00	30.00
Pocono	0.00	100.00
Northeastern	0.00	60.00
Ridge and Valley	53.33	61.54
Allegheny Forest	28.57	83.33
Western	47.62	52.50
Average	21.85	62.08

Source: See Table 40.

Huntingdon received much more support from all regions enabling the company to acquire its charter. Appropriating funds for lines that would compete with the public works was anathema to most legislators; authorizing the construction of the same line by the private sector, on the other hand, was merely accepting the inevitable.

Indeed, support for the three acts of incorporation or charter extensions for privately-owned railroad companies was much more universal than was support for publicly-owned or mixed routes. (See Table 43.) Once again, Northeastern and Allegheny Forest representatives voted consistently in favor of all of the proposed routes, as did the Pocono Region member. Legislators from the Anthracite, Ridge and Valley and Western regions likewise supported these policies on the average of sixty-five to seventy percent of the time, while the Southeastern members cast roughly sixty percent of their votes in favor of the corporations. As on the public works and mixed enterprise roll-calls, regional self-interest was evident in the voting patterns for some regions and not for others. Allegheny Forest legislators voted unanimously in favor of incorporating the railroad which would traverse their region. The Western Region members, too, demonstrated a good deal of support when voting for their area's Freeport and New Castle line. But once again, the Ridge and Valley representatives failed to put up a unified front when voting for their own route and, in fact, seemed able to agree more on transportation

TABLE 43

PERCENT IN FAVOR OF GRANTING CHARTERS TO RAILROAD COMPANIES BY REGION, 1838-39

Rte.	Reg. Lctn.	Region 1	2	3	4	5	6	7	Ave.
Hollidaysbrg. & Huntngdn.	5	47.22	30.00	100.00	60.00	61.54	83.33	52.50	62.08
Freeport & New Cstle.	7	69.70	83.33	---	100.00	75.00	100.00	76.19	84.03
Loyalsock	6	65.71	100.00	100.00	100.00	71.43	100.00	72.22	87.05
Ave. All Rtes.		60.87	71.11	100.00	86.67	69.32	94.44	66.97	

Source: See Table 40.

proposals which affected markets far removed from their own terrain.

The patterns for the commercial-economic and commercial-economic aggregate groups reinforce the regional trends on public works, mixed enterprise, and private corporation roll-calls. (See Table 44.) For the most part, support for all types of routes was lodged in the least-developed commercial-economic group and in the two most developed groups. Commercial-economic group 4 representatives supported appropriations to mixed corporations and charters to private railroad companies more than did group 5 legislators. The middle commercial-economic group members, on the other hand, remained, as in 1829, the least supportive.

Similar trends are evident among the commercial-economic aggregate groups. Representatives from the three less-developed groups consistently supported all types of transportation improvements, and were frequently more in favor of appropriations and charters than members from group 5. Once again, it was the commercial-economic aggregate group 4 legislators that persistently opposed an expansive transportation policy.

One can only speculate upon the reasons for the resolute resistance to transportation improvements by commercial-economic group 3 and commercial-economic aggregate group 4 members. These counties had apparently attained a rather comfortable, middle-of-the road commercial

TABLE 44

PERCENT IN FAVOR OF PUBLIC WORKS, MIXED ENTERPRISE AND PRIVATE INCORPORATION ROUTES BY COMMERCIAL-ECONOMIC AND COMMERCIAL-ECONOMIC AGGREGATE GROUPS, 1838-39

Type of Route	Commercial-Economic Group					
	1	2	3	4	5	Ave.
Public Works	46.60	38.83	30.48	47.47	48.89	42.45
Mixed Enterprises	56.28	50.83	48.57	63.53	60.38	55.92
Private Incorporations	71.03	46.67	48.60	79.00	75.44	64.15
Average All Types	54.36	47.02	43.93	58.95	57.45	
	Commercial-Economic Aggregate Group					
	1	2	3	4	5	Ave.
Public Works	47.02	47.66	49.05	32.26	46.95	44.59
Mixed Enterprises	68.75	57.80	63.81	46.28	57.40	58.81
Private Incorporations	100.00	73.22	77.90	41.85	67.59	72.11
Average All Types	56.99	55.85	58.39	41.34	55.30	

Source: See Table 40.

and economic existence. Unlike the counties in the less-developed groups, these districts did not actively seek additional transportation routes. And unlike the counties in the more-developed groups, they either feared or had no use for improvements that might open up competing markets and put an increased strain on their pocketbooks. Not only did the representatives from these groups oppose the state's involvement in the public works and in mixed enterprises, but they also voted against the generally popular acts of incorporation for private companies.

The issues debated during the 1838-39 session did not augur well for the future of either the public works or the state's subsidization of mixed corporations. Support for appropriations had declined since 1829 in the face of endlessly rising construction costs and mounting repair and operating expenses. The railroad, moreover, continued to compete with the canal system until it virtually swallowed the public works in the 1850s. Within four years of the close of the 1838-39 session, the commonwealth liquidated over four million dollars of its publicly held stock. And in 1844, the question of whether or not to sell the Main Line was put to a popular vote. It passed by a vote of 146,748 to 124,598.[33] However, it would take the commonwealth thirteen years to find a buyer for this outmoded project.

IV

By the 1849 session it was all too clear that the state-owned canal system was on its last legs. Only three proposals for new construction were seriously entertained, although the legislature continued to appropriate large sums for repairs, damages, and general operating costs.[34] The major debate revolved around the completion of the North Branch Extension. The original North Branch Canal, which ran from the basin which united the Susquehanna River and the West Branch Division at Northumberland to the Lackawanna Creek, had been in operation since 1834. In 1836, work was begun on the second, longer portion of the branch canal which was to continue from the Lackawanna Creek northward to the New York state line. Construction on the canal proceeded slowly, and was finally abandoned completely in 1841 when the state's financial condition became so tenuous.[35]

In 1849, the movement to complete this section was revived and a separate bill was proposed asking for an allocation of $1.2 million. Finishing the canal, it was argued, had "become a matter of positive necessity. . . . Nearly two millions and a half of dollars have been expended on that part of the North Branch Canal . . . when this work is completed, it passes directly through the heart of the Wyoming and Lackawanna coal fields."[36] Another advocate argued that the canal had received

> more than twenty years since, Legislative sanction; . . . we subscribe most fully to the proposition, that there is an implied pledge existing on the part of the State, to carry out its original design in regard to this work. . . . This improvement, three-fourths complete, mars for its hundred miles in length, the fine fertile valley in which it is located. The farms of the citizens of this valley have been divided--roads destroyed--and, instead of bringing promised blessings and benefits, it is, in its present condition, an eye-sore, if not a curse. . . . this work ought to be completed with as little delay as the exigencies of the Commonwealth will permit.[36]

Opponents of the project argued that "the internal improvement system of Pennsylvania has been abandoned--abandoned by common consent. The practical working of it has not met the expectations of its friends, nor have the advantages resulting therefrom convinced the people of its utility and the propriety of its continuance."[37] If the North Branch Extension bill passes, they warned, "it will at once plunge us into a further system of internal improvements, and consequently will indefinitely increase our State debt, State taxes, and all the other evils which always attend a system of making appropriations without first considering where the money is to come from, or how it is to be paid when it falls due."[38]

In the end, the separate bill authorizing completion of the North Branch Extension was defeated, but the crusade to recommence work on the canal was partially successful. As part of the general act "to provide for the ordinary expenses of the government, the repair of the canals and railroads of the commonwealth, and the payment of other claims due by the same," the Canal Commissioners were authorized to appoint a competent engineer to superintend the completion of the branch line. The funds, however, were rather vaguely to come from "whatever balance of money remains in the treasury unappropriated, after the payment of the August and February interest in each current year." No engineer or superintendent was to be appointed until there was $150,000 in the treasury that was not already appropriated.[39] Work continued slowly on the line, which was never wholly completed, until 1856.[40]

The attempt to secure funds for a railroad to avoid the inclined plane on the Philadelphia and Columbia Railroad, the first leg of the Main Line in the east, was more successful. An effort was made to slip a $400,000 appropriation for this purpose into the original North Branch Extension bill, which was defeated. This amount was eventually awarded in the general fiscal act. The proposal to appropriate $20,000 to complete the reservoir on the western side of the Allegheny mountain, however, was resoundingly defeated.

As in 1839, there was a movement to investigate the conduct of the Canal Commissioners (who were, by this time, elected by the people), and to require them to give formal depositions explaining their actions. In addition, yet another vote was taken in the House on the sale of the public works. Even though the plebiscite of 1844 had gone in favor of the sale of the Main Line, no bidders were willing to meet the $20 million dollar price tag set by the legislature. Moreover, as the financial crisis lessened, there was a slight revival of hope that the state system might someday turn a profit.

The regional voting patterns on these issues revive some familiar themes. (See Table 45.) The North Branch Extension cut directly through both the Anthracite and the Northeastern regions and explains the strong support of the representatives from these areas. While the route did not directly traverse the Pocono Region, the hope of tapping into the trade of this north-south line, given its close proximity, motivated the Pocono legislator to vote in favor of its completion. Support from all other regions for the North Branch Extension was moderate at best. Already saddled with a publicly-owned transportation system that drained their pocketbooks but did not wholly satisfy their commercial needs, these legislators were reluctant to authorize funds for such an open-ended undertaking, no matter how important the route might be.

Although regional self-interest is not evident in the Southeastern support of the inclined plane proposal nor in the percentage voting in favor of the reservoir among Western members, the Northeastern, Allegheny Forest, and Anthracite representatives demonstrated above-average support on at least one of these votes. As in the 1838-39 session, these were the three regions which continually tended to vote in favor of most internal improvements, even those which did not directly benefit their area.

What about the pressure to interrogate the Canal Commissioners and to sell the public works? One would expect the less populated regions to be the most critical of a Board over which they had little control and of a public works system that had failed to meet their demands. Actually, just the reverse was true. The regions demonstrating the most dissatisfaction with the canal system and its administration continued to be the most populous, prosperous Southeastern and Western regions. Those areas most reluctant to attack the commissioners or to push for the sale of the system were the least populated, interior regions. Although these regions had not benefited nearly as much from the system, they lacked the private capital to construct transportation routes on their own. While there was dissatisfaction with the public system, as the debate over the North Branch Extension indicated, representatives from these areas were not yet prepared to throw the whole system away.

The voting patterns for the commercial-economic and commercial-economic aggregate groups on the appropriations roll-calls are difficult to decipher. In previous sessions, support for internal improvements had been strongest in the lower and upper commercial-economic and commercial-economic aggregate groups, while the middle groups had been less enthusiastic. On these appropriations issues, however, the middle commercial-economic groups were most enthusiastic, while support at the upper and lower ends of the spectrum

TABLE 45

PERCENT IN FAVOR OF PUBLIC WORKS ROUTES, CANAL BOARD DEPOSITIONS, AND THE SALE OF THE PUBLIC WORKS, 1849

Route/Issue	Regions 1	2	3	4	5	6	7	Ave.
North Branch	57.47	73.27	75.00	86.00	47.32	44.83	54.24	62.59
Inclined Plane	53.70	53.19	---	91.30	44.68	66.67	57.02	61.09
Reservoir	11.54	60.00	---	0.00	25.00	50.00	33.33	29.98
Depositions	39.44	16.67	---	10.00	20.00	0.00	51.11	22.87
Sale	34.62	33.33	0.00	0.00	22.22	0.00	28.57	16.96

Route/Issue	Commercial-Economic Groups 1	2	3	4	5	Ave.
North Branch	56.25	46.40	67.44	52.43	61.10	56.72
Inclined Plane	45.45	58.02	65.82	58.70	51.16	55.83
Reservoir	50.00	28.57	36.36	18.18	19.23	30.47
Depositions	33.33	25.00	33.33	7.69	49.32	39.60
Sale	33.33	7.14	28.57	9.09	40.00	29.73

Route/Issue	Commercial-Economic Aggregate Groups 2	3	4	5	Ave.
North Branch	48.92	58.71	48.58	67.00	55.80
Inclined Plane	58.49	69.89	51.85	49.71	57.49
Reservoir	36.84	27.27	13.33	21.05	24.62
Depositions	40.48	10.34	6.25	58.33	28.85
Sale	22.22	6.25	17.65	52.38	24.63

Source: Pennsylvania, House of Representatives, Legislative Journal, Vol. 1, 1849.

often fell below average. Similarly, commercial-economic aggregate group 4 which had been so noticeably opposed to any appropriations in previous sessions supported funds at least for the North Branch and inclined plane projects.

Trends on the deposition and sale issues are easier to explain. As with the regions, the greatest pressure to investigate the Board's conduct and to sell the public works came from the most affluent, and populous counties, or those in both commercial-economic and commercial-economic aggregate group 5. While the lower and middle level groups may still have hoped to benefit from the state-owned system, the more prosperous districts were already deeply involved in the next phase of the transportation revolution--privately-funded railroads.

Sixty-two transportation companies were incorporated during the 1849 session, yet of that number, only two--both railroad companies--came to a final vote in the House of Representatives.[41] This ratio is in itself instructive: voting for these charters among the regions and both sets of commercial-economic groups is further proof of the overall support for private railroad companies. Proposals to incorporate these railways won majorities in all regions and groups; on only two occasions, did this support dip below seventy percent.[42] While issues involving privately-owned railroads created problems for future legislators, the private companies incorporated during the 1849 session aroused no significant opposition.

V

In the second roll-call during the 1859 session the legislature abolished the Board of Canal Commissioners by an almost unanimous vote.[43] This act marked a new chapter in Pennsylvania transportation history that revolved around long distance railroad companies and the local passenger railway.

The Pennsylvania Railroad, which had purchased the Main Line in 1857, succeeded the public works as the new focus of debate. The issue which aroused the most discussion involved the tonnage tax which had been imposed upon the railroad in its original 1846 charter. Since the railroad competed directly with the Main Line prior to the 1857 sale, the legislature levied a five-mill tonnage tax on the Pennsylvania Railroad to be collected between March 10th and December 1st each year. This tax was eventually lowered to three mills in 1848, but was collected all year long.[44]

Never happy about the tax, the Pennsylvania believed it had scored a major victory in 1857 when the legislature included a proviso in the Main Line sale bill stating that if the Pennsylvania Railroad purchased the works for $9 million, the company would be released forever from the tonnage tax and all state taxation on capital stock, bonds, dividends, and other property. In 1858, the state Supreme Court promptly declared this exemption unconstitutional, but the railroad, claiming that the tax was in violation of federal law, continued to withhold payment of the tonnage duty.[45] The debate during the 1859 session revolved around whether or not to repeal the railroad's charter since it persisted in its refusal to pay the tax.[46]

Buoyed by the Supreme Court's decision, the legislature attempted to impose similar taxes on two other major railways in 1859, the Philadelphia and Reading and the Philadelphia and Trenton. The House voted to levy these duties even though some objected on the grounds that the original intent of the tax was to recoup losses resulting from the competition with the public works, which were no longer in operation.[47]

Table 46 provides the voting patterns on the tonnage tax roll-calls for each railroad. The average percent voting in favor of the tax was much higher for the Pennsylvania Railroad than it was on the other two lines. Moreover, with the exception of the Southeastern Region, commercial-economic group 5, and commercial-economic aggregate group 5, support for retaining the tax was overwhelming. These results emphasize beyond a doubt from which region and types of counties the Pennsylvania drew its support. The legislators from the Southeastern Region and the upper-level groups were clearly watching out for interests and investments that would have suffered from the payment of additional duties.

Support for taxing the other railroads was not as great and was more evenly distributed among the regions and

TABLE 46

PERCENT IN FAVOR OF TONNAGE TAXES, 1859

Railroad	Region 1	2	3	4	5	6	7	Ave.
Pennsylvania RR	55.74	92.31	100.00	89.29	64.00	95.45	92.66	84.21
Phila/Reading	50.00	62.50	44.44	56.52	58.33	63.16	47.47	54.63
Phila/Trenton	52.94	40.00	0.00	50.00	0.00	50.00	31.82	32.11
Ave. All Routes	52.89	64.94	48.15	65.27	40.78	69.54	57.32	

	Commercial-Economic Groups 1	2	3	4	5	Ave.
Pennsylvania RR	92.86	87.14	97.10	85.00	52.06	82.82
Phila/Reading	60.00	50.85	56.72	58.90	48.09	54.91
Phila/Trenton	50.00	27.27	23.08	28.57	55.26	36.84
Ave. All Routes	67.62	55.09	58.97	57.49	51.80	

	Commercial-Economic Aggregate Groups 2	3	4	5	Ave.
Pennsylvania RR	86.42	97.96	82.22	45.33	77.98
Phila/Reading	59.72	57.30	54.88	44.97	54.22
Phila/Trenton	30.77	29.41	29.41	58.06	36.91
Ave. All Routes	58.97	61.56	55.50	49.45	

Source: Pennsylvania, House of Representatives, Legislative Journal, Vol. 1, 1859.

groups. The regions most in favor of imposing the tax--the Anthracite, Northeastern, and Allegheny Forest regions--were precisely those that had continually supported state involvement in both the public works and mixed ventures. Similarly, the lower commercial-economic and commercial-economic aggregate groups which had voted consistently to support the public works also voted to tax the railroads. These regions and groups, then, continued to believe that some sort of state involvement with the transportation system was desireable, or at the very least, that the commonwealth should reap some financial benefit from the railroad companies it chartered. The top commercial-economic and commercial-economic aggregate groups had also supported the public works. By 1859, however, these counties had made the transition to a different kind of transportation system which relied solely on private capital and was much less dependent upon the state than the previous system had been.

Clamor to construct passenger railways in the commonwealth's two major cities also generated new issues. Indeed, the incorporation of passenger railroads dominated the transportation discussion. Several companies frequently competed with one another to secure the right of way on the most desireable thoroughfares. Early in the session, proposals were made to have maps of Philadelphia and Pittsburgh printed along with two-hundred copies of all passenger railroad bills for the use of the railroad committee and the House. The maps, it was argued, were necessary because "more than half of the Committee on Railroads are not citizens of Philadelphia and the proposition to build Passenger Railroads in that place seems to be a very important one just now." House members, too, should be provided with maps, for as one member put it, "we have to vote on those bills, and in order to vote intelligently, it is necessary that we know the exact location of [sic] the two cities."[48]

Although the resolution to provide the maps lost by one vote, the motion to print copies of the bills carried by five votes, but not without a good deal of debate. Those opposed to the idea complained that this was a local matter, an enormous expense would be incurred, and the printing of passenger railway bills would set a dangerous precedent that would lead to the printing of many other types of bills. Others, however, argued that it had "been difficult, if not impossible, to obtain clear information upon the subject. The discrimination between these routes should not be left to the Railroad Committee, . . . It is not a mere local question as Philadelphia is the commercial metropolis of the State, we are all directly or indirectly interested in that which interests her."[49]

Despite this appeal, there were those who clearly remained disgruntled over the amount of time spent debating passenger railroads. "For two weeks past," one opponent complained,

> there has been but one question considered in this House and that has been that of passenger railways. We have now been in session six weeks, and not a single bill of public importance has been considered, much less acted upon. . . . It seems they must be considered in this House, in preference to every other subject; they overshadow everything and all our time is taken up to consider whether a horse-railroad shall run along certain streets of Philadelphia.[50]

This same legislator proposed that night sessions be held several times a week solely for the purpose of considering these bills, but the resolution was not adopted. The Pennsylvania Daily Telegraph, on the other hand, realistically recommended that the legislature pass a general incorporation law which would give control over the location and all minor details to the City Councils "who are the immediate representatives of city interests, and are presumed to be best acquainted with city wants."[51] Although dissatisfaction over the preoccupation with passenger railroads continued to mount, the legislature never seriously considered the Telegraph's suggestion. Most charters required the railway to obtain the consent of the City Council before commencing construction and to pay the city a certain annual fee for the use of the route. The power to incorporate, however, was jealously guarded by the General Assembly.

Acts of incorporation or charter alterations for eleven passenger railways came to a vote during the 1859 session. Ten were located in Philadelphia, and one in Pittsburgh.[52] Table 47 lists the percent voting in favor of the various passenger railway issues by region, commercial-economic and

TABLE 47

PERCENT IN FAVOR OF PASSENGER RAILROAD ISSUES AND INCORPORATIONS, 1859

Issue	Region							
	1	2	3	4	5	6	7	Ave.
Maps	60.00	25.00	0.00	60.00	40.00	75.00	39.13	42.71
Printing Bills	55.84	67.35	16.67	68.96	23.06	15.00	65.71	44.66
Incorporations	62.35	72.96	33.33	78.13	53.13	67.09	60.70	61.10

	Commercial-Economic Groups					
	1	2	3	4	5	Ave.
Maps	50.00	46.15	30.77	26.67	61.70	43.06
Printing Bills	18.18	60.27	56.14	36.84	62.39	46.76
Incorporations	58.00	70.51	58.10	71.94	65.44	64.80

	Commercial-Economic Aggregate Groups				
	2	3	4	5	Ave.
Maps	46.67	36.84	5.26	78.38	41.79
Printing Bills	56.96	47.67	39.56	67.04	52.81
Incorporations	57.09	70.94	65.68	67.12	65.21

Source: See Table 46.

commercial-economic aggregate group. Given the preoccupation of the legislature with the issue of passenger railroads, one would expect to find very pronounced hostility on the part of the less-developed regions and groups, or in other words, from those counties that had virtually no interest in how Philadelphia and Pittsburgh moved its citizens about. While such animosity is evident on some roll-calls, it is not a persistent trend across all issues. Strong opposition can be detected, for instance, on the map issue from Anthracite and Pocono representatives, and to a slightly lesser extent, from Ridge and Valley and Western members. Legislators from the Northeastern and Allegheny Forest regions, however, were quite favorably disposed to printing the maps.

The roll-calls on the printing of passenger railway bills, however, produced slightly different results. Here, with the exception of the Northeastern Region, the pattern looks more like one would expect. The regions most interested in passenger rail lines--the Southeastern, Western, and Anthracite[53] regions--were most favorable to printing the bills, while the Pocono, Ridge and Valley, and Allegheny Forest regions were decidedly opposed. Voting patterns on both distributing maps and printing bills among the commercial-economic and commercial-economic aggregate groups are more clear cut. In both cases, the upper-level groups were most favorable, while the remaining groups fluctuated in their response. Support for the incorporation of passenger railways was greatest in the most-developed groups. Whereas the least-commercial groups had been quite enthusiastic about transportation improvements in past sessions, their representatives were much less interested in passenger transportation in the two major cities in 1859.

As on other transportation issues, evidence of strong, regional self-interest is lacking. The representatives from the two regions one would expect to show the most support for passenger railways--the Southeastern and Western regions--did not vote in favor of these acts as frequently as members from other regions. Anthracite, Northeastern, and Allegheny Forest legislators voted to incorporate or expand the charters of passenger railroad companies the greatest percentage of the time. The representative from the Pocono Region continued to oppose the extension of any route which did not directly cut through his own backyard, while members from the Ridge and Valley area voted in between these two extremes. Thus, even though transportation issues had changed dramatically by the 1859 session, regional voting patterns remained surprisingly consistent. While interior region representatives were dissatisfied with the monopolization of the legislative agenda on the part of passenger railway advocates, when the time came to decide for or against incorporation, they voted along the same lines as their predecessors.

VI

State involvement in creating a transportation network for antebellum Pennsylvania had come full circle by the eve of the Civil War. In the early years of the century, the commonwealth had limited its role to granting charters and making fairly minimal investments in strategically important lines. As the demands for cheaper, longer, more accessible routes accelerated, and as Pennsylvania watched neighboring states expand their markets, the commonwealth became more engrossed in building a transportation system. While the construction of the public works did create new market opportunities for many communities the state's experiment with a publicly-owned network was a failure. Pennsylvania had over-extended itself financially for a canal system that was technologically outmoded before it was completed. By the 1850's, the legislature was actively seeking ways to divest the state of its financial involvement in transportation. With the passage of an anti-investment constitutional amendment and the sale of the Main Line in 1857, the commonwealth effectively restricted its role to guiding transportation development by incorporating private companies.

Throughout the antebellum period, the legislature was, in fact, very interested in granting charters to private companies. The percent voting in favor of acts of incorporation for all regions, as Table 48 indicates, was

TABLE 48

REGIONAL AVERAGE PERCENT VOTING IN FAVOR OF PUBLIC WORKS, MIXED ENTERPRISE, AND PRIVATE CORPORATION ROUTES BY SESSION

Session	Public Works	Mixed	Private
1828-29	59.70	66.82	---
1838-39	44.03	60.46	77.08
1849	54.03	---	82.55
1859	---	---	61.10

Source: Pennsylvania, House of Representatives, Legislative Journal, vol. 1, 1828-29, 1838-39, 1849, 1859.

very high. Even mixed enterprises remained quite popular through the late 1830's. But there was increasing disillusionment with the publicly-owned system. While an average of close to 60% of the legislators in all regions voted in favor of the project in 1829, support had dipped well below the necessary majority one decade later. Although support rose slightly by 1849, the construction of only one route was under consideration, and that route was already partially completed. Legislators were not opposed to expanding the transportation system per se, especially through private charters which they handed out quite freely with relatively little dissent. The problems arose when numerous routes competed for increasingly limited public funds.

The debacle of the public works experiment has been blamed on precisely these grounds. Pennsylvanians, unlike New Yorkers, could never come to any agreement on which transportation lines were the most important. Rather than concentrating their efforts on one or two crucial routes, the legislators caved into selfish, sectional demands and authorized the building of a widely scattered transportation network which, in the end, satisfied few and drove the commonwealth to the brink of bankruptcy.

How debilitating were these regional and local demands? Regional interests did figure prominently in legislative decision-making for some regions, on some issues, some of the time. For the most part, the smaller, more geographically and economically homogeneous regions--the Northeastern, Pocono, Anthracite, and Allegheny Forest regions--demonstrated the most consistency when voting on transportation issues. Not only did representatives from these areas vote overwhelmingly to support the routes which traversed their own region, but, with the exception of the Pocono member, they voted in favor of appropriating funds or for granting charters for all routes with remarkable constancy. Representatives from the regions that were more geographically and economically complex, on the other hand, had difficulty presenting a united front. Southeastern, Western, and Ridge and Valley members rarely voted together to support their own region's routes, and demonstrated equally divided views on lines to be constructed in other parts of the state.

These divided regions suffered from what might be called an acute case of sectionalism. As Louis Hartz so perceptively put it, "The truth is that the idea of regional self-interest had no area around which it could effectively come to a focus. If it could be used on the state level it could also be used on the sectional level, and if it could be used there, it could also be invoked to rationalize the ambitions of one hamlet as against another within a section."[34] While representatives from the more homogeneous regions arrived at a consistent policy of general support for transportation improvements, legislators from the three more complex areas fell prey to competing demands from within their own region and clashed with each other as frequently as they conflicted with members from distant parts of the commonwealth.

Within all regions, certain types of counties were more likely to support the promotion of transportation improvements than were others. Less-developed districts, for example, were the most desperate for improved routes and generally voted in favor of extending and constructing new lines. Representatives from the more commercially-oriented areas also threw their support behind the majority of the bills as they pursued wider market opportunities and cheaper forms of transportation. Between these two extremes, however, was a bloc of counties that was consistently opposed to the financing and construction of new routes. Apparently fearful of the increased competition these new avenues of trade might bring and apprehensive over the mounting state debt, opposition to the public works, to mixed ventures, and to the granting of new charters remained centered in these districts throughout the antebellum period.

Unlike the sources of banking and business corporation support which shifted among regions and commercial-economic groups over time, certain areas consistently favored the expansion of the commonwealth's transportation network. Yet this support was not always a manifestation of a well-defined regional self-interest. Rampant localism prevented a cohesive regional approach from developing in

Pennsylvania's most populous areas and, in the end, seriously undermined the efforts of the legislature to create an efficient transportation network. Deprived of its power to finance and construct the routes, the commonwealth accepted the alternative role of guiding the private sector's attempts to create a workable transportation system.

FOOTNOTES

[1]See Table 5.

[2]William Miller, "A Note on the History of Business Corporations in Pennsylvania, 1800-1860," Quarterly Journal of Economics 55(November 1940): 154. Hartz has expanded Miller's data to include the decade of the 1790's. See Louis Hartz, Economic Policy and Democratic Thought: Pennsylvania, 1776-1860 (Cambridge: Havard University Press, 1948; reprint ed., Chicago: Quadrangle Paperback Books, Inc., 1968), p.38.

[3]Hartz, Economic Policy, pp. 83-86.

[4]The most in depth discussion of Pennsylvania's decision to build the canal can be found in Julius Rubin, Canal or Railroad? Imitation and Innovation in the Response to the Erie Canal in Philadelphia, Baltimore, and Boston (Philadelphia: The American Philosophical Society, 1961); and Julius Rubin, "An Imitative Public Improvement: The Pennsylvania Mainline," in Carter Goodrich, ed., Canals and American Economic Development (New York and London: Columbia University Press, 1961), pp. 67-114.

[5]Avard L. Bishop, "The State Works of Pennsylvania," Transactions of the Connecticut Academy of Arts and Sciences 13(November 1908): 208-9; Hartz, Economic Policy, pp. 148-50.

[6]Hartz, Economic Policy, pp. 103-04; 124-25, 164-65.

[7]For a discussion of the effects of sectional demands on the development of transportation policy, see Bishop, "The State Works of Pennsylvania," pp. 189-201; Hartz, Economic Policy, pp. 14, 42-44, 94-95, 132-36, 148-50; Michael F. Holt, Forging a Majority: The Formation of the Republican Party in Pittsburgh, 1848-1860 (New Haven: Yale University Press, 1969), p. 112; Philip S. Klein, Pennsylvania Politics, 1817-1832: A Game Without Rules (Philadelphia: Historical Society of Pennsylvania, 1940), pp. 195-7; H. Benjamin Powell, Philadelphia's First Fuel Crisis: Jacob Cist and the Developing Market for Pennsylvania Anthracite (University Park, PA: Pennsylvania State University Press, 1979), pp. 122-23; Charles M. Snyder, The Jacksonian Heritage: Pennsylvania Politics, 1833-1848 (Harrisburg: Pennsylvania Historical and Museum Commission, 1958), p. 12; George Rogers Taylor, The Transportation Revolution, 1815-1860 (New York: Holt, Rinehart and Winston, 1951; reprint ed., New York: M. E. Sharpe, Inc., 1977), pp. 43-45; Peter Andrew Wallner, "Politics and Public Works: A Study of the Pennsylvania Canal System, 1825-1857," (Ph.D. dissertation, Pennsylvania State University, 1973), pp. 109, 115, 122-23.

[8]Bishop, "The State Works of Pennsylvania," p. 190.

[9]Pennsylvania, Laws of the Commonwealth of Pennsylvania, 1828-29, pp. 2-4.

[10]Harrisburg Chronicle, 14 December 1828.

[11]Laws of the Commonwealth of Pennsylvania, 1828-29, p. 252.

[12]Harrisburg Chronicle, 19 March 1829.

[13]Pennsylvania, House of Representatives, Legislative Journal, Vol. 1, 1828-29, pp. 901-2.

[14]Marguerite Bartlett, Chief Phases of Pennsylvania Politics in the Jacksonian Period (Allentown, PA: H. Ray Hass & Company, 1919), pp. 112-13; Bishop, "The State Works of Pennsylvania," p. 209-11; Hartz, Economic Policy, p. 149.

[15]Hartz has suggested that certain farming groups feared the competition from the West that might result from the completion of a successful east-west transportation system. See Hartz, Economic Policy, pp. 134-35.

[16]Laws of the Commonwealth of Pennsylvania, 1828-29, pp. 200-201.

[17]The nine routes voted upon were (1) a turnpike road between Potter's Old Fort in Centre County to the Juniata turnpike in Huntingdon County; (2) a turnpike road from the York and Conewago turnpike to the Harrisburg bridge; (3) a state road from Wattsburg to Erie; (4) a state road from Franklin to Warren; (5) a state road from White Horse tavern to the Virginia state line; (6) a state road from Rodger's Ferry to Sunbury; (7) a state road from the Kiskiminetas salt works through Greensburg, Mt. Pleasant, and Conellsville to the Virginia state line; (8) a road adjoining the canal in Columbia County; and (9) for the improvement of Penn's Creek in Centre County.

[18]Harrisburg Chronicle, 30 March 1829. In his attacks upon the commonwealth, Moore is referring to the land policy developed by the state during the two decades following the Revolutionary War. Although the state made some attempt to promote the rapid settlement of the northwest corner by providing generous terms to settlers, a loophole in the 1792 land act resulted in massive land speculation schemes which ultimately obstructed the orderly settlement of the area. For a discussion of post-Revolutionary land policy, see Paul D. Evans, The Holland Land Company (Buffalo: Buffalo Historical Society, 1924); pp. 87-177; Solon J. Buck and Elizabeth H. Buck, The Planting of Civilization in Western

Pennsylvania (Pittsburgh: University of Pittsburgh Press, 1939), pp. 135-37, 204-14.

[19]Pennsylvania Reporter, 21 April 1829.

[20]Appropriations for the following public works routes were voted upon during the 1838-39 session:

1. North Branch Canal
2. Erie Extension
3. Railroad from the Philadelphia and Columbia Railroad to connect with the Lancaster and Harrisburg Railroad.
4. Hollidaysburg and Huntingdon Railroad
5. Allegheny Feeder
6. Improvement of the Allegheny River from Pittsburgh to Warren
7. Wiconisco Canal
8. New Canal from the West Branch to the Allegheny River
9. Railroad or macademized road from Chambersburg to Pittsburgh
10. Gettysburg-York Railroad
11. Sinnemahoning Extension
12. Inclined plane on the Philadelphia and Columbia Railroad
13. Railroad from Philadelphia to Pittsburgh
14. Allegheny River Reservoir

The mixed enterprise routes voted upon were:

1. Monongahela Navigation Company
2. Pennsylvania and Ohio Canal Company
3. Bald Eagle and Spring Creek Railroad
4. Union Canal Company
5. Danville and Pottsville Railroad
6. Lancaster Bridge
7. Williamsport and Elmira Railroad
8. Franklin Railroad
9. Sunbury and Erie Railroad
10. Danville and Northumberland Bridges
11. Baltimore and Ohio Railroad
12. Monongahela Bridge
13. Somerset and Conemaugh Turnpike Company
14. Milesburg and Smethport Turnpike Company
15. Doylestown and Willow Grove Turnpike Company
16. Lackawaxen Turnpike Company

Three railroad companies applied for charters during the 1838-39 session: the Hollidaysburg and Huntingdon Railroad, the Freeport and New Castle Railroad, and theh Loyalsock Railroad. In addition, the Philadelphia and Trenton applied for permission to extend their route.

[21]Laws of the Commonwealth of Pennsylvania, 1838-39, pp. 631-34.

[22]Ibid., pp. 8-9.

[23]Wallner, "Politics and Public Works," p. 197.

[24]Laws of the Commonwealth of Pennsylvania, 1838-39, pp. 631-34.

[25]Keystone, 3 July 1839; Wallner, "Politics and Public Works," pp. 179-80, 196-99.

[26]Hartz, Economic Policy, pp. 150-51.

[27]Laws of the Commonwealth of Pennsylvania, 1838-39, pp. 631-34. The six routes which ultimately received some appropriation from the legislature were (1) a route to avoid the inclined plane on the Columbia and Philadelphia Railroad; (2) the Allegheny River reservoirs; (3) New locomotives for the portage railroads; (4) the Erie Extension; (5) the North Branch Extension; and (6) the Wiconisco Canal.

[28]House of Representatives, Legislative Journal, Vol. 1, 1838-39, pp. 884-90; Keystone, 15 May 1839.

[29]Rubin, Imitation or Innovation, passim; and Rubin, "An Imitative Public Improvement," passim.

[30]Laws of the Commonwealth of Pennsylvania, 1838-39, pp. 346-47; Keystone, 26 June 1839.

[31]Laws of the Commonwealth of Pennsylvania, 1838-39, pp. 355-60.

[32]Pennsylvania Telegraph, 9 February 1839.

[33]Hartz, Economic Policy, pp. 104, 163.

[34]Laws of the Commonwealth of Pennsylvania, 1838-39, pp. 631-45.

[35]Pennsylvania Telegraph, 14 February 1849.

[36]Ibid., 21 February 1849.

[37]Ibid., 28 February 1849.

[38]Ibid., 3 March 1849.

[39]Laws of the Commonwealth of Pennsylvania, 1849, p. 642.

[40]Bishop, "The State Works of Pennsylvania," pp. 199-200.

[41]Miller, "A Note on the History of Business Corporations," p. 157. The two acts of incorporation for railroad companies which came to a roll-call vote in the 1849 session were the Middle Coal Field Railroad and the Broad Top Railroad. Votes on charter incorporations for combined coal and railroad companies, which in reality were more involved in mining that in long-range transportation, were included in the previous chapter.

[42]The percent voting in favor of the 1849 railroad incorporations was as follows:

Region	Percent in favor
Southeastern	98.33
Anthracite	79.17
Pocono	100.00
Northeastern	50.00
Ridge/Valley	88.20
Allegheny Forest	100.00
Western	87.50
Ave.	86.17

Commercial-Economic Group	
1	66.67
2	90.00
3	90.91
4	84.29
5	96.52
Ave.	85.68

Commercial-Economic Aggregate Group	
2	90.00
3	82.50
4	87.01
5	100.00
Ave.	89.88

[43]Laws of the Commonwealth of Pennsylvania, 1859, pp. 6-7; House of Representatives, Legislative Journal, Vol. 1, 1859, p. 28.

[44]Wallner, "Politics and Public Works," p. 257.

[45]Hartz, Economic Policy, pp. 267-69.

[46]Pennsylvania Daily Telegraph, 23 March 1859.

[47]House of Representatives, Legislative Journal, Vol. 1, pp. 548-49.

[48]Pennsylvania Daily Telegraph, 18 January 1859.

[49]Ibid., 3 February 1859.

[50]Ibid., 15 February 1859.

[51]Ibid., 18 February 1859.

[52]Passenger railroads which applied for incorporation and were voted upon during the 1859 session are listed below. All lines were located in Philadelphia, unless otherwise noted.

1. Germantown Railroad
2. Green and Coates Street Railroad
3. Citizen's Passenger Railroad (Pittsburgh)
4. Citizen's Railway
5. Richmond and Schuylkill Railroad
6. Philadelphia and Trenton Railroad
7. Philadelphia City Passenger Railroad
8. Thirteenth and Fifteenth Street Railroad
9. Seventeenth and Nineteenth Street Railroad
10. Twelfth and Thirteenth Street Railroad
11. Passayunk and Penn Township Railroad

[53]Suggestions were made that the lines of some railroads, most notably the Phildelphia and Reading be extended into the Anthracite Region's major city, Pottsville, for passenger purposes. These proposals, however, never came to a vote.

[54]Hartz, Economic Policy, p. 14.

CHAPTER SEVEN

PARTIES, REGIONS, AND COMMERCIAL-ECONOMIC DEVELOPMENT

The foregoing chapters have demonstrated that regional location and relative level of commercial and economic development were formative influences in economic policy during the antebellum decades.[1] These aspects of antebellum society all too often have been absorbed by a discussion of party politics. This is not to suggest that parties were irrelevant to legislative decision-making. What it does suggest is that when an era spans such a period of party formation and partisan fluctuation, factors other than party affiliation must be brought into play.

The emergence of the Democrats and Whigs during the 1830s as the first modern political parties and their rather premature demise two decades later have captured the fascination of several generations of American scholars. Most recent literature on antebellum politics involves parties as agents of voter mobilization and legislative action at both the state and national levels.[2] This obscures equally important, non-partisan factors. How are we to analyze legislative voting in the years preceding full-blown party development? How do we explain roll-call patterns that don't neatly fit the partisan formula?

Political parties are often described as autonomous; yet, like the policies dealt with in the preceding chapters, they were the result of conflicting impulses emanating from the various consitituencies. Parties should be viewed as <u>dependent</u> variables fashioned, at least in part, out of the uneven pace of economic growth and settlement which characterized antebellum America. Once formed, parties brought together voters and leaders alike, reinforcing some societal divisions while alleviating others. Parties were the product of and not the initial creators of these divisions.

The relationships between the regions, the two sets of commercial-economic groups, and the political parties must now be explored. The dominant regional and economic characteristics of Pennsylvania society go far to explain why some districts were Whig and others Democratic, why some issues divided the parties while others defied a simple partisan classification, and allow us to trace patterns of continuity and disruption into later years.

II

Creating and maintaining a two-party system in Pennsylvania remained a very uneven process throughout much of the antebellum period. During the 1820s there were no political parties in their modern version. Referring to Pennsylvania politics in the 1820s as "a game without rules," historian Philip Klein observed that national, state, and local partisan units were all based upon different considerations and "in each of these three fields there were, in addition, factional divisions. In such circumstances, it was impossible to determine where any man stood politically."[3] The outlines of a Jacksonian party and an opposition emerged after the presidential election of 1828, but the political affiliation of many did not solidify until over a decade later. "In no state, surely," stated Richard P. McCormick in his multi-state study of party development, "did political parties present such indistinct outlines as in Pennsylvania. . . . The manifestations of instability persisted until 1840. Party formation in Pennsylvania, then, cannot be portrayed in terms of sharp and durable alignments, nor can transitions in political patterns be dated with precision."[4]

Acute factionalism continued to delay the unification of both major parties throughout the 1830s. The Democrats, or the Jacksonians, were the first to emerge after the 1828 election. Jackson's veto of the Second Bank of the United States, however, seriously undermined progress which had been made toward uniting earlier factions. The bank, after all, was a Pennsylvania institution and one in which Pennsylvanians took enormous pride. State party officials were forced to decide whether or not to uphold the decision of the president. The resulting schism allowed the opposition to gain control of the governor's seat in the 1835 election.[5]

The opposition, however, was even less unified. Throughout the 1830s, it was uncertain whether the

Antimasons or the Whigs would emerge as the leading competitor of the Jacksonians. The high point of Antimasonic influence came in 1835 when Joseph Ritner, an Antimason, endorsed also by the Whigs, was elected governor. Capitalizing on the 1835 merger, the Whigs gained steadily in strength until they had eclipsed the Antimasons by 1840.[6]

Despite the Whig-Antimasonic victory of 1835, Democrats continued to dominate Pennsylvania politics for the next two decades. A Whig was successful in securing the governor's chair only once more, and then only because the Democratic governor, Francis R. Shunk, was too ill to continue in office. In a special election in the fall of 1848, Speaker of the Senate and Acting Governor William F. Johnston managed to defeat his Democratic opponent by a margin of but three-hundred votes. This was the Whigs' first and last successful, single-party bid for the governorship.[7]

The Democrats also dominated both houses of the legislature. Although the Whigs came closer to challenging their opponents here, elections were not always resolved peacefully. The beginning of the 1838-39 legislative session, for example, was delayed for almost a month due to contested election returns and the outbreak of the "Buckshot War." After the fall election of 1838, the returns from the town of Northern Liberties in Philadelphia County, the outcome of which would determine which party gained control of the House of Representatives, were contested. Both parties sent their delegates to Harrisburg, creating two competing Houses, each of which elected a Speaker. The Whigs dominated the Senate and were thus expected to grant official recognition to the Whig-controlled House. An emotionally charged mob attempted to invade the Senate chambers when the General Assembly convened in early December. Fearing for the safety of himself and other prominent Whig leaders, Governor Ritner called out the state militia who arrived five days later armed with "thirteen rounds of buckshot cartridges." Meanwhile, both Houses continued to meet until Christmas day when five members of the Whig-Antimason coalition in the Senate joined the opposition to recognize the Democratic representatives, who then dominated the House by a margin of 56-44.[8]

One decade later, the Whigs managed to gain more equal representation in the House with a good deal less fanfare. Benefiting from Johnston's victory in the special gubernatorial election held in the fall of 1848, the Whigs sent forty-five representatives to Harrisburg in January of 1849. In addition, five Native American party candidates, all from Philadelphia County, were elected. Since these men usually sided with the Whigs, the 1849 legislature was split between fifty Democrats and fifty Whig-Nativist members.[9]

Despite the ability of the Whigs to present a respectable challenge to the Democracy in Pennsylvania, the party, as elsewhere in the nation, underwent rapid erosion and ceased to function by 1853. The remainder of the 1850s was vaguely reminiscent of the 1830s. The Democrats struggled to maintain party unity and their hold over state politics while various factions competed to control the other major party. By the final years of the decade, the Republican party, which frequently used the allegedly less-objectionable name of the People's party, had eclisped the Know-Nothing and Temperance groups to become not only the dominant opposition force, but the dominant party in the commonwealth.[10] Indeed, during the fall election of 1859, the Republicans won sixty-seven seats in the House of Representatives, while the Democrats secured but thirty-three.[11]

What distinguished Whigs from Democrats and Democrats from Republicans and how did these differences manifest themselves in the halls of the House of Representatives? In their notions about the role of government and society, the two parties differed markedly. The Whigs favored an active role for government in economic development. Government aid to corporations, banks and transportation endeavors, they argued, would benefit all of society. To Democrats, on the other hand, these actions were nothing less than sheer favoritism. Privileges, they argued, were being given to the few at the expense of the many only to undermine the general welfare. Government action of the Democratic variety should be virtually nonexistent, or minimal at best.[12]

These perceptions of the proper role of government were reflected in the voting patterns of legislators. The Whigs supported a wide array of promotional policies much more consistently than did their Democratic counterparts. Whig and Democratic legislators clashed most openly over banking and corporation policies and, to a lesser degree, over internal improvements. Whigs tended to favor legislation which granted lenient charters and financial assistance, while Democrats remained more reluctant to grant what they viewed as special privileges to an elite few.[13]

Many of these distinctions carried over into the Republican-Democratic battles of the 1850s. Republican leaders soft-pedaled the paternalistic, positive government appeals of the Whigs and talked more of individual rights than had their predecessors. Democrats, on the other hand, became less reluctant to appeal directly to particular economic interests. In spite of these rhetorical sleights of hand, however, Republicans supported broad use of governmental power while the Democrats opposed liberal grants of authority to banks and corporations.[14]

This study reinforces these traditional views about differences between the parties. We are left, however, with a curious inconsistency. Given the supposed opposition of the Democrats to government involvement, why were so many Whig policies enacted? Pennsylvania's banking system, its increasing affirmation of the corporation as an acceptable means of business organization, and its massive expenditures on the public works all smack of Whiggery much more than the cherished ideals of individual liberty espoused by the

Democracy. How are we to explain the success of the Whig program in a state that was governed predominantly by the opposition?

The regional and economic divisions which underlay both the legislative process and party formation help to provide the answer. Real differences did indeed exist between Whig and Democratic representatives, and these differences are reflected in the voting behavior. Whigs, however, tended to come from more homogeneous districts than did their opponents. The Democrats who ultimately voted with the Whigs, and thus assured the success of their program, tended to come from counties which were very much like the Whig districts. Consequently, while they expressed opposition to pro-corporation policies in general, they often supported them in practice. Democratic party voting was often shaped by a favorable attitude toward economic development. Such factors also help explain the rapid growth of the Republican party.

III

Although Whigs and Democrats had different ideas about the role of government in antebellum society, the Whigs were more cohesive in their attempt to implement their ideas as legislation in the Pennsylvania General Assembly. As the comparison of the Rice Indexes in Table 49 indicates, Whig cohesion levels were significantly higher than those of the Democrats. Democratic indexes, on the other hand, were not

TABLE 49

RICE INDEXES OF COHESION BY ISSUE, REGION, COMMERCIAL-ECONOMIC GROUP, COMMERCIAL-ECONOMIC AGGREGATE GROUP AND PARTY

BANKING

	1839	1849	1859
Democrats	45.36	56.26	58.80
Whigs or Repubs.	85.88	83.10	45.56
Native Americans		76.51	
Regional Average	47.05	50.24	50.86
Com-Econ.Gp.Ave.	39.75	34.77	41.65
Com-Econ.Ag.Gp.Ave.	45.21	39.64	35.13
Random Indexes	31.49	22.34	28.32

BUSINESS

	1839	1849	1859
Democrats	25.54	66.65	38.80
Whigs or Repubs.	67.91	72.73	63.04
Native Americans		73.33	
Regional Average	53.88	51.40	63.55
Com-Econ.Gp.Ave.	34.79	45.20	49.33
Com-Econ.Ag.Gp.Ave.	41.75	47.75	49.11
Random Indexes	28.70	33.06	45.63

TRANSPORTATION

	1839	1849	1859
Democrats	42.27	57.84	56.46
Whigs or Repubs.	67.70	61.35	44.62
Native Americans		68.09	
Regional Average	49.88	51.40	62.64
Com-Econ.Gp. Ave.	37.24	41.99	53.20
Com-Econ.Ag.Gp.Ave.	37.83	43.74	45.88
Random Indexes	25.45	29.18	37.22

ALL ROLL CALLS

Democrats	46.77	53.55	54.57
Whigs or Repubs.	68.12	64.11	46.63
Native Americans		74.03	
Regional Average	50.41	50.27	58.47
Com-Econ.Gp.Ave.	39.14	41.42	50.65
Com-Econ.Ag.Gp.Ave.	40.18	41.50	43.50
Random Indexes	29.57	27.88	36.48

Source: Pennsylvania, House of Representatives, Legislative Journal, Vol. 1, 1838-39, 1849, and 1859.

only lower than the opposition party's, but also fell below the regional averages during the 1838-39 session. While Democratic cohesion had increased somewhat by 1849, it was still markedly below Whig levels. By 1859, this situation had changed dramatically. The Democrats were the minority party by the late 1850s, and their cohesiveness as the "out" party had increased accordingly. Now it was the Republican party that had difficulty achieving cohesion levels that exceeded the regional averages, and in some cases, the commercial-economic group averages.

No issue divided Whigs and Democrats more than the question of banking.[15] In almost all cases, however, Whigs demonstrated greater cohesion when supporting pro-bank policies than the Democrats did in opposing them. The Whigs, in fact, approached unanimity on major banking decisions in both the 1838-39 and 1849 sessions. (See Table 50.) Democratic representatives, on the other hand, were more divided. As the 1849 issue break-down indicates, Democrats displayed stronger cohesion on the more controversial questions of banking privileges such as limited liability, length of the terms of the charter, directorial borrowing, and small note circulation. Many Democrats, however, could not bring themselves to vote on the final roll-calls against incorporation of the bank or for extension of an existing bank's charter. Motivated at least in part by constituency demand,[16] the Democrats that defected from the party line in the eleventh hour helped to

TABLE 50

PERCENT IN FAVOR OF BANKS BY ISSUE, PARTY AND SESSION

1838-39 Session

Issue	Demos	Whigs	Natives
Final Incorp. Votes	46.44	96.44	
Limited Liability	51.11	97.06	

1849 Session

Issue	Demos	Whigs	Natives
Final Incorp. Votes	40.20	92.11	85.71
Limited Liability	17.46	94.57	100.00
Collection frm. Stockholders	22.50	94.44	100.00
Charter Length	14.38	96.98	79.41
Par Value	34.31	93.75	53.33
Director's Borrowing	8.56	77.17	40.00
Specie Redemption	19.51	90.19	50.00
Small Note Issue	3.19	87.95	55.56

1859 Session

Issue	Demos	Whigs	Natives
Final Incorp. Votes	17.91	71.57	
General Banking	35.99	68.84	

Source: See Table 49.

perpetuate a banking system strongly advocated by the opposition party.

These trends continued after the party restructuring of the 1850s. Although Republican representatives did not display the high degree of unanimity on banking issues as had the Whigs, they were still overwhelmingly in favor of granting bank charters and only slightly less enthusiastic about the general banking law. The Democrats, on the other hand, were solidly opposed to bank incorporations and only somewhat more inclined to support the free banking bill.

Voting patterns on business corporation issues closely parallel those on banking. (See Table 51.) During both the 1838-39 and 1849 sessions, Whigs were more in favor of granting charters with liberal corporation privileges than were the Democrats. The latter, once again, were overwhelmingly opposed to the concept of limited liability and were also hesitant to support a general incorporation law that would result in a proliferation of these objectionable organizations. Yet, on the final votes, enough Democrats joined forces with their opponents to assure the perpetuity of the corporation. As on the banking roll-calls, Democrats remained more opposed to granting charters of incorporation in 1859 than did their Republican counterparts.

Other studies of state legislative behavior have downplayed party differences on transportation or internal improvements issues and have stressed, instead, the

TABLE 51

PERCENT IN FAVOR OF BUSINESS CORPORATIONS BY ISSUE, PARTY, AND SESSION

Issue	Demos	Whigs	Natives
1838-39 Session			
Final Incorp. Votes	54.13	81.41	
Limited Liability	38.36	84.63	
1849 Session			
Final Incorp. Votes	40.74	97.39	94.12
Limited Liability	4.04	89.87	69.57
General Laws	7.14	100.00	100.00
1859 Session			
Final Incorp. Votes	44.39	85.89	

Source: See Table 49.

importance of sectional influences.[17] The previous chapter, however, indicated that regional interests were not always reliable predictors of legislative behavior. While the differences between Whigs and Democrats and between Democrats and Republicans on transportation roll-calls were not as striking as on banking and business questions, there are some important divisions.

Political party voting patterns on transportation issues represent an interesting mix between political expediency and traditonal partisan stands. Despite their official pronouncement in favor of minimal state involvement, the Democrats were the godfathers of the public works system. Plans for the Main Line, it will be recalled, had been launched long before party lines had hardened during the 1830s. As the dominant party in Pennsylvania, the Democrats became the heirs to a publicly-owned and administered transportation system.[18] Their dilemma is readily apparent in the voting patterns on transportation roll-calls, particularly during the busy 1838-39 session. (See Table 52.) On the more general votes, such as those for system-wide appropriations or for the popular election of Canal Commissioners, a majority of Democrats voted to appropriate the funds necessary to continue the public works just as they voted against a popular election that could wrest control of Canal Commissioner appointments away from the party. The Whigs, on the other hand, found themselves in the enviable position of being able to criticize the

TABLE 52

PERCENT IN FAVOR OF INTERNAL IMPROVEMENTS BY ISSUE, ROUTE AND PARTY, 1838-39

Public Works

Issue/Route	Demos	Whigs
General Appropriations	63.37	24.92
Election/Commissioners	24.34	69.39
North Branch Canal	73.28	35.47
Erie Extension	63.90	41.13
Phila./Lancaster	22.84	62.30
Hollidaysburg & Huntingdon	5.05	55.70
Allegheny Feeder	22.55	28.36
Allegheny R.Imp.	20.41	9.38
Wiconisco Canal	31.63	100.00
West Branch/New Canal	39.80	55.56
Chambersburg/Pittsburgh	51.05	74.44
Gettysburg/York	0.00	60.00
Sinnemahoning Ext.	64.08	34.25
Phila/Pittsbrgh RR	28.26	84.85
Allegh. R. Reservoirs	6.00	100.00
Inclined Plane	35.48	47.66
Average	33.17	56.36

Mixed Enterprises

Issue/Route	Demos	Whigs
Mon.Navigation Co.	52.83	16.67
PA/Ohio Canal Co.	52.48	84.85
Bald Eagle/Sprg.Crk.	46.53	66.67
Union Canal Co.	75.00	87.14
Danville/Pottsville	66.43	84.40
Lancaster Bridge	39.02	81.48
Wmsport/Elmira	25.47	88.28
Franklin RR	74.49	33.80
Sunbury/Erie	21.74	26.47
Danville/Nrthmbrlnd	47.83	87.10
B & O RR	47.34	70.59
Mon. Bridge Relief	65.12	85.19
Somerset/Conemaugh	54.76	93.75
Milesburg/Smethport	56.25	93.10
Doylestwn/WillowGrve	50.00	65.22
Lackawaxen	31.71	0.00
Ave.	50.44	66.54

Private Incorporations

Hollidaysburg & Huntingdon	26.74	85.25
Freeport/Newcastle	58.14	100.00
Loyalsock	53.66	100.00
Ave.	46.18	95.08

Source: See Table 49.

administration of a public works system that was in deep financial trouble. Predictably, they voted overwhelmingly against granting additional funds for general purposes and for the popular election of the commissioners.

Votes on the specific routes, however, tell a much different story. Despite Whig opposition to increased general appropriations, they favored more than did the Democrats funds for the construction of specific routes in ten out of fourteen cases. Democrats threw their support behind routes which were partially constructed and to which the state had already pledged their aid, such as the North Branch Canal and the Erie Extension. Whigs favored assistance to longer range routes and, significantly, to railroads. Routes such as that proposed from Chambersburg to Pittsburgh, the Hollidaysburg and Huntingdon Railroad, and a railroad from Philadelphia to Pittsburgh would open up new markets and speed the transportation of agricultural and manufactured products.

Similar trends are apparent in the votes for mixed enterprise routes and on the incorporation of private companies. Democrats favored these types of ventures more than they had public routes, yet the Whigs almost unanimously favored charters to private corporations and were more inclined than their opponents to grant aid to mixed enterprises in thirteen out of sixteen cases.[19]

These patterns continued into the 1849 session. (See Table 53.) As in 1839, the Democrats remained exceedingly

TABLE 53

PERCENT IN FAVOR OF INTERNAL IMPROVEMENTS BY ISSUE, ROUTE, AND PARTY, 1849 AND 1859

1849 Session
Public Works

Issue/Route	Demos	Whigs	Natives
Mismanagement of	7.06	62.86	87.50
Sale of	0.00	61.29	0.00
North Branch	44.65	72.08	41.18
Inclined Plane	66.11	50.23	4.55
Alleg. Reservoir	15.15	39.29	0.00
Route Ave.	41.97	53.87	15.24
Private Incorporations -- Railroads			
Middle Coal Field	75.00	100.00	100.00
Broad Top	86.21	100.00	100.00
Ave.	80.61	100.00	100.00

1859 Session

Passenger Railroads

Maps	35.71	54.84
Printing Bills	33.33	65.03
Incorporations	52.90	71.83
Ave.	40.65	63.90
Tonnage Tax		
Pennsylvania RR	92.31	66.22
Philadelphia/ Reading	61.34	48.35
Philadelphia/ Trenton	12.50	53.70
Ave.	55.38	56.09

Source: See Table 49.

loyal to a public works system that bore their party stamp and voted overwhelmingly against both the sale of the public project and against attempts to investigate the alleged mismanagement of the system. Whigs and Nativists, on the other hand, were more interested in unloading a transportation network that had become little more than a financial burden to the commonwealth. Once again, however, the Whigs showed more interest in completing and bankrolling long-range routes, in this case the North Branch Extension, that would present new commercial opportunities. By the end of the 1840s, Democrats were more disposed to incorporate private railroad companies than they had been a decade before while Whigs and Nativists had achieved total unanimity in support of such charters.

Voting trends on the 1859 transportation issues are much more in line with the party differences noted on the banking and business roll-calls. (See Table 53.) The Democrats, in keeping with their distrust of corporations favored the tonnage tax more than did the Republicans, particularly against the egregious Pennsylvania Railroad. Although the Democrats eventually mustered a slight majority in support of the passenger railroad incorporations, they were less enthusiastic about using legislative funds to supply maps of Philadelphia and Pittsburgh for the use of the railroad committee and to print the passenger railroad bills. In contrast, the Republicans were sympathetic to the needs created by the new passenger railways and gave their overwhelming support to the incorporation of these companies.

Whigs and Republicans, therefore, tended to be more tenancious and consistent in their support of legislation that would promote economic development. While Democrats undoubtedly held strong feelings about corporate privilege and extending the arm of the state, they frequently succumbed on the final votes to give Whigs, and later Republicans, the edge they needed to enact their policies. Hence they perpetuated a vision of government and society that was markedly at odds with Democratic rhetoric.

IV

The ability of the Whigs to present a consistent and cohesive front stemmed, in large part, from the fact that Whig legislators tended to come from regions and counties with fairly homogeneous commercial-economic characteristics. Their opponents came from more disparate districts. Figures 18 and 19 indicate which counties sent Democrats and which Whigs to the legislature during the 1838-39 and 1849 sessions while Tables 54 through 56 give the distribution of parties by region, commercial-economic and commercial-economic aggregate group.

Whig counties tended to cluster along the major avenues of transportation, and especially along the primary public works routes. These patterns are indicated in the accompanying tables. Whig legislators came from districts

FIGURE 18

POLITICAL PARTY AFFILIATION OF MEMBERS OF THE HOUSE OF REPRESENTATIVES BY COUNTY, 1838-39

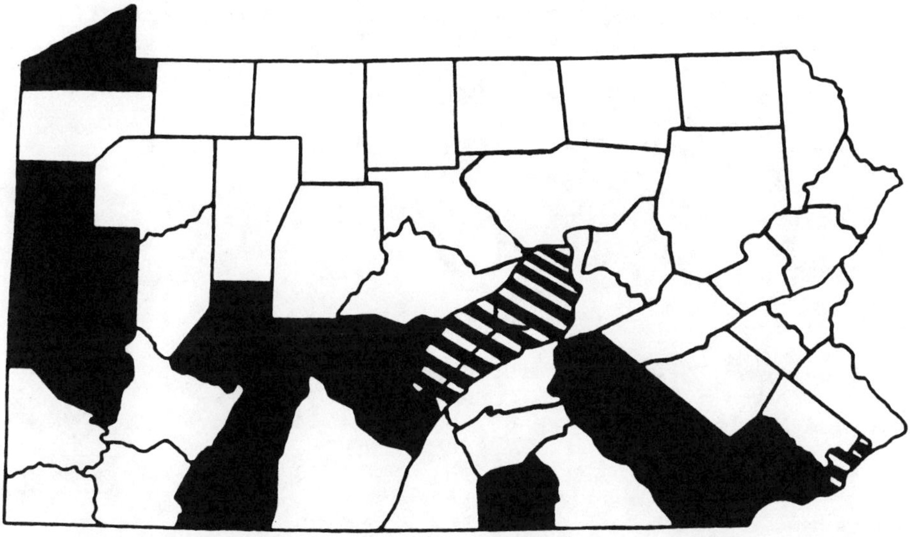

FIGURE 19

POLITICAL PARTY AFFILIATION OF MEMBERS OF THE HOUSE OF REPRESENTATIVES BY COUNTY, 1849

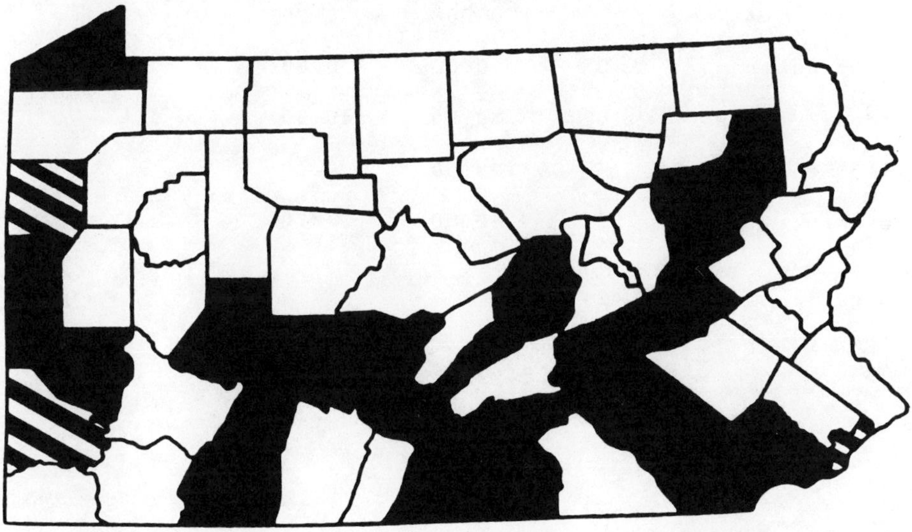

Note: Whig counties are shaded.

TABLE 54

NUMBER AND PERCENT OF REPRESENTATIVES IN EACH PARTY BY REGION, 1838-39 AND 1849

1838-39 Session

Region	#Reps	%Demo	%Whig	%Ntve.
Southeastern	49	59.18	40.82	
Anthracite	9	66.67	33.33	
Pocono	1	100.00	0.00	
Northeastern	3	100.00	0.00	
Ridge & Valley	9	55.56	44.44	
Allegheny Forest	4	100.00	0.00	
Western	25	44.00	56.00	
		1849 Session		
Southeastern	45	42.22	46.67	11.11
Anthracite	9	22.22	77.78	
Pocono	1	100.00	0.00	
Northeastern	5	100.00	0.00	
Ridge & Valley	10	60.00	40.00	
Allegheny Forest	5	100.00	0.00	
Western	25	48.00	52.00	

Source: See Table 49.

TABLE 55

NUMBER AND PERCENT OF REPRESENTAIVES IN EACH PARTY BY COMMERCIAL-ECONOMIC GROUP, 1838-39 AND 1849

Com-Econ Group	#Reps	%Demo	%Whig	%Ntve.
		1838-39 Session		
1	10	60.00	40.00	
2	16	56.25	43.75	
3	15	86.67	13.33	
4	20	75.00	25.00	
5	39	41.03	58.97	
		1849 Session		
1	3	66.67	33.33	
2	15	80.00	20.00	
3	18	50.00	50.00	
4	19	73.68	26.32	
5	45	28.89	60.00	11.11

Source: See Table 49.

TABLE 56

NUMBER AND PERCENT OF REPRESENTATIVES IN EACH PARTY BY COMMERCIAL-ECONOMIC AGGREGATE GROUP, 1838-39 AND 1849

Com-Econ Group	#Reps	%Demo	%Whig	%Ntve.
		1838-39 Session		
1	1	100.00	---	
2	15	46.67	53.33	
3	21	80.95	19.05	
4	22	72.73	27.27	
5	41	43.90	56.10	
		1849 Session		
1	---	---	---	---
2	22	63.64	36.36	
3	18	77.78	22.22	
4	23	65.22	34.78	
5	37	18.92	67.57	13.51

Source: See Table 49.

which were disproportionately represented in the upper commercial-economic and commercial-economic aggregate groups and which were located in the more populous, most economically developed regions: The Southeastern, Anthracite, Western and Ridge and Valley regions. This concentration, moreover, increased between 1839 and 1849. In other words, as counties became more economically developed and commercially involved, they tended increasingly to select Whig legislators. This trend is most evident in the Anthracite Region. As the upper anthracite fields became more fully integrated into a wider commercial network, Whigs rather than Democrats were sent to represent the region's interests in the state legislature.

The idea that Whigs came from the most commercially-oriented areas is not a new one. At the end of the nineteenth century, Frederick Jackson Turner suggested that the more economically developed districts tended to support Whigs. Several decades later, Thomas P. Abernethy also argued that Whig centers of strength followed the lines of communication, an idea more recently upheld by James Roger Sharp and Harry Watson, both of whom have emphasized the importance of trade routes as influential determinants of partisan affiliation.[20] As early as the 1920's, Henry R. Mueller's study of the Whig party in Pennsylvania offered evidence that Whigs came from counties with the highest property valuations. Using similar evidence, Donald Ratcliffe substantiated these conclusions for Ohio and, along the same lines as the conclusions presented in this study, found that support for the Jackson party tended to diminish as property valuations increased.[21]

Although the present study examines the partisan affiliation of state representatives in only two selected sessions, it is more multi-dimensional and more systematic than many of the above studies. Recognizing the limitations of property valuation as a measure, I have used a variety of economic, commercial, and communications measures to provide a more complete description of each district's relative level of economic development and commercial involvement. Given the belief that the state representative spoke for the dominant economic interests of the county, the findings presented here strongly lend further credence to these earlier works.[22]

If Whig representatives tended to come from select regions and from districts with similar commercial-economic outlooks, Democratic legislators were more widely dispersed throughout the commonwealth. The Democracy was, in fact, the dominant party among state representatives in all regions, except the Western, during the 1838-39 session, an edge that it lost to the Whigs in the Anthracite Region and to a Whig-Nativist combination in the Southeastern Region by 1849. Democrats were also usually dominant in all commercial-economic and commercial-economic aggregate groups with the notable exception of the <u>most</u> developed groups which sent Whigs rather than Democrats to Harrisburg.

Most interesting, however, is the strong Democratic majority in the second most developed group, or in commercial-economic and commercial-economic aggregate groups 4 for both the 1838-39 and 1849 sessions. Given the Whig dominance of the uppermost groups, one would expect to see greater Whig strength in the next tier of counties. Instead, we find pockets of strong Democratic influence. It was, however, precisely this group of Democrats that was most likely to abandon the party line and vote with the Whigs particularly on the more controversial issues like banking and corporate policy.

The near unanimous support of banking and business incorporations on the part of the Whigs during the 1838-39 and 1849 sessions allows us to compare the percent voting in favor of these measures with the percent Whig in each commercial-economic group to indicate which types of Democrats were likely to forsake the party standard to join the opposition. While there were some Democrats from all commercial-economic groups who voted with the Whigs, Tables 57 and 58[23] demonstrate that it was the Democrats in the upper commercial-groups, and particularly from commercial-economic group 4, who were most likely to change their stand on the final incorporation votes, thus assuring the success of policies that were perceived as much more Whiggish than Democratic. Despite their avowed aversion to the odious privileges of corporations such as limited liability, Democrats, like Whigs, were, in the final

TABLE 57

PERCENT IN FAVOR OF BUSINESS CORPORATIONS ON FINAL VOTES COMPARED TO PERCENT WHIG BY COMMERCIAL-ECONOMIC GROUP, 1838-39

Com-Econ Group	% Pro	% Whig	Difference*
1	55.49	40.00	15.49
2	50.40	43.75	6.65
3	55.25	13.33	41.92
4	70.72	25.00	45.72
5	73.34	58.97	14.37

*The difference is calculated by subtracting the percent Whigs from the percent voting in favor of business corporations for each group. The groups which most pro-business Democrats came from are reflected by the highest values in this column. Whigs were 81.41% in favor of business corporations on the final votes while Democrats were 54.13% in favor.

Source: See Table 49.

TABLE 58

PERCENT IN FAVOR OF BANKS ON FINAL VOTES COMPARED TO PERCENT WHIG BY COMMERCIAL-ECONOMIC GROUP, 1849

Com-Econ Group	% Pro	% Whig*	Difference**
1	47.22	33.33	13.89
2	49.04	20.00	29.04
3	59.90	50.00	9.90
4	63.29	26.32	36.97
5	77.86	71.11	6.75

*Includes Native Americans.

**The difference is calculated by subtracting the percent of Whigs from the percent voting in favor of banks for each group. The groups which most pro-bank Democrats came from are reflected by the highest values in this column. Whigs were 92.11% in favor of banks on the final votes and Democrats were 40.20% in favor.

Source: See Table 49.

analysis, motivated by the needs of their districts. While they continued to oppose the most objectionable measures, those from the more developed areas seemed to believe that some banks and corporations were better for society than none at all.

Although the party positions on the transportation roll-calls were not as clear cut as on banking and corporation questions, the regional and commercial-economic group voting patterns help to explain why parties were not as unified on these issues and allow us to isolate districts which persistently deviated from the party norm. The Northeastern, Allegheny Forest, and Anthracite representatives, it will be remembered, not only displayed obvious regional self-interest when casting their votes, but also tended to demonstrate consistent support for all types of internal improvements, both public and private.[34] Of the three supporting regions, two--the Northeastern and Allegheny Forest regions--sent only Democratic representatives to Harrisburg. The Anthracite Region, on the other hand, elected a majority of Democratic legislators in 1838-39 and an even greater majority of Whigs a decade later. The remaining regions, in contrast, were more evenly balanced in the number of Whigs and Democrats they sent to the House, an element which contributed to the competitiveness within each area.

It may be that party was a more important factor in influencing transportation policy than has been previously thought, but not in precisely the same way. Those regions with fewer representatives and a clearly dominant party were able to arrive at a more unified position on internal improvements issues than their counterparts from more populous areas with roughly an equal number of legislators from each party. Whereas regional self-interest and the needs of similar commercial-economic groups had worked to the Whigs' advantage in these populous regions on banking and corporate questions, this was not always the case on transportation issues which involved dividing up a limited amount of public resources. In addition, the enormous degree of state involvement in the public works and the close association of the Democrats with the administration of the system exacerbated the political connotations of some issues just as it muddied traditional partisan positions on others.

In short, the regions which tended to be more economically homogeneous also tended to elect the majority of their representatives from one party. These legislators generally managed to arrive at a broad, consistent, and highly favorable position toward all types of transportation improvements. Representatives from the more populous, economically diverse regions, on the other hand, had more difficulty supporting even those routes which would directly benefit their areas. It may be that the absence of a clearly dominant party in these regions tended to heighten the conflict over a decision-making process that involved increasingly limited resources. Freed from party opposition within their own region on issues that were frequently discussed in sectional terms, representatives from the more homogeneous areas felt more comfortable pursuing transportation policies that, at times, countered the party's traditional position. Legislators from regions with more competitive party structures, on the other hand, perhaps felt compelled to adhere to a more consistent party position even when it involved sacrificing the interests of the region as a whole.

These banking, business, and transportation voting patterns go far to explain the realignment process of political parties in the 1850s. As Figure 20 demonstrates, the distribution of Republican and Democratic members of the House of Representatives presents a very different picture from that of the Whigs and Democrats a decade before. A closer comparison of Table 59 with Tables 54 through 56, however, reveals more continuity than is apparent at first glance. Like the Whigs, Republicans were in the majority in the most commercially involved and economically developed districts while the Democrats dominated areas which which were less developed.

Those regions and types of commercial-economic districts that had elected Democratic representatives who had shown the greatest propensity to break with traditional party positions and to vote along Whig lines in 1838-39 and 1849, however, were precisely those areas which demonstrated

FIGURE 20

POLITICAL PARTY AFFILIATION OF MEMBERS OF THE HOUSE OF REPRESENTATIVES BY COUNTY, 1859

Note: Republican counties are shaded.

TABLE 59

NUMBER AND PERCENT OF REPRESENTATIVES IN EACH PARTY BY REGION, COMMERCIAL-ECONOMIC GROUP, AND COMMERCIAL-ECONOMIC AGGREGATE GROUPS, 1859

Region	#Reps	%Democrat	%Republican
Southeastern	44	36.36	63.64
Anthracite	12	41.67	58.33
Pocono	2	100.00	0.00
Northeastern	6	0.00	100.00
Ridge & Valley	6	0.00	100.00
Allegheny Forest	5	60.00	40.00
Western	25	28.00	72.00
Com-Econ Group			
1	3	100.00	0.00
2	16	12.50	87.50
3	15	60.00	40.00
4	18	22.22	77.78
5	48	31.25	68.75
Com-Econ Ag Group			
1	-----		
2	18	50.00	50.00
3	22	27.27	72.73
4	21	38.09	61.90
5	3	25.64	73.36

Source: See Table 49.

the greatest Republican gains by 1859. Both commercial-economic and commercial-economic aggregate groups 4 had been predominantly Democratic during the earlier legislative sessions, but had tended to vote with the Whigs on final business and banking roll-calls. These groups had become overwhelmingly Republican by 1859. Similarly, the regions whose Democratic representatives had displayed the greatest willingness to support internal improvements in 1838-39 and 1849--the Northeastern and Allegheny Forest regions--also demonstrated significant shifts toward the Republican party during the 1850s.

Some partisan shifts occurred that are difficult to explain in regional or commercial-economic terms. The Anthracite Region, for example, had become a bastion of Whiggery by the late 1840s as well as one of the most commercially-involved areas of the commonwealth. By all accounts, one would expect the region to become solidly Republican by 1859, a shift that did not take place. Quite clearly, non-economic influences were extremely influential in determining which types of representatives were sent to Harrisburg. The Republican party did, after all, emerge as a fusion of various economic and ethno-religious thrusts that had achieved political saliency by the early 1850s. Other historians have stressed the ethno-religious elements of the Republican-Democratic two-party system, often to the exclusion of economic factors.[25] The foregoing demonstrates that regional, commercial, and economic influences go far in explaining the shifts in the partisan affiliation of members of the Pennsylvania House of Representatives during the 1850s. If anything, the challenge is to explain those instances, like the shift in Anthracite Region support, which run counter to the prevailing pattern.

V

The formation of banking, business, and transportation policies in antebellum Pennsylvania was a very complex process which defies a simple party explanation. Political parties--Whigs and Democrats, and then Democrats and Republicans--did indeed differ in their views on economic policy and representatives cast their votes accordingly more often than not. Yet the differences between the parties was more one of degree rather than kind. If the Democrats who dominated Pennsylvania politics from the 1830s until the mid-1850s had been truly committed to minimal state involvement, the commonwealth never would have created a well-developed banking system, accepted the corporation as the principal form of business organization by mid-century, nor continued the construction and administration of a massive, rapidly outmoded public-works project. In the past, scholars have frequently explained the success of these more "Whiggish" policies in terms of sectional, or to use my term, regional self-interest. Local needs and "sectional passions," it is argued, prevented party cohesion and rendered the development of a consistent Democratic party program impossible.[26]

While regional aggrandizement did influence the outcome of many legislative decisions, party and section alone cannot explain the process of economic policy formation in antebellum Pennsylvania. Equally, if not more important, was the relative level of commercial and economic development of the representative's district. Including this economic dimension does add an additional level of complexity to the analysis of the policy process. Yet understanding the uneven and diverse economic and settlement patterns of antebellum Pennsylvania helps to clarify many legislative voting trends that can not be explained in sectional or partisan terms.

Relying on an "economic" explanation, however, does not imply that legislators were acting out of a simple, Beardian type of self-interest. The foregoing suggests a much more subtle, yet broader type of economic influence. From all available evidence, the men elected to the Pennsylvania House of Representatives during the first half of the nineteenth century were local elites.[27] As such, these men arrived at a perception of their own county's position vis a vis the other counties in the commonwealth, a perception shaped by patterns of regional development, the county's specific agricultural and manufacturing mix, its accessibility to transportation and communications networks, and its particular financial needs. An attempt has been made to include all of these factors in the preceding analysis through a combination of the regional configuration and the commercial-economic continua. Accusations of log-rolling, corruption, and voting for personal self-aggrandizement should not be dismissed lightly.[28] Yet the consistency demonstrated by most legislators on <u>all</u> roll-calls on a given issue regardless of whether or not their particular district was affected suggests that most legislators had developed a world view with fairly consistent ideas about economic progress and the role of government that was shaped largely by their perception of the relative position of their own district. More often than not, these legislators acted in accordance with these general perceptions and views when casting their roll-call votes in the state legislature on a wide array of economic issues.

The parties that emerged in the 1830s were fashioned to a large degree out of these various regional and commercial-economic impulses and perceptions. The editorials, the speeches, and the platforms which accompanied the rise of these organizations were an attempt to give these impulses a cohesion that could be harnessed for the use of the party. The Whigs were the most successful at creating a consistent party position due to the fact that they tended to come from districts which were much more homogeneous regionally, commercially, and economically than those of their opponents, and hence, had similar needs and demands. Democratic legislators, on the other hand, came from more disparate backgrounds and had more difficulty maintaining party unity. When Whig interests converged with the regional and commercial-economic group interests of the more populous districts as they frequently did on banking and corporate issues, the Whigs were able to get their policies enacted with the help of the Democratic representative from the counties most similar to theirs. When regional or commercial-economic group cohesion broke down as it did in the face of rampant localism on transportation issues, neither party was able to garner the support necessary to enact a more coherent program.

By the late 1850s, regional and commercial-economic factors still exerted a good deal of influence over legislative voting on economic issues. The emergence and eventual absorption of other viable political organizations like the Know-Nothing and the Temperance parties, however, injected a new element into the game of party politics. While the regional location and relative level of commercial-economic development of a representative's district still helped to predict which party he belonged to, there were glaring exceptions which served to indicate that non-regional and non-economic factors were becoming increasingly important aspects of political life.

Throughout the 1830s and 1840s, however, the creation of economic policies as well as the formation of the two political parties turned largely on these regional, commercial and economic concerns. Significant regional and commercial-economic patterns of legislative cohesion on these issues were already evident during the late 1820s. Both Democrats and Whigs responded to these divisions and used them to aid in the process of party building during the 1830s. While party positions were never totally dichotomous and were frequently muddied by a peculiar conversion of national and state circumstances particularly on banking and transportation issues, party rhetoric as well as party behavior on legislative roll-calls was deeply rooted in the regional, commercial, and economic differences of antebellum Pennsylvania.

FOOTNOTES

[1] Other historians have also pointed to the significance of sectional and economic factors as important legislative influences. See Louis Hartz, Economic Policy and Democratic Thought: Pennsylvania, 1776-1860 (Cambridge: Harvard University Press, 1948; reprint ed., Chicago: Quadrangle Paperback Books, Inc., 1968); Michael Holt, Forging a Majority: The Formation of the Republican Party in Pittsburgh, 1848-1860 (New Haven: Yale University Press, 1969); Philip S. Klein, Pennsylvania Politics, 1817-1832: A Game Without Rules (Philadelphia: Historical Society of Pennsylvania, 1940); James W. Livingood, The Philadelphia-Baltimore Trade Rivalry, 1780-1860 (Harrisburg: Pennsylvania Historical and Museum Commission, 1947); Charles M. Snyder, The Jacksonian Heritage: Pennsylvania Politics, 1833-1848 (Harrisburg: Pennsylvania Historical and Museum Commission, 1958).

[2]For a summary of recent literature and a good discussion of the importance of political parties in the antebellum period, see Joel H. Silbey, The Partisan Imperative: The Dynamics of American Politics before the Civil War (New York and Oxford: Oxford University Press, 1985).

[3]Klein, Pennsylvania Politics, p. 188. Due to the difficulty of determining partisan affiliation during the 1820s, the roll-calls have not been analyzed on the basis of party for the 1828-29 session.

[4]Richard P. McCormick, The Second American Party System: Party Formation in the Jacksonian Era (Chapel Hill: University of North Carolina Press, 1966; reprint ed., New York: W. W. Norton and Company, 1973), p. 134.

[5]For a discussion of the difficulties faced by the Democrats following Jackson's veto of the Second Bank of the United States, see Marguerite Bartlett, Chief Phases of Pennsylvania Politics in the Jacksonian Period (Allentown: H. Ray Hass & Company, 1919), pp. 62-63, 82-83; Snyder, Jacksonian Heritage, pp. 35-68; Peter Andrew Wallner, "Politics and Public Works: A Study of the Pennsylvania Canal System, 1825-1857" (Ph.D. dissertation, Pennsylvania State University, 1973), pp. 130-31.

[6]For a discussion of the emergence of the Whig party, see Bartlett, Chief Phases of Pennsylvania Politics, pp. 16-29, 72-81; Henry R. Mueller, The Whig Party in Pennsylvania (New York: Columbia University, 1922), pp. 11-91; Snyder, Jacksonian Heritage, pp. 64-81.

[7]John F. Coleman, The Disruption of the Pennsylvania Democracy, 1848-1860 (Harrisburg: Pennsylvania Historical and Museum Commission, 1975), pp. 26; Mueller, Whig Party, pp. 149-58; Snyder, Jacksonian Heritage, pp. 215-18; Wallner, "Politics and Public Works," pp. 244-45.

[8]Douglas E. Bowers, "The Pennsylvania Legislature, 1815-1860: A Study of Democracy at Work" (Ph.D. dissertation, University of Chicago, 1974), pp. 75-76; Richard Nelson Current, Old Thad Stevens: A Story of Ambition (Madison: University of Wisconsin Press, 1942), pp. 65-68; Snyder, Jacksonian Heritage, pp. 131-35.

The fifty-six Democrats and forty-four Whigs in the 1838-39 session were identified by using roll-call votes relating to the Buckshot War which were referred to by the Pennsylvania Telegraph, 26 January 1839, as straight party votes. See Journal of the House of Representatives, vol. 1, p. 176. See also, Snyder, Jacksonian Heritage, pp. 132-34.

[9]The roll-call votes recorded for the election of the State Treasurer were used to determine party affiliation for the 1849 session. See Journal of the House of Representatives, vol. 2, p. 165.

[10]For a discussion of the decline of the Whig party and the rise of the Republican party in Pennsylvania, see Coleman, Disruption of the Pennsylvania Democracy; Holt, Forging a Majority; Holt, The Political Crises of the 1850s (New York: John Wiley & Sons, 1978); Philip S. Klein and Ari Hoogenboom, A History of Pennsylvania, 2nd ed. (University Park, PA: Pennsylvania State University Press, 1980), pp. 160-179.

[11]The election of State Treasurer was again used to determine party affiliation during the 1859 session. See Legislative Record, 1859, p. 56.

[12]For a discussion of differences between Whigs and Democrats, see Herbert Ershkowitz and William G. Shade, "Consensus or Conflict? Political Behavior of State Legislative Parties during the Jacksonian Era," Journal of American History 58 (December 1971): 614-19; Holt, Forging a Majority, pp. 47-49; Holt, Political Crisis, pp. 32-35; Daniel Walker Howe, The Political Culture of the American Whigs (Chicago: University of Chicago Press, 1979);Marc W. Kruman, Parties and Politics in North Carolina: 1836-1865 (Baton Rouge: Louisiana State University Press, 1983), pp. 5-6; Joel H. Silbey, The Shrine of Party: Congresional Voting Behavior, 1841-1852 (Pittsburgh: University of Pittsburgh Press, 1967), pp. 26-28.

[13]Numerous studies have come to similar conclusions with respect to the issues which strongly differentiated

Whigs from Democrats in both Congress and the various state legislatures studied. See Rodney Owen Davis, "Illinois Legislators and Jacksonian Democracy, 1834-1841," (Ph.D. dissertation, University of Iowa, 1966); Ershkowitz and Shade, "Consensus or Conflict?"; Peter Levine, The Behavior of State Legislative Parties in the Jacksonian Era: New Jersey, 1829-1844 (Rutherford-Teaneck, N.J.: Fairleigh Dickenson Press, 1977); Peter Levine, "State Legislative Parties in the Jacksonian Era: New Jersey, 1829-1844," Journal of American History 62 (December 1975): 591-608; Stephen E. Maizlish, The Triumph of Sectionalism: The Transformation of Ohio Politics, 1844-1856 (Kent, Ohio: Kent State University Press, 1983); William G. Shade, Banks or No Banks: The Money Issue in Western Politics, 1832-1865 (Detroit: Wayne State University Press, 1972); James R. Sharp, The Jacksonians Versus the Banks: Politics in the States after the Panic of 1837 (New York: Columbia University Press, 1970); Silbey, Shrine of Party.

[14]Bruce Collins, "The Democrats' Loss of Pennsylvania in 1858," Pennsylvania Magazine of History and Biography 109 (October 1985): 506-7, 509, 512; Holt, Forging a Majority, pp. 289-90, 310-11.

[15]Ershkowitz and Shade, "Consensus or Conflict?"; Levine, Behavior of State Legislative Parties, pp. 112-50; Shade, Banks or No Banks; Sharp, Jacksonians Versus the Banks.

[16]See Chapter 5.

[17]Ershkowitz and Shade, "Consensus or Conflict?", pp. 604-6; Davis, "Illinois Legislators and Jacksonian Democracy," pp. 217-21.

[18]For a discussion of the Democrats' association with the public works system, see Wallner, "Politics and Public Works," particularly, pp. 285-87.

[19]This is in sharp contrast to the findings of Ershkowitz and Shade, "Consensus or Conflict?", p. 604, who found that, "Democrats were even more willing than Whigs to charter transportation corporations" during the late 1830s and early 1840s.

[20]For a discussion of these earlier works, see Edward Pessen, Jacksonian America: Society, Personality, and Politics, revised ed., (Homewood, Illinois: The Dorsey Press, 1978), pp. 245-49. See also Sharp, Jacksonians Versus the Banks, pp. 160-89; 325-26; Harry L. Watson, Jacksonian Politics and Community Conflict: The Emergence of the Second American Party System in Cumberland County, North Carolina (Baton Rouge: Louisiana State University Press, 1981), pp. 13-16, 322-23.

[21]Mueller, Whig Party in Pennsylvania, pp. 244-45; Donald J. Ratcliffe, "Politics in Jacksonian Ohio: Reflections on the Ethnocultural Interpretation," Ohio History 88 (1979): 32-33.

[22]See Chapter 3.

[23]The final votes on business incorporations during the 1838-39 session and on banking charters during the 1849 session were selected as the most representative bloc of roll-calls on these issues. Questions surrounding the nature of the business corporation were most hotly contested during the 1838-39 session just as banking issues dominated the legislative agenda one decade later.

[24]Due to the fact that the Pocono Region sent only one representative to the legislature in both the 1838-39 and 1849 sessions, it has been omitted from this discussion.

[25]See, for example, Walter Dean Burnham, Critical Elections and the Mainspring of American Politics (New York: W. W. Norton & Company, Inc., 1970), pp. 35-38; Holt, Forging a Majority, Paul Kleppner, The Cross of Culture: A Social Analysis of Mid-Western Politics, 1850-1900 (New York, 1970).

[26]Hartz, Economic Policy and Democratic Thought, pp. 42-48, 62-64.

[27]Edward J. Davies, II, "Political Careers and Social Origins of Pennsylvania Legislators, 1848-52, 1870-75, 1890-95," (Unpublished paper, University of Utah, 1985).

[28]For a discussion of lobbying and logrolling techniques in Pennsylvania, see Douglas E. Bowers, "From Logrolling to Corruption: The Development of Lobbying in Pennsylvania, 1815-1861," Journal of the Early Republic 3 (Winter 1983): 439-74; Hartz, Economic Policy and Democratic Thought, pp. 44-45.

CHAPTER EIGHT

CONCLUSION

The antebellum Pennsylvania legislature performed a vital function as it responded to a rapidly expanding society by integrating political and economic change. We have learned a good deal, of late, about how socio-economic and cultural factors were translated into political expression by individual voters on election day. We know far less, however, about how conflicting demands were molded into public policy. By focusing on the interaction of policy formation and the economic characteristics of Pennsylvania's legislative districts, I have demonstrated that legislation was not a result of capricious personal interests, but was deeply rooted in the economic experiences of home districts. The outlook of most lawmakers reflected the peculiar commercial and economic climate of their districts and in that sense, Pennsylvania government in the first half of the nineteenth century was responsible government.[1]

Most representatives, moreover, arrived at the state capital with fairly well-established ideas about the relationship between government and the economy. As a result, persistent patterns of legislative behavior developed within each legislative session that reflected both regional and commercial-economic differences. By and large, however, regional influences were not nearly as prevalent as previous interpretations have led us to believe. Those who have studied Pennsylvania politics in the past have over-emphasized the staying power of coalitions that developed during battles over specific, highly controversial issues. Conflicts which clearly pitted one section against another did occur. Indeed, the battle between the Pennsylvania Railroad and the Baltimore and Ohio for railway rights through the western half of the state became so intense during the mid-1840s that, at one point, the western counties threatened to secede from the commonwealth altogether.[2]

But this kind of sectional rivalry was the exception, not the rule. Distinct regional patterns did emerge on certain roll-call votes, but only the less populous, less economically diverse regions were able to achieve any significant overall degree of cohesion when it came to voting on economic policies. Louis Hartz was precisely right when he argued that "the idea of regional self-interest had no area around which it could effectively come to focus."[3] Most legislation affected much smaller localities making the development of a cohesive, persistent regional consciousness exceedingly difficult.

For these reasons, then, legislative behavior was more firmly grounded in the level of economic development and degree of commercial involvement of Pennsylvania's counties. Commercial-economic group voting patterns frequently overlapped with sectional interests and contributed to stronger regional cohesion. A district's economy and the extent of its commercial network, however, was ultimately a more reliable predictor of a representative's stand than the geographical location of his home on most economic issues.

Since the positions adopted by the legislators reflected the economic conditions of their districts, views on development tended to shift with the prevailing economic climate. During the 1820s, members from the less-developed counties in the state enthusiastically supported charters for new banks and actively campaigned for the construction of transportation routes. By the 1840s, however, representatives from these same areas had soured on the very concept of the corporation in the face of repeated bank suspensions and business bankruptcies which spelled financial ruin for hundreds of innocent creditors. These less-developed areas had been hardest hit by the economic downturn of the late 1830s. Although their representatives continued to lobby for transportation improvements, banks in particular, and corporations more generally, became the objects of their economic frustration. The legislators from the most-developed areas of the state became the ardent supporters of more lenient banking and corporation measures just as they continued to sponsor both private and public efforts to improve the commonwealth's transportation system.

The political parties which emerged during the 1830s picked up on these commercial-economic differences and reinforced them through their rhetoric, platforms, and party doctrine. These new organizations assiduously downplayed regional or sectional divisions, for they could too easily fragment party unity. Differing perceptions of the economic future and the appropriate role of the state, however, were already emerging and the parties exploited these in their attempt to create state-wide organizations that transcended regional boundaries.

Legislative behavior continued to reflect earlier economic divisions which were now heightened and given more concrete expression by the two emerging major parties. Although the Democrats dominated Pennsylvania politics throughout the 1830s and 1840s, the most economically developed and commercially active districts in the commonwealth ususally chose to send Whig representatives to Harrisburg. Whig doctrine allowed for a more active government and party representatives openly supported intervention in the economy. Democratic legislators, on the other hand, tended to come from the less-developed areas of the state. Ever-vigilant of individual liberty, these representatives perceived much governmental activity as sheer favoritism which accorded privileges to the few at the expense of the many.

All too frequently, however, Democratic party discipline was undermined by the same commercial and economic characteristics it sought to exploit. Democratic members from districts that were in the process of developing and expanding increasingly had difficulty supporting party policies that inhibited the commonwealth's economic growth. Representatives from these developing districts abandoned the party line to support policies that were more in line with Whig beliefs, and ultimately contributed to the evolution of a more active and involved state government.

Throughout these decades, economic policy dominated the legislative agenda in Pennsylvania and occupied center stage in the debate over the role of the state. The first half of the nineteenth century was, indeed, a period of experimentation as the legislature struggled to arrive at responsible political answers to new economic questions. Uncertain as to the distinction between the public and private spheres of economic life, state involvement ran the gamut from the cautious chartering of early corporations that were perceived as quasi-public institutions, to a more active role as a major stockholder in various banks and transportation companies, to full-fledged public ownership with the construction of the Pennsylvania canal system. By the eve of the Civil War, many of the questions concerning the role of the state and the division between public and private interests had been worked out in the debates over countless bank charters, internal improvements proposals, and acts of incorporation. The financial debacle resulting from the construction of the public works system caused the state to retreat from its most public and involved role. At the same time, the corporation slowly gained greater acceptance as a legitimate institution, thus creating a more strictly private area of economic life. Throughout the latter half of the nineteenth century, the state increasingly took up the role of regulator rather than that of prime instigator of economic change.

As the legislators reached accommodations on the economic issues that had dominated their agenda for over half a century, they increasingly began to confront non-economic questions that also demanded the reconciliation between public and private interests. Although never a dominant legislative topic, the number of laws passed on public health and welfare issues, for example, climbed steadily during the sessions examined in this study.[4] While comparable data for Pennsylvania are unavailable, Ballard Campbell's work on midwestern legislatures in the late 1880s and 1890s suggests an increasing preoccupation with what he terms "community mores". Indeed, the number of roll-call votes taken on these issues in the Illinois, Iowa, and Wisconsin legislatures slightly surpassed the number taken on economic topics.[5] Campbell, moreover, found that the ethnic composition of the legislative districts, not the economic characteristics, stood out as the best indicator of the partisan affiliation of elected representatives.[6]

This changing preoccupation of state legislatures tells us a great deal about the role of the state and people's expectations and perceptions of government, and raises the critical question about the connection between electoral behavior, legislative behavior, and policy concerns. Historians and political scientists are not exactly certain how or if these aspects of politcal life fit together. Did voting at the grass-roots level have anything to do with governance, and if it did, precisely how were those political impulses transferred to the policy debates and outcomes of nineteenth century legislatures?

State politics in the first half of the nineteenth century seemed to be driven by the divisions created by the rapid, yet uneven pace of economic development. The Pennsylvania legislature's agenda was overwhelmingly dominated by economic issues. Legislative behavior as well as the party affiliation of these lawmakers was also deeply rooted in the commercial and economic structure of Pennsylvania society. Although some scholars have asserted that ethnocultural distinctions were the most important determinant of partisan choice among the electorate during these years,[7] recent studies have suggested that "previous interpretations . . . have seriously erred in minimizing the role of economic issues and economic conditions."[8] The response of the electorate, in other words, may have been shaped just as much by the nature of the economy in which the voter lived as by his ethnic and religious heritage.

Ethnocultural differences, however, did become increasingly important electoral and legislative influences with the advent of the third party system. This shift to a different social context for political conflict was already apparent in Pennsylvania in 1859. Although it was still possible to predict the party affiliation of representatives by the commercial-economic characteristics of their districts, significant exceptions to this pattern emerged which indicated that the socio-economic foundations of party support were in transition. Paul Kleppner and others have amply demonstrated that ethnic and religious factors became the most important determinants of electoral behavior in the latter half of the nineteenth century.[9] Ballard Campbell has added another dimension to this interpretation by emphasizing the importance of cultural issues and by linking legislative partisanship to the ethnocultural characteristics of the various constituencies.

One must exercise a great deal of caution when noting this shift from economic to cultural concerns. Early nineteenth century state legislatures, for example, did confront pressing social issues just as late nineteeth century representative bodies continued to perform important economic functions. Yet a decided shift from a dominant preoccupation with economic policies to cultural issues seems to have taken place, and may have affected several levels of political life simultaneously.

While broad patterns such as these can be detected, the reasons for this trend and the relationships between public policy, legislative behavior, party politics, and the electorate are not easy to isolate. These are the kinds of connections, however, that must be explored in much greater depth. "If political history has a core subject," Richard L. McCormick argued, "that subject is the political system as a whole, including the methods and patterns of political participation and the decisions and actions of government. And if political history has a core purpose, that purpose is to explain the course of politics and government by relating each to the larger environment and each in turn to each other."[10]

State legislatures were a critical link in the nineteenth century political chain as they absorbed the demands that emanated from the larger society and fashioned them into policies that structured the daily economic and social lives of their constituents. We know, as yet, far too little about their activities and how they changed in response to the socio-economic forces exogeneous to parties and government. The issues debated in these assemblies, the types of laws enacted, and the behavior of elected representatives must continue to be examined in their broader social and economic context if we hope to gain a more comprehensive understanding of America's political past.

FOOTNOTES

[1]Others have also concluded that nineteenth legislatures, for the most part, conformed to a responsible government model. See, in particular, Ballard Campbell, Representative Democracy: Public Policy and Midwestern Legislatures in the Late Nineteenth Century (Cambridge, Mass.: Harvard University Press); Richard L. McCormick, The Party Period and Public Policy: American Politics from the Age of Jackson to the Progressive Era (New York: Oxford University Press, 1986), pp. 214-15.

[2]Louis Hartz, Economic Policy and Democratic Thought: Pennsylvania, 1776-1860 (Cambridge, Mass.: Harvard University Press, 1948; reprint ed. Chicago: Quadrangle Paperback Books, Inc., 1968), pp. 43-44.

[3]Ibid., p. 14.

[4]See Table 5.

[5]Campbell, Representative Democracy, p.58.

[6]Ibid., pp. 15-24.

[7]Lee Benson, The Concept of Jacksonian Democracy: New York as a Test Case (Princeton: Princeton University Press, 1961); Ronald P. Formisano, The Birth of Mass Political Parties: Michigan, 1827-1861 (Princeton: Princeton University Press,1971); William G. Shade, "Pennsylvania Politics in the Jacksonian Period: A Case Study, Northampton County, 1824-1844," Pennsylvania History 39 (July 1972): 313-33.

[8]Michael F. Holt, "The Election of 1840, Voter Mobilization, and the Emergence of the Second American Party System: A Reappraisal of Jacksonian Voting Behavior," in A Master's Due: Essays in Honor of David Herbert Donald, eds. William J. Cooper, Michael F. Holt, John McCarder (Baton Rouge: Louisiana State University Press, 1985), p. 19. See also Kim T. Phillips, "The Pennsylvania Origins of the Jackson Movement," Political Science Quarterly 91 (Fall 1976): 489-508; Donald J. Ratcliffe, "Politics in Jacksonian Ohio: Reflections on the Ethnocultural Interpretation, " Ohio History 88 (1979): 5-35; Harry L. Watson, Jacksonian Politics and Community Conflict: The Emergence of the Second American Party System in Cumberland County, North Carolina (Baton Rouge: Louisiana State University Press, 1981).

[9]Paul Kleppner, The Cross of Culture: A Social Analysis of Midwestern Politics, 1850-1900 (New York: Free Press, 1970).

[10]McCormick, Party Period and Public Policy, p. 16.

APPENDICES

APPENDIX A

THE POLICY CATEGORIES

The Pennsylvania General Assembly considered a wide array of economic, social, administrative and private issues during the antebellum years. In order to get a sense of the relative importance of these various concerns and how the emphasis of legislative activity shifted over time, the following policy classification scheme has been devised.

POLICY CATEGORIES

1. Procedural

   a. motions regarding adjournment
   b. election of house offices
   c. miscellaneous

2. Private

   a. divorces
   b. estates
   c. relief/reimbursement
   d. miscellaneous

3. Government

   a. counties, cities, towns, townships
   b. fiscal/taxation
   c. elections
   d. courts
   e. militia
   f. miscellaneous

4. Transportation

   a. turnpikes
   b. state roads
   c. canals
   d. railroads
   e. public works
   f. rivers/bridges
   g. miscellaneous

5. Business and Commerce

   a. corporations
   b. regulatory

c. government promotion
d. labor
e. miscellaneous

6. Banking

a. banks
b. savings institutions
c. general laws
d. miscellaneous

7. Public Health and Welfare

a. prisons/punishment
b. cemeteries
c. hospitals and asylums
d. public health
e. charitable and voluntary associations
f. poor laws
g. liquor control
h. miscellaneous

8. Education

a. private schools and academies
b. common (or public) schools
c. miscellaneous

9. Religion

a. churches
b. religious societies
c. miscellaneous

11. Agriculture, Forestry, Fishery, etc.

12. Miscellany

POLICY CATEGORY DESCRIPTION

1. Procedural: The majority of the roll calls that were classified as procedural were taken on motions to adjourn the legislature for that particular day, or were votes to decide when the legislative session should terminate. If

the motion to adjourn appeared to be used as a stalling technique to buy more time for the discussion of a particular bill or to delay the final vote on an issue, the roll call was classifed with the bill in the appropriate policy category.

Other issues which fell in the procedural category included the election of state printer, debate over the number of copies of bills and reports to print, and the question of repairing the legislative halls.

2. Private: Roll calls and session laws placed in the Private category, with few exceptions, dealt with a specific individual or individuals. These roll calls and laws included divorce decrees, estate settlements, relief and pension payments, and settlements of claims against the commonwealth frequently incurred by employees or contractors working on the Pennsylvania public works.

3. Government: This category included a broad range of legislative, administrative, and judicial issues. The antebellum Pennsylvania legislature was responsible for creating new counties, chartering cities, boroughs, and towns as well as monitoring the activities of these local governmental organizations. The legislature was also called upon to settle local election disputes and determined the geographical limits of the election districts every seven years. In accordance with the changes mandated by the

Constitution of 1838, the General Assembly passed legislation which provided for the election of a number of local officials, and established a classification system for the state's asssociate judges. In addition, the legislature eventually debated a constitutional amendment making supreme court judges and judges of the court of common pleas elective.

It is difficult to identify an annual fiscal policy, or budget. For the most part, legislation having to do with the state's fiscal affairs was intimately intertwined with the debate over the construction and administration of the public works. Legislators did, on occasion, debate their own salary and frequently argued over printing costs. By the 1849 and 1859 sessions, bills dealing with the creation of a sinking fund, and more sweeping legislation providing for "the ordinary expenses of the government" had become the rule.

4. Transportation: All roll calls and laws pertaining to both public and private transportation endeavors were included in this category. The public works was, not surprisingly, consistently the largest sub-category until the system was sold in 1857. All votes and bills relating to the financing, construction, administration and ultimate dissolution of the combined canal and railroad system were placed in this policy category.

Acts of incorporation for privately financed turnpike companies, bridge companies and increasingly for both freight and passenger railroads were classified under the appropriate sub-category.

5. Business and Commerce: This rather broad policy category includes all acts of incorporation, supplements to previous acts of incorporation, regulatory measures, and promotional activities dealing with business and commerce undertaken by the General Assembly during the four legislative sessions. All private corporations, with the exception of those formed for transportation, banking, or non-economic purposes were classified in this category. Attempts by the legislature to regulate the quality, movement, or size and weight of various commodities were also included as were efforts to encourage certain types of business endeavors the legislators believed would benefit the state's economy. Finally, the relatively small number of laws and roll calls pertaining to child labor restrictions and mechanics' liens against employers are listed here.

6. Banking: All session laws and roll calls dealing with acts of incorporation or alterations thereon of banks and savings institutions are included in this category, as are those laws and legislative votes pertaining to the

denominational limit of paper money and the proposed bill to enact a general incorporation law for all banks.

7. Public Health and Welfare: This broad category includes both public and private attempts to address health and welfare issues. The administration of the eastern and western state penitentiaries as well as bills establishing appropriate punishment for a variety of crimes became heated topics during several of the legislative sessions under examination. Other bills provided for the erection and administration of county poor houses, houses of refuge, asylums for the deaf and dumb, and the Penn Industrial Reform School. Privately sponsored charitable and voluntary associations which received charters of incorporation from the state were also placed in this category.

Other issues in this policy classification included attempts to restrict or control the sale of intoxicating liquor, to prevent the carrying of concealed weapons, to protect the estates of widowed and single women, to establish a health office in Philadelphia, and to provide for the registration of marriages, births and deaths.

8. Education: Included in this category were all laws and roll calls pertaining to the incorporation or subsequent alteration of laws establishing private academies or educational institutions and all laws regarding the

allocation and disbursement of the common school fund and the delineation of school district boundaries. Occasionally, the legislature debated whether or not certain textbooks should be purchased by the state and furnished to each school district.

9. Religion: This policy includes issues dealing with the incorporation of churches and voluntary associations established for specifically religious purposes, such as bible societies.

10. Agriculture: The relatively few number of votes and session laws pertaining to agriculture, fisheries, or forestry were classified in this category.

11. Miscellany: This category includes resolutions regarding national issues that the legislature felt compelled to address such as the abolition of slavery in the District of Columbia, the Maine-Great Britain boundary dispute, and the tariff.

At the beginning of the 1838-39 legislative session, the Buckshot War erupted between two factions vying for control of the legislature, each claiming to have been legitmately elected. This violent and embarassing confrontation generated numerous propositions and roll calls designed to ferret out and punish the perpetrators. All of these votes have been classified in this category.

All other roll calls and session laws which do not fit easily into any of the above policies have been included in this category.

APPENDIX B

THE ROLL CALL SELECTION

Several steps, procedures, and sources were used to make the final selection of the 875 roll calls used for more detailed analysis. Ballard Campbell has cautioned the researcher who attempts roll call analysis to be as systematic and rigorous as possible when selecting the sample[1]. Precise, "scientific" sampling by definition, however, assumes that all units, in this case roll calls, of the larger population are equal. Unfortunately, such is not the case when dealing with antebellum recorded legislative votes. All too frequently the Journal of the Pennsylvania House of Representatives simply did not provide enough information for the researcher to determine exactly what issue was being debated and what the roll call vote was for, thus making the roll call selection process outlined below more problematic, but not insurmountable.

Initially, the contested issue which generated each roll call taken during the four legislative sessions was recorded on a note card and assigned to a policy category. The roll calls were kept in chronological order and an attempt was made to follow the debates through the Harrisburg newspapers[2]. A large portion of these newspapers was dedicated to providing an accurate account of the legislative proceedings in both houses on a day to day basis. It was thus possible to supplement the rather sketchy information provided by the Journal and to gain a better understanding of many of the questions that required a roll call vote. In addition, the title of each bill under consideration was matched with a list of the laws passed during that session. If the bill had, in fact, been enacted, the session law itself frequently gave further insight into the terms of the debate.

Once these three sources--the Journal, the newspapers, and the session laws--had been searched, the first roll call selection was made. Several guidelines were followed when making this first cut. To begin with, no attempt was made to omit what others have termed "unanimous" roll calls. Some roll call analysists have automatically eliminated all votes which did not pass a pre-determined "conflict" or "cleavage" test such as a minimum of 10-15 percent voting in the minority.[3] While we are certainly interested in how legislators differed in their responses to various issues, we are also interested in those questions which generated greater consensus.[4]

Other types of roll calls, however, were omitted immediately. All procedural roll calls such as motions to adjourn, or resolutions regarding final adjournment of the session were eliminated unless they were clearly ploys to buy more time for further legislative debate or to stall the final vote on a particular issue. In addition, all strictly personal roll calls were discarded.

Supplements to laws enacted during previous sessions were particularly problematic. Frequently, reference was made to the supplement only through the title of the new bill and no indication was given as to the actual substance of the law. As a general rule of thumb, roll calls on supplements were only included if the bill was actually passed and the session law could be consulted, unless, of course, the supplement generated enough interest to occasion debate and a mention in the press.

Votes on bills from previous sessions returned by the Governor were not included. If the bill was returned within the same session, however, and voted on again, the roll call was included in the first selection. Towards the end of each session, the legislature frequently voted to postpone consideration of many non-pressing bills. The roll calls on these postponements rarely reflected the legislator's true feelings on the issue but were deemed expedient to bring the session to a close. As such, these votes were also eliminated.

The roll calls that survived this first selection process were then arranged by bill. It was not uncommon for discussion of a bill to emerge several times throughout the session, and numerous roll calls were often taken on a single bill. Generally, the most heated debate and the most crucial decisions were made during the second reading of the bill. Indeed, the third reading and final vote on a bill was often little more than a pro forma acceptance of the terms that had been decided during the second reading. Once the roll calls were arranged by bill and analyzed for their content, it was possible to eliminate certain redundant votes which elicited virtually the same yea-nay division, such as motions to reconsider a particular vote, motions to proceed to the third reading, and so on. While every effort was made to keep all roll calls that had any substantive bearing on the bill, it was possible to omit certain superfluous votes.

The 875 roll calls that survived the first and second selection process thus constitute those used in the select roll call analysis.

APPENDIX C

ASSIGNMENT OF REPRESENTATIVES TO REGION AND COMMERCIAL-ECONOMIC GROUPS AND COMMERCIAL-ECONOMIC AGGREGATE GROUPS

The Journal of the House of Representatives lists the representatives by county at the beginning of each legislative session. Based upon the county, each representative was assigned a regional, commercial-economic group, and commercial-economic aggregate group code number. In each session, there were several legislators who represented multi-county districts. If all counties in the district were in the same region, the same commercial-economic group, and the same commercial-economic aggregate group, there was no problem assigning the appropriate codes. This consistency, however, rarely occurred. When the counties in a single district came from different regions or registered different commercial-economic values, assignment of the regional, continuum, and aggregate codes was made on the basis of the county populations taken from the decennial census conducted the year following the legislative session. If only two counties were in the district, the codes were assigned on the basis of the most populous county. If more than two counties were in the district, the regional code was assigned to the region most frequently represented, while the two commercial-economic codes were calculated as an average of the individual county's scores weighted according to population.

Multi-county districts most frequently combined a number of lightly populated, less developed counties. As a result, some of the regions and commercial-economic groups had noticeably few legislators representing them in the House of Representatives. The Pocono Region, for example, had no representatives in 1828-29, one in 1838-39 and 1849, and two by 1859. Similarly, the Northeastern Region had only one representative in 1828-29, but had acquired six by 1859. Meanwhile, the vast Allegheny Forest Region remained so sparsely populated that it only sent five legislators to Harrisburg by 1859. Likewise, once the commercial-economic continua scores were averaged the least developed commercial-economic aggregate group was only represented during the 1838-39 session, and then by only one legislator!

The following tables list the number of legislators representing each region, commercial-economic group and commercial-economic aggregate group for each session.

Number of Representatives by Region and Legislative Session

	Region						
	1	2	3	4	5	6	7
1828-29	53	10	---	1	11	2	23
1838-39	49	9	1	3	9	4	25
1849	45	9	1	5	10	5	25
1859	44	12	2	6	6	5	25

Number of Representatives by Commercial-Economic Group

	Commercial-Economic Group				
	1	2	3	4	5
1828-29	8	10	17	22	43
1838-39	10	16	15	20	39
1849	3	15	18	19	45
1859	3	16	15	18	48

Number of Representatives by Commercial-Economic Aggregate Group

	Commercial-Economic Aggregate Group				
	1	2	3	4	5
1828-29	---	13	17	29	41
1838-39	1	15	21	22	41
1849	---	22	18	23	37
1859	---	18	22	21	39

FOOTNOTES

[1]Ballard Campbell, "The State Legislature in American History: A Review Essay," Historical Methods Newsletter 9(September 1976): 186.

[2]The newspapers consulted were The Harrisburg Chronicle, 1 December 1828-20 April 1829; Pennsylvania Reporter and Democratic Herald, 7 April 1829-15 May 1829; Pennsylvania Telegraph, 1 December 1838-3 April 1839; Keystone, 8 May 1839-31 July 1839; Pennsylvania Telegraph, 1 January 1849-9 May 1849; Pennsylvania Daily Telegraph, 3 January 1859-18 April 1859. In addition, the Legislative Record, 1859 was consulted. This volume was published by the commonwealth beginning in the mid-1850s and was designed to provide a much more detailed account of the legislative debates in much the same fashion as the Harrisburg newspapers.

[3]See, for example, Ballard Campbell, Representative Democracy: Public Policy and Mid-Western Legislatures in the Late Nineteenth Century (Cambridge: Harvard University Press, 1980), p. 207; Peter D. Levine, The Behavior of State Legislative Parties in the Jacksonian Era: New Jersey, 1829-1844 (Rutherford-Teaneck, N.J.: Fairleigh Dickinson University Press, 1977), p. 99.

[4]Richard I. Hofferbert, The Study of Public Policy (Indianapolis: Bobbs-Merrill, 1974), pp. 39-40. Hofferbert cautions against eliminating "unanimous" votes. While he concedes that this procedure is acceptable when dealing with a single state, he advises retention of unanimous roll calls when doing a comparative multi-state analysis. Given the built-in comparative nature of this study's research design, it seemed wise to avoid immediately tossing all "unanimous" votes. Retaining even the less divisive roll calls will help to determine which regions or commercial-economic groups exhibited the most cohesive legislative behavior and on which issues.

B I B L I O G R A P H Y

BIBLIOGRAPHY

Official Documents

"A Tabular Statement relating to the tax on real and personal estate, for State purposes . . . " Pennsylvania, House of Representatives, Legislative Journal, vol. 2, 1846, pp. 346-65.

"Communication from the Auditor General, accompanied with a Statement of the Certain Banks, Read December 30, 1826." Pennsylvania, House of Representatives, Legislative Journal, vol. 2, 1826, pp. 89-115.

"Communication from the Auditor General, accompanied by a Statement of the Certain Banks, read January 5, 1836." Pennsylvania, House of Representatives, Legislative Journal, vol. 2, 1835, pp. 144-93.

"Communication from the Auditor General transmitting Quarterly Statements of the Several Banks and Savings Institutions." Pennsylvania, House of Representatives, Legislative Journal, vol. 2, 1846.

"Communciation from the Auditor General, transmitting the Returns of the Several Banks and Savings Institutions of this Commonwealth." Pennsylvania, House of Representatives, Legislative Journal, vol. 2, 1856, p. 255.

Pennsylvania, General Assembly, Laws of the Commonwealth of Pennsylvania, 1828-29, 1838-39, 1849, 1859.

Pennsylvania, General Assembly, Legislative Record: Proceedings of the General Assembly of the Commonwealth of Pennsylvania for the session commencing January 4, 1859. Harrisburg: Patriot and Union Office, 1859.

Pennsylvania, House of Representatives, Legislative Journal, Vol. 1, 1828-29, 1838-39, 1849, 1859.

Register of All Officers and Agents, Civil, Military, and Naval in the Service of the United States, 1845, 1855.

"Report of the State Treasurer on the Finances of the State." Pennsylvania, General Assembly, Legislative Documents, 1855, pp. 40-41.

"Returns of the County Commissioners. Increase of county rates and levies for the use of the commonwealth, per act of 25th March, 1831." Pennsylvania, House of Representatives, Legislative Journal, vol. 2, 1832-33, pp. 189-231.

U. S. Congress. House of Representatives. Executive Documents, 1861-62. "Railroads of the United States." 37th Congress, 2nd session.

U. S. Congress, Postage at Each Office in 1825 and 1826. H.Doc. 35, 19th Congress, 2nd session.

U. S. Congress, Postage Accruing at Each Office, 1835. H.Doc. 262, 24th Congress, 1st session.

Census Documents

Fourth Census of the United States, 1820. Washington: Gales & Seaton, 1821.

Fourth Census of the United States, 1820. Book II: Digest of the Accounts of Manufacturing Establishments in the United States and of their Manufactures. Washington: Gales & Seaton, 1823.

Sixth Census of the United States, 1840. Compendium of Enumeration of Inhabitants and Statistics of the United States. Washington: Thomas Allen, 1841.

Statistical View of the United States . . . Being a Compendium of the Seventh Census. Washington: 1854.

Agriculture of the United States in 1860; Compiled from the Original Returns of the Eighth Census. Washington: Government Printing Office, 1864.

Manufactures of the United States in 1860; Compiled from the Original Returns of the Eighth Census. Washington: Government Printing Office, 1865.

Ninth Census of the United States, 1870. Vol. 1: Population. Washington: Government Printing Office, 1871.

Sixteenth Census of the United States: Agriculture, Vol. 1, Part 1. Washington: Government Printing Office, 1942.

Newspapers

The Harrisburg Chronicle, 1 December 1828-20 April 1829.

Hazard's Register of Pennsylvania, 1828-1835.

Keystone, 8 May 1839-31 July 1839.

Pennsylvania Reporter and Democratic Herald, 7 April 1829-15 May 1829.

Pennsylvania Daily Telegraph, 3 January 1859-18 April 1859.

Pennsylvania Telegraph, 1 December 1838-3 April 1839; 1 January 1849-9 May 1849.

County Histories, Gazetteers, etc.

Africa, J. Simpson. History of Huntingdon and Blair Counties, Pennsylvania. Philadelphia: L. H. Everts, 1883.

Agnew, Daniel. A History of the Region of Pennsylvania North of the Ohio and West of the Allegheny River. Philadelphia: Kay and Brother, 1887.

Albert, George Dallas. History of the County of Westmoreland, Pennsylvania. Philadelphia: L. H. Everts, 1882.

Aldrich, Lewis Cass. History of Clearfield County, Pennsylvania. Syracuse: D. Mason and Co., 1887.

Appel, John C. History of Monroe County, Pennsylvania: 1725-1976. East Stroudsburg, Pa.: Bicentennial Project of the Pocono Hospital Auxiliary, 1976.

Armstrong County, Pennsylvania: Her People, Past and Present . . . Chicago: J. H. Beers & Co., 1914.

Ashmead, Henry Graham. History of Delaware County, Pennsylvania. Philadelphia: L. H. Everts, 1884.

Battle, J. H. History of Columbia and Montour Counties. Chicago: A. Warner & Co., 1887.

Bausman, Joseph H. History of Beaver County, Pennsylvania. 2 vols. New York: Knickerbocker Press, 1904.

Beebe, Victor Llewellyn. History of Potter County, Pennsylvania. Coudersport, Pa.: Potter County Historical Society, 1934.

Bell, Herbert C., ed. History of Venango County, Pennsylvania. Chicago: Brown, Runk & Co., 1890.

Blackman, Emily C. History of Susquehanna County, Pennsylvania. Philadelphhia: Claxton, Remsen and Haffelfinger, 1873.

Blair County Historical Society. Blair County's First Hundred Years: 1846-1946. Altoona, Pa.: The Mirror Press, 1945.

____________. History of Bradford County, Pennsylvania. Chicago: S. B. Nelson & Co., 1891.

Bradsby, Henry C. History of Luzerne County, Pennsylvania. Chicago, 1893.

Brown, Robert C. History of Butler County, Pennsylvania. Chicago: R. C. Brown and Co., 1895.

Buck, William Joseph. History of Montgomery County within the Schuylkill Valley . . . Norristown, Pa.: E. L. Acker, 1859.

Burrowes, Thomas. A State-Book of Pennsylvania. Philadelphia: U. Hunt & Son, 1846.

Crumrine, Boyd, ed. History of Washington County, Pennsylvania. Philadelphia: L. H. Everts & Co., 1882.

Cushing, Thomas, et al. History of Allegheny County, Pennsylvania. Chicago: A. Warner & Co., 1889.

Davis, Aaron J. History of Clarion County, Pennsylvania. Syracuse: D. Mason & Co., 1887.

Davis, Tarring S., ed. A History of Blair County, Pennsylvania. 2 vols. Harrisburg: National Historical Association, 1931.

Davis, William Watts Hart. The History of Bucks County, Pennsylvania. Doylestown, Pa.: Democrat Book & Job Office, 1876.

Donheoo, George P. Harrisburg and Dauphin County: A Sketch of the History for the Past Twenty-five Years, 1900-1925. Dayton, Ohio: The National Historical Association, 1925.

Durant, Samuel W. _History of Allegheny County_. Philadelphia: L. H. Everts, 1876.

Eaton, Rebecca. _A Geography of Pennsylvania_. 2d ed. Philadelphia: Edward C. Biddle, 1837.

Eaton, Samuel John Mills. _Centennial Discourse: A Sketch of the History of Venango County, Pennsylvania_. Franklin, Pa.: Venango Spectator Job Office, 1876.

Egle, William Henry. _History of the Counties of Dauphin and Lebanon in the Commonwealth of Pennsylvania_. Philadelphia: Everts & Peck, 1883.

Ellis, Franklin, ed. _History of Fayette County, Pennsylvania_. Philadelphia: L. H. Everts & Co., 1882.

________, and Evans, Samuel. _History of Lancaster County, Pennsylvania_. Philadelphia: Everts & Peck, 1883.

________. _History of Northampton County, Pennsylvania_. Philadelphia: P. Fritts, 1877.

________, and Hungerford, A. N., eds. _History of that Part of the Susquehanna and Juniata Valleys Embraced in the Counties of Mifflin, Juniata, Perry, Union and Snyder in the Commnwealth of Pennsylvania_. Philadelphia: Everts, Peck, & Richards, 1886.

Forrest, Earle R. _History of Washington County, Pennsyvlania_. Chicago: S. J. Clarke Publishing Co., 1926.

Futhey, John Smith. _History of Chester County, Pennsylvania_. Philadelphia: L. H. Everts, 1881.

Gordon, Thomas F. _A Gazetteer of the State of Pennsylvania_. Philadelphia: T. Belknap, 1833.

Hain, Harry Harrison. _History of Perry County, Pennsylvania_. Harrisburg: Harn-Moore, Co., 1922.

Harvey, Oscar Jewell. _A History of Wilkes-Barre, Luzerne County, Pennsylvania_. 3 vols. Wilkes-Barre, Pa.: Raeder Press, 1909.

History of Butler County, Pennsylvania. Chicago: Waterman, Watkins & Co., 1883.

History of Crawford County, Pennsylvania. Chicago: Warner, Beers & Co., 1885.

History of Cumberland and Adams Counties, Pennsylvania. Chicago: Warner, Beers & Co., 1886.

History of Erie County, Pennsylvania. Chicago: Warner, Beers & Co., 1884.

History of Luzerne, Lackawanna, and Wyoming Counties, Pennsylvania. New York: W. W. Munsell & Co., 1880.

History of Schuylkill County, Pennsylvania. New York: W. W. Munsell & Co., 1881.

History of Tioga County, Pennsylvania. New York: W. W. Munsell & Co., 1883.

Hunsicker, Clifton S. Montgomery County, Pennsylvania: A History. 3 vols. New York: Lewis Historical Publishing Company, 1923.

Klein, Frederic Shriver. Old Lancaster: Historic Pennsylvania Community from its Beginning to 1865. Lancaster: Early American Series, Inc., 1964.

Klein, Harry Martin John. Lancaster County, Pennsylvania: A History. New York: Lewis Historical Publishing Company, 1924.

Kriebel, H. W. A Brief History of Montgomery County, Pennsylvania. Norristown, Pa.: The School Directors' Association, 1923.

Kurtz, Paul. Blair, Main Line: A History of the Tuckahoe Valley. Bellwood, Pa.: Bicentennial of the Bellwood Antis Area, 1976.

Leeson, Michael A. History of the Counties of McKean, Elk, Cameron and Potter, Pennsylvania. Chicago: J. H. Beers, 1890.

Lytle, Milton Scott. History of Huntingdon County, in the State of Pennsylvania. Lancaster, Pa.: William H. Roy, 1876.

McCauley, I. H. Historical Sketch of Franklin County, Pennsylvania. Chambersburg, Pa.: D. F. Pursel, 1878.

McKnight, William James. A Pioneer History of Jefferson County, Pennsylvania. Philadelphia: J. B. Lippincott, Co., 1898.

Mathews, Alfred, and Hungerford, Austin N. History of the Counties of Lehigh and Carbon, in the Commonwealth of Pennsylvania. Philadelphia: Everts & Richards, 1884.

Meginness, John Franklin. Lycoming County: Its Origins and Condensed History for 100 Years. Williamsport, Pa.: n.p., 1895.

_________. Otzinachson, Or A History of the West Branchh Valley of the Susquehanna. Philadelphia: H. B. Ashmed, 1857; revised ed., Williamsport, Pa.: Gazette & Bulletin Printing House, 1889.

Montgomery, Morton L. History of Berks County in Pennsylvania. Philadelphia: Everts, Peck & Richards, 1886.

Morgan, George H. Centennial: The Settlement, Formation and Progress of Dauphin County, Pennsylvania from 1785 to 1876. Harrisburg: Telegraph Steam Book and Job Printing House, 1877.

National Historical Association. A History of the Juniata Valley. 3 vols. Harrisburg: Telegraph Press, 1936.

Nelson's Biograpical Dictionary and Historical Referernce Book of Erie County, Pennsylvania. Erie, Pa.: S. B. Nelson, 1896.

Palmer, Charles Palmer, ed. A History of Delaware County, Pennsylvania. 3 vols. Harrisburg: National Historical Association, 1932.

Pitt, Thomas A., comp. History and Progress of Chester County. Westchester, Pa.: Commissioners of Chester County, 1962.

Reed, John Elmer. History of Erie County, Pennsylvania. Topeka, Indianapolis: Historical Publishing Co., 1925.

Rupp, Israel D. History and Topography of Dauphin, Cumberland, Franklin, Bedford, Adams and Perry Counties. Lancaster, Pa.: n.p., 1846.

_________. The History and Topography of Dauphin, Cumberland, Franklin, Bedford, Adams, Perry, Somerset, Cambria, and Indiana Counties . . . Lancaster: Gilbert Hills, 1848.

_________. History and Topography of Northumberland, Huntingdon, Mifflin, Centre, Union, Columbia, Juniata and Clinton Counties, Pennsylvania. Lancaster: Gilbert Hills, 1847.

_________. History of Northampton, Lehigh, Monroe, Carbon and Schuylkill Counties. Harrisburg: Hickok & Cantine, 1845.

Sanford, Laura G. The History of Erie County, Pennsylvania. Philadelphia: J. B. Lippincott & Co., 1862.

Schell, William P. The Annals of Bedford County, Pennsylvania, . . . Bedford, Pa.: Gazette Publishing Co., 1907.

Schenck, J. S., ed. History of Warren County, Pennsylvania. Syracuse: D. Mason & Co., 1887.

Scott, Kate M., ed. History of Jefferson County, Pennsylvania. Syracuse: D. Mason & Co., 1888.

Sipe, Chester Hale. History of Butler County, Pennsylvania. Topeka, Indianapolis: Historical Publishing Co., 1927.

Smith, George. History of Delaware County, Pennsylvania. Philadelphia: H. B. Ashmead, 1862.

Stewart, Joshua T. Indiana County, Pennsylvania. 2 vols. Chicago: J. H. Beers & Co., 1913.

Storey, Henry Wilson. History of Cambria County, Pennsylvania. 3 vols. New York, Chicago: Lewis Publishing Company, 1907.

Thomson, Wilmer W. Chester County and Its People. Chicago, New York: Union History Co., 1898.

Trego, Charles B. A Geography of Pennsylvania. Philadelphia: E. C. Biddle, 1843.

Walton, D. L., ed. Beaver County Bicentennial Atlas. Beaver County Bicentennial Commission, 1976.

Weigley, Russell F., et al. Philadelhia: A 300 Year History. New York: W. W. Norton & Co., 1982.

Wright, Silas. History of Perry County, in Pennsylvania, from the Earliest Settlement to the Present Time. Lancaster: Wylie & Griest, 1873.

Books and Articles

Agriculture, Its Early History and Development in Pennsylvania, and its Present Status. Harrisburg: Bureau of Industrial Statistics, 1875.

Akagi, Roy H. "The Pennsylvania Constitution of 1838." Pennsylvania Magazine of History and Biography 48 (1924): 301-33.

Alwin, John A. "Post Office Locations and the Historical Geographer: A Montana Example." The Professional Geographer 26 (1974): 183-86.

Anderson, Lee F., Watts, Meredith W. Jr., and Wilcox, Allen R. Legislative Roll-Call Analysis. Evanston: Northwestern University Press, 1966.

Baer, Christopher T. Canals and Railroads of the Mid-Atlantic States, 1800-1860. Greenvillle, Wilmington, Dela.: Regional Economic History Research Center, Eleutherian Mills-Hagley Foundation, 1981.

Baker, Reginald Paul. "Economic Development and Rural Social Structure: Pennsylvania in 1860." Ph.D. dissertation, University of Pittsburgh, 1977.

Bartlett, Marguerite. Chief Phases of Pennsylvania Politics in the Jacksonian Period. Allentown, Pa.: H. Ray Hass & Co., 1919.

Bender, Thomas. "The New Political History--Then and Now. Reviews in American History 12 (December 1984).

Benson, Lee. The Concept of Jacksonian Democracy: New York as a Test Case. Princeton: Princeton University Press, 1961.

Bidwell, Percy W. and Falconer, John I. History of Agriculture in the Northern United States, 1620-1860. Washington: Carnegie Institution of Washington, 1925.

Billinger, Robert D. Pennsylvania's Coal Industry. Gettysburg: Pennsylvania Historical Association, 1954.

Binder, Frederick Moore. Coal Age Empire: Pennsylvania Coal and its Utilization to 1860. Harrisburg: Pennsylvania Historical and Museum Commission, 1974.

Bining, Arthur C. Pennsylvania's Iron and Steel Industry. Gettysburg: Pennsylvania Historical Association, 1954.

Bishop, Avard L. "The State Works of Pennsylvania." Transactions of the Connecticut Academy of Arts and Sciences. 13 (1908): 149-297.

Bogen, J. The Anthracite Railroads. New York: Ronald Press, 1927.

Bourke, Paul F. and Debats, Donald A. "Restoring Politics to Political History." Journal of Interdisciplinary History 15(Winter 1985): 459-66.

Bogue, Allan. "American Historians and Legislative Behavior." In American Political Behavior: Historical Essays and Readings, pp. 99-118. Edited by Lee Benson, et al. New York: Harper & Row, 1974.

_________. Clio and the Bitch Goddess: Quantification in American Political History. Beverly Hills: Sage Publication, Inc., 1983.

Bowers, Douglas E. "From Logrolling to Corruption: The Development of Lobbying in Pennsylvania, 1815-1861." Journal of the Early Republic 3 (Winter 1983): 439-74.

_________. "The Pennsylvania Legislature, 1815-1860: A Study of Democracy at Work." Ph.D. dissertation, University of Chicago, 1974.

Branning, Rosalind L. Pennsylvania Constitutional Development. Pittsburgh: University of Pittsburgh Press, 1960.

Brown, Richard D. "The Emergence of Urban Society in Rural Massachusetts, 1760-1820." Journal of American History 61(June 1974): 29-51.

Bruchey, Stuart. The Roots of American Economic Growth, 1607-1861: An Essay in Social Causation. New York: Harper & Row, 1965.

Buck, Solon J. and Buck, Elizabeth H. The Planting of Civilization in Western Pennsylvania. Pittsburgh: University of Pittsburgh Press, 1939.

Burnham, Walter Dean. Critical Elections and the Mainspring of American Politics. New York: W. W. Norton & Co., 1970.

Cadman, John W., Jr. The Corporation in New Jersey: Business and Politics, 1791-1875. Cambridge, Ma.: Harvard University Press, 1949.

Campbell, Ballard. Representative Democracy: Public Policy and Midwestern Legislatures in the Late Nineteenth Century. Cambridge, Ma.: Harvard University Press, 1980.

_________. "The State Legislature in American History: A Review Essay. Historical Methods Newsletter 9 (September 1976): 185-194.

Carlson, Robert E. "The Pennsylvania Improvement Society and its Promotion of Canals and Railroads, 1824-26." Pennsylvania History 31 (July 1964): 295-310.

Clark, Joseph S., Jr. "The Railroad Struggle for Pittsburgh: Forty-three years of Philadelphia-Baltimore Rivalry, 1838-1871." *Pennsylvania Magazine of History and Biography* 48 (1924): 1-37.

Cochrane, Willard W. *The Development of American Agriculture: A Historical Analysis*. Minneapolis: University of Minneapolis Press, 1979.

Coleman, John F. *The Disruption of the Pennsylvania Democracy, 1848-1860*. Harrisburg: Pennsylvania Historical and Museum Commission, 1975.

Collins, Bruce. "The Democrats' Loss of Pennsylvania in 1858." *Pennsylvania Magazine of History and Biography*. 109 (October 1985): 499-536.

Cox, Thomas R. "Transition in the Woods: Log Drivers, Raftsmen, and the Emergence of Modern Lumbering in Pennsylvania." *Pennsylvania Magazine of History and Biography* 104 (January 1980): 345-64.

Current, Richard Nelson. *Old Thad Stevens: A Story of Ambition*. Madison: University of Wisconsin Press, 1942.

Davies, Edward J., II. "Elite Migration and Urban Growth: The Rise of Wilkes-Barre in the Northern Anthracite Region, 1820-1880. *Pennsylvania History* 45 (October 1978): 291-314.

__________. "Political Careers and Social Origins of Pennsylvania Legislators, 1848-53, 1870-75, 1890-95." Unpublished paper, University of Utah, 1985.

Davis, Rodney O. "Illinois Legislators and Jacksonian Democracy, 1834-1841." Ph.D. dissertation, University of Iowa, 1966.

__________. "Partnership in Jacksonian State Politics: Party Divisions in the Illinois Legislature, 1834-1841." In *Quantification in American History*, pp. 149-62. Edited by Robert Swierenga. New York: 1970.

Dawson, Richard and Robinson, James A. "Inter-party Competition, Economic Variables and Welfare Policies in the American States." *Journal of Politics* 25 (1963): 265-89.

Defebaugh, James Elliott. *History of the Lumber Industry of America*. Vol. 2. Chicago: The American Lumberman, 1906-09.

Dye, Thomas R. "Politics Versus Economics: The Development of the Literature on Policy Determination." Policy Studies Journal 7 (1979): 652-662.

Fenton, J. H. and Chamberlayne, D. W. "The Literature Dealing with the Relationships between Policy Processes, Socioeconomic Conditions, and Public Policies in the American States: A Bibliographic Essay." Polity 1 (Spring 1969): 388-404.

Eavenson, Howard N. The Pittsburgh Coal Bed: Its Early History and Development. New York, 1938.

Egle, William H. An Illustrated History of the Commonwealth of Pennsylvania: Civil, Political, and Military . . . . Harrisburg: DeWitt C. Goodrich & Co., 1876.

Ershkowitz, Herbert and Shade, William G. "Consensus or Conflict?: Political Behavior of State Legislative Parties during the Jacksonian Era." Journal of American History 58 (December 1971): 591-621.

Evans, Paul D. The Holland Land Company. Buffalo: Buffalo Historical Society, 1924.

Fletcher, Stevenson Whitcomb. Pennsylvania Agriculture and Country Life, 1640-1840. Harrisburg: Pennsylvania Historical and Museum Commission, 1950.

__________. Pennsylvania Agriculture and Country Life, 1840-1940. Harrisburg: Pennsylvania Historical and Museum Commission, 1955.

Florin, John William. The Advance of Frontier Settlement in Pennsylvania, 1638-1850: A Geographic Interpretation. University Park, Pa.: Department of Geography, Pennsylvania State University, 1977.

Folsom, Burton W., Jr. Urban Capitalists: Entrepreneurs and City Growth in Pennsylvania's Lackawanna and Lehigh Regions, 1800-1920. Baltimore, London: Johns Hopkins Press, 1981.

Formisano, Ronald P. The Birth of Mass Political Parties: Michigan, 1827-1861. (Princeton: Princeton University Press, 1971).

________. "Toward a Reorientation of Jacksonian Politics: A Review of the Literature, 1959-1975." Journal of American History 63 (1976): 42-65.

Fuller, Wayne E. The American Mail: Enlarger of the Common Life. Chicago: University of Chicago Press, 1972.

Gates, Paul. The Farmer's Age: Agriculture, 1815-1860. White Plains, NY: M.E. Sharpe, Inc., 1960.

Gerrity, Frank. "The Masons and the Antimasons, and the Pennsylvania Legislature, 1834-1836." Pennsylvania Magazine 99 (April 1975): 180-207.

Gienapp, William E. "Nebraska, Nativism, and Rum: The Failure of Fusion in Pennsylvania, 1854." Pennsylvania Magazine of History and Biography 109 (October 1985): 425-71.

Godcharles, Frederic A. Pennsylvania: Political, Governmental, Military, and Civil. New York: American Historical Society, 1933.

Goodrich, Carter. "American Development Policy: The Case of Internal Improvements." Journal of Economic History 16 (December 1956): 449-60.

_________, ed. Canals and American Economic Development. New York: Columbia University Press, 1961.

_________. Government Promotion of American Canals and Railroads, 1800-1890. New York: Columbia University Press, 1960.

_________. "Internal Improvements Reconsidered." Journal of Economic History 30 (June 1970): 289-311.

Gray, Ralph D. "Philadelphia and the Chesapeake and Delaware Canal, 1769-1823." Pennsylvania Magazine of History and Biography 84 (October 1960): 401-424.

Gunn, L. Ray. "Crisis of Authority in the Antebellum States: New York, 1820-1860." Review of Politics 41 (April 1979): 273-97.

_________. "The New York State Legislature: A Developmental Perspective." Social Science History 4 (August 1980): 267-94.

_________. "Political Implications of General Incorporation Laws in New York to 1860." MidAmerica 59 (October 1977): 171-91.

Hall, Van Beck. "A Fond Farewell to Henry Adams: Ideas on Relating Political to Social Change in the Early National Period." In The Human Dimensions of Nation Making: Essays on Colonial and Revolutionary America, pp. 323-61. Edited by James Kirby Martin. Madison: University of Wisconsin Press, 1976.

__________. Politics Without Parties: Massachusetts, 1780-1791. Pittsburgh: University of Pittsburgh Press, 1972.

Hammond, Bray. Banks and Politics in America: From the Revolution to the Civil War. Princeton: Princeton University Press, 1957.

__________. "Long and Short Term Credit in Early American Banking." Quarterly Journal of Economics 49 (November 1934): 79-103.

Handlin, Oscar and Handlin, Mary Flug. Commonwealth; A Study of the Role of Government in the American Economy: Massachusetts, 1774-1861. New York: New York University Press, 1947.

__________. "Origins of the American Business Corporation." Journal of Economic History 5 (May 1945): 1-23.

Hartz, Louis. Economic Policy and Democratic Thought: Pennsylvania, 1776-1860. Cambridge: Harvard University Press, 1948; reprint ed., Chicago: Quadrangle Paperback Books, Inc., 1968.

Hays, Samuel P. American Political History as Social Analysis. Knoxville: University of Tennessee Press, 1980.

__________. "Political Parties and the Community-Society Continuum." In The American Party Systems: Stages of Political Development, 2d ed., pp. 152-181. Edited by William Nesbitt Chambers and Walter Dean Burnham. New York: Oxford University Press, 1975.

__________. "Politics and Society: Beyond the Political Party." In The Evolution of American Electoral Systems. Edited by Paul Kleppner, et al. Westport, Conn.: Greenwood Press, 1982.

__________. "Society and Politics: Politics and Society." Journal of Interdisciplinary History 15 (Winter 1985): 481-99.

Heath, Milton Sydney. Constructive Liberalism: The Role of the State in Economic Development in Georgia to 1860. (Cambridge: Harvard University Press, 1954).

Hewitt, Warren F. "The Know-Nothing Party in Pennsylvania." Pennsylvania History 2 (April 1935): 69-85.

Hofferbert, Richard I. "Socioeconomic Dimensions of the American States, 1890-1960." Midwest Journal of Political Science 12 (1968): 405-409.

________. "State and Community Policy Studies: A Review of Comparative Input-Output Analyses." Political Science Journal 3 (1972): 3-72.

________. The Study of Public Policy. Indianapolis: Bobbs-Merrill, 1974.

Hogan, Joseph John, Jr. "The Social Economy of a Country Town: Montrose, Pennsylvania, 1800-1840." Ph.D. dissertation, State University of New York at Binghamton, 1975.

Holdsworth, John Thomas. Financing an Empire: History of Banking in Pennsylvania. Vols. 1 and 2. Chicago and Philadelphia: S. J. Clarke Publishing Co., 1928.

Holt, Michael F. Forging a Majority: The Formation of the Republican Party in Pittsburgh, 1848-1860. New Haven, Conn.: Yale University Press, 1969.

________. "The Election of 1840, Voter Mobilization, and the Emergence of the Second American Party System: A Reappraisal of Jacksonian Voting Behavior." In A Master's Due: Essays in Honor of David Herbert Donald, pp. 16-58. Edited by Willliam J. Cooper, Michael F. Holt, and John McCarder. Baton Rouge: Louisiana State University Press, 1985.

________. The Political Crises of the 1850s. New York: John Wiley & Sons, 1978.

Howe, Daniel Walker. The Political Culture of the American Whigs. Chicago: University of Chicago Press, 1979.

Huston, James L. "The Demise of the Pennsylvania American Party, 1854-1858." Pennsylvania Magazine of History and Biography 109 (October 1985): 473-98.

Johnson, George Fiske. "Agriculture in Pennsylvania: A Study of Trends, County and State Since 1840." Pennsylvania Department of Agriculture, General Bulletin, No. 484. Harrisburg: Department of Agriculture, 1929.

Jones, Chester Lloyd. The Economic History of the Anthracite-Tidewater Canals. Philadelphia: University of Pennsylvania Press, 1908.

Kelly, Clyde. United States Postal Policy. New York: D. Appleton & Co., 1932.

Klechner, Clyde I. "Constitutional History of Pennsylvania with Particular Reference to Taxation." Ph.D. dissertation, Cornell University, 1939.

Klein, Philip S. and Hoogenboom, Ari. A History of Pennsylvania. 2nd ed. University Park, Pa.: Pennsylvania State University, 1980.

________. Pennsylvania Politics, 1817-1832: A Game Without Rules. Philadelphia: Historical Society of Pennsylvania, 1940.

Klein, Theodore B. The Canals of Pennsylvania and the System of Internal Improvements. Harrisburg: William Stanley Ray, State Printer, 1901.

Kleppner, Paul. The Cross of Culture: A Social Analysis of Midwestern Politics, 1850-1900. New York: Free Press, 1970.

Kousser, Morgan J. "Are Political Acts Unnatural?" Journal of Interdisciplinary History 15 (Winter 1985): 467-80.

__________. "Restoring Politics to Political History." Journal of Interdisciplinary History 12 (Spring 1982): 569-95.

Kruman, Marc W. Parties and Politics in North Carolina: 1836-1865. Baton Rouge: Louisiana State University Press, 1983.

Latner, Richard B. and Levine, Peter D. "Perspectives on Antebellum Pietistic Politics." Reviews in American History 4 (March 1976): 15-34.

Lemon, James T. The Best Poor Man's Country: A Geographical Study of Early Southeastern Pennsylvania. New York: W. W. Norton & Co., Inc., 1972.

Leuchtenberg, William. "The Pertinence of Political History: Reflections on the Significance of the State in America." Journal of American History 73 (December 1986): 585-600.

Levine, Peter D. The Behavior of State Legislative Parties in the Jacksonian Era: New Jersey, 1829-1844. Rutherford-Teaneck, N.J.: Fairleigh Dickenson Press, 1977.

________. "State Legislative Parties in the Jacksonian Era: New Jersey, 1829-1844 ." Journal of American History 62 (December 1975): 591-608.

Lindstrom, Diane. "American Economic Growth Before 1840: New Evidence and New Directions." Journal of Economic History 39 (March 1979): 289-301.

________. Economic Development in the Philadelphia Region, 1810-1850. New York: Columbia University Press, 1978.

Livingood, James W. The Philadelphia-Baltimore Trade Rivalry, 1780-1860. Harrisburg: Pennsylvania History and Museum Commission, 1947.

Lowi, Theodore H. "Business, Public Policy, Case Studies, and Political Theories." World Politics 16 (July 1964): 677-715.

McCormick, Richard L. "Ethno-Cultural Interpretations of Nineteenth Century American Voting Behavior." Political Science Quarterly 89 (June 1974): 351-77.

________. The Party Period and Public Policy: American Politics from the Age of Jackson to the Progressive Era. New York: Oxford University Press, 1986.

________. "The Party Period and Public Policy: An Exploratory Hypothesis." Journal of American History 56 (September 1979): 279-98.

________, ed. Political Parties and the Modern State. (New Brunswick: Rutgers University Press, 1984).

McCormick, Richard P. "New Perspectives on Jacksonian Politics." American Historical Review 65 (January 1960): 288-301.

________. The Second American Party System: Party Formation in the Jacksonian Era. Chapel Hill: University of North Carolina Press, 1966.

McFaul, John M. The Politics of Jacksonian Finance. Ithaca: Cornell University Press, 1972.

Maizlish, Stephen E. and Kushma, John J., eds. Essays in American Antebellum Politics, 1840-1860. College Station, Tx.: A & M University Press, 1982.

________. The Triumph of Sectionalism: The Transformation of Ohio Politics, 1844-1856. Kent, Ohio: Kent State University Press, 1983.

Meyers, Marvin. The Jacksonian Persuasion: Politics and Belief. Stanford: Stanford University Press, 1957.

Meyers, Richmond E. "The Development of Transportation in the Susquehanna Valley: A Geographical Study, 1700-1900." Ph.D. dissertation, Pennsylvania State University, 1951.

Miller, Eugene Willard. _An Economic Atlas of Pennsylvania_. Harrisburg: Commonwealth of Pennsylvania, State Planning Board, 1964.

Miller, Frederic K. "The Rise of an Iron County: An Economic History of Lebanon County from 1740 to 1865." Ph.D. dissertation, University of Pennsylvania, 1948.

Miller, Harry E. _Banking Theories in the United States Before 1860_. Cambridge: Harvard University Press, 1927.

Miller, Nathan. _The Enterprise of a Free People: Aspects of Economic Development in New York State during the Canal Period, 1792-1838_. Ithaca: Cornell University Press, 1962.

Miller, William. "A Note on the History of Business Corporations in Pennsylvania, 1800-1860." _Quarterly Journal of Economics_ 55 (November 1940): 150-160.

Mueller, Harry R. _The Whig Party in Pennsylvania_. New York: Columbia University, 1922.

Murphy, Raymond E. and Murphy, Marion. _Pennsylvania: A Regional Geography_. Harrisburg: The Pennsylvania Book Service, 1937.

__________. _Pennsylvania Landscapes: Geography of the Commonwealth_. State College, PA: Penns Valley Publishers, 1951.

Niemi, Albert, Jr. _State and Regional Patterns in American Manufacturing, 1860-1900_. Westport, Conn.: Greenwood Press, 1974.

North, Douglass C. _The Economic Growth of the United States, 1790-1860_. New York: W. W. Norton & Co., 1966.

Paskoff, Paul F. _Industrial Evolution: Organization, Structure, and Growth of the Pennsylvania Iron Industry, 1750-1860_. Baltimore and London: Johns Hopkins University Press, 1983.

Pavick, Thomas Peter. "An Economic History of Southwestern Pennsylvania, 1850-1860." Ph.D. dissertation, West Virginia University, 1973.

Pessen, Edward. _Jacksonian America: Society, Personality, and Politics_. Revised ed. Homewood, Ill.: The Dorsey Press, 1978.

__________. "Social Structure and Politics in American History." American Historical Review 87 (December 1982): 1291-1335.

Phillips, Kim T. "The Pennsylvania Origins of the Jackson Movement." Political Science Quarterly 91 (Fall 1976): 489-508.

Pool, J. Lawrence. America's Valley Forges and Valley Furnaces. Published by the author, 1982.

Powell, H. Benjamin. "The Pennsylvania Anthracite Industry, 1769-1976." Pennsylvania History 47 (January 1980): 3-28.

________. Philadelphia's First Fuel Crisis: Jacob Cist and the Developing Market for Pennsylvania Anthracite. University Park, PA: Pennsylvania State University Press, 1979.

Pred, Allan R. Urban Growth and the Circulation of Information: The United States System of Cities, 1790-1840. Cambridge, Mass.: Harvard University Press, 1973.

Primm, James Neal. Economic Policy in the Development of a Western State: Missouri, 1820-1860. Cambridge, 1954.

Phillips, Mary Viola. Teaching Pennsylvania Geography: A Teacher's Manual for the Aero Relief Map of Pennsylvania. Philadelphia: Aero Service Corporation, 1957.

Pritchard, Linda. "Religious Change in a Developing Region: The Social Contexts of Evangelicalism in Western New York and the Upper Ohio Valley during the Mid-Nineteenth Century." Ph.D. dissertation, University of Pittsburgh, 1980.

Ratcliffe, Donald J. "Politics in Jacksonian Ohio: Reflections on the Ethnocultural Interpretation." Ohio History 88 (1979): 5-35.

Reiser, Catherine Elizabeth. Pittsburgh's Commercial Development, 1800-1850. Harrisburg: Pennsylvania Historical and Musuem Commission, 1951.

Rice, Stuart A. Quantitative Methods in Politics. New York: Alfred A. Knopf, 1928.

Rubin, Julius. "Canal or Railroad? Imitation and Innovation in Response to the Erie Canal in Philadelphia, Baltimore and Boston." Transactions of the American Philosophical Society vol. 51, Part 7, 1961.

Schaefer, Donald F. "A Quantitative Description and Analysis of the Growth of the Pennsylvania Anthracite Coal Industry, 1820 to 1865." Ph.D. dissertation, University of North Carolina, 1967.

Scheiber, Harry N. "Federalism and the American Economic Order, 1789-1910." Law and Society Review 10 (Fall, 1975): 57-118.

________. "Government and the Economy: Studies of the 'Commonwealth' Policy in Nineteenth Century America." Journal of Interdisciplinary History 3 (Summer 1972): 135-51.

________. Ohio Canal Era: A Case Study of Government and Economy, 1820-1861. Athens, Ohio: Ohio University Press, 1969.

Schlesinger, Arthur M., Jr. The Age of Jackson. Boston: Little, Brown & Co., 1945.

Schotter, Howard W. The Growth and Development of the Pennsylvania Railroad Company. Philadelphia: Press of Allen, Lane and Scott, 1927.

Shade, William. Banks or No Banks: The Money Issue in Western Politics, 1832-1865. Detroit: Wayne State University Press, 1972.

________. "Pennsylvania Politics in the Jacksonian Period: A Case Study, Northampton County, 1824-1844." Pennsylvania History 39 (July 1972): 313-333.

________. "Politics and Parties in Jacksonian America." Pennsylvania Magazine of History and Biography 110 (October 1986): 483-507.

Shank, William H. The Amazing Pennsylvania Canals. York, Pa.: Historical Society of York County, 1965.

Sharp, James R. The Jacksonians Versus the Banks: Politics in the States after the Panic of 1837. New York: Columbia University Press, 1970.

________. "The Political Culture of Middle-Period United States." Canadian Review of American Studies 15 (Spring 1984): 49-62.

Shortridge, James R. "The Post Office Frontier in Kansas." Journal of the West 13 (July 1974): 83-97.

Silbey, Joel H. The Partisan Imperative: The Dynamics of American Politics Before the Civil War. New York: Oxford University Press, 1985.

_________. The Shrine of Party: Congressional Voting Behavior, 1841-1852. Pittsburgh: University of Pittsburgh Press, 1967.

Sipes, William B. The Pennsylvania Railroad: Its Origins, Construction, Condition and Connection. Philadelphia: Pennsylvania Railroad Company, Passenger Department, 1875.

Smith, Chester, and Kay, John L. Pennsylvania Postal History. Lawrence, Mass.: Quarterman Publications, Inc. 1976.

Snyder, Charles M. The Jacksonian Heritage: Pennsylvania Politics, 1833-1848. Harrisburg: Pennsylvania Historical and Museum Commission, 1958.

Stevens, Sylvester Kirby. Exploring Pennsylvania: Its Geography, History and Government. New York: Hartcourt Brace, 1953.

_________. Pennsylvania: Titan of Industry. 3 vols. New York: Lewis Historical Publishing Co., 1948.

Stradley, Leighton P. Early Financial and Economic History of Pennsylvania. New York: Commerce Clearing House, Inc., 1942.

Taylor, George Rogers. "American Urban Growth Preceding the Railway Age." Journal of Economic History 27 (September 1967): 309-39.

_________. The Transportation Revolution, 1815-1860. New York: Holt, Rinehart & Winston, 1951; reprint ed., Armonk, NY: M. E. Sharpe, Inc., 1977.

Van Fenstermaker, Joseph. The Development of American Commercial Banking, 1782-1837. Kent, Ohio: Kent State University Press, 1965.

Wallner, Peter Andrew. "Politics and Public Works: A Study of the Pennsylvania Canal System, 1825-1857." Ph.D. dissertation, Pennsylvania State University, 1973.

Watson, Harry L. Jacksonian Politics and Community Conflict: The Emergence of the Second American Party System in Cumberland County, North Carolina. Baton Rouge: Louisiana State University, 1981.

Wilentz, Sean. "On Class and Politics in Jacksonian America." Reviews in American History 10 (December 1982): 45-63.

Williams, Charles A. "The History and Operations of the Pennsylvania Turnpike System." Ph.D. dissertation: University of Pittsburgh, 1954.

Wilson, William Bender. History of the Pennsylvania Railroad. Philadelphia: H. T. Coates and Co., 1899.

Wittlinger, Carlton O. "Early Manufacturing in Lancaster County, Pennsylvania, 1710-1840." Ph.D. dissertation, University of Pennsylvania, 1953.

Yearley, C. K., Jr. Enterprise and Anthracite: Economics and Democracy in Schuylkill County, 1820-1875. Baltimore: Johns Hopkins Press, 1961.

Zelinsky, Wilbur. "What Are the Regions of Pennsylvania?" Paper presented at the 78th annual meeting of the Pennsylvania Federation of Historical Societies, Bethlehem, Pa., April 12, 1985.